LIVING BIOGRAPHIES OF
Great Poets

By HENRY THOMAS AND
DANA LEE THOMAS

(Henry Thomas Schnittkind and
Dana Arnold Schnittkind)

Illustrations by
GORDON ROSS

Essay Index Reprint Series

BOOKS FOR LIBRARIES PRESS
FREEPORT, NEW YORK

Copyright 1941, 1959 by
Doubleday and Company, Inc.

Reprinted 1972 by arrangement

Library of Congress Cataloging in Publication Data

Thomas, Henry, 1886-
    Living biographies of great poets.

    (Essay index reprint series)
    1. Poets, English--Biography. 2. Poets,
American--Biography. I. Thomas, Dana Lee, 1918-
joint author. II. Title.
PR105.T5 1972   821'.009 ⌐B⌐   79-167415
ISBN 0-8369-2626-9

PRINTED IN THE UNITED STATES OF AMERICA
BY
NEW WORLD BOOK MANUFACTURING CO., INC.
HALLANDALE, FLORIDA 33009

LIVING BIOGRAPHIES OF
Great Poets

Contents and Illustrations

CONTENTS

Introduction

IT IS A COMMON ERROR to suppose that a poet is merely a rhymester. He is much more than that. The term *poet* is derived from the Greek *poietes*, which means *a maker*, *a designer*, a weaver of musical words and a creator of musical thoughts.

The true poet is a creator—and more. He is a prophet. Indeed the ancient Romans used the same word, *vates*, to signify both prophet and poet. "The prophet," as Carlyle reminds us, "is a revealer of what we are to do; the poet, of what we are to love." He is the Seeker and the Seer—"a blessed heaven-sent bringer of light." He can see more clearly than the rest of us— not only into the progress of Man, but into the purpose of God. He can "dip into the future"—to paraphrase Lord Tennyson— far as human eye can see, and behold the Final Vision and the wonder that will be, when the war drum throbs no longer and the battle flags are furled in the Parliament of nations, the Republic of the world.

The true poet is a creator and a prophet. And he is something even beyond that—a teacher. He not only sees the light but he also guides our steps in its direction. While the scholar sits quietly in his ivory tower of sheltered speculation, the poet is generally to be found fighting in the vanguard of human progress. We see few poets among the reactionaries, but many among the rebels. The great poets try to eliminate the injustices of the world and to perpetuate its beauties. They form the closest link between the men of today and the supermen of tomorrow. They are "our loftier brothers" who take us by the hand and lead us over "the great world's altar stairs that slope through darkness up to God."

The poet, therefore, is God's ambassador of good will to men—a loftier brother with a seeing eye, a singing voice and a hopeful heart. And of all the superior types of men, the poet is perhaps the most universally understood. For, to quote Carlyle again, "a vein of poetry exists in the hearts of all men." We are all poets when we understandingly read a great poem.

In this volume—which, like the other volumes in the present series, is designed to be biographical rather than critical—we have invited a group of our superior fellow poets to come into the circle of our intimate friends.

*   *   *

A word as to the omission of three of the greatest poets—Homer, Shakespeare and Goethe—from this volume. Homer was not an individual poet. The so-called "Homeric Poems" are the combined work of a number of poets who succeeded one another over a period of several centuries and whose lives are today unknown. As for Shakespeare and Goethe, we are planning to include these two poet playwrights in another volume of our present series—*Living Biographies of Great Dramatists*.

H. T

D. L. T

DANTE

Great Poems by Dante

The Divine Comedy: Inferno, Purgatorio, Paradiso.	*Eclogues.*
	Songs.
Vita Nuova.	*Sonnets.*
The Banquet.	*Ballata.*

Dante Alighieri

1265–1321

IN THE MONTH OF AUGUST 1264 a comet appeared in the skies over the city of Florence. Its trail, as it moved from east to west, spread out into a fanlike radiation of splendor that turned the night into day. "This comet," said the citizens of Florence to one another, "foretells the coming of a great man." And a few months later, at the end of May 1265, a man-child was born to Signor Alighiero and Madonna Gabriella. They named him Durante—Dante for short.

He was a sad child, and he had good reason for his sadness. For he lost his mother at five and his father at twelve. His pale, thin face, his auburn-golden hair and his dark, questioning, melancholy eyes gave him an eerie look. They called him "the little poet of the other world." He gave people a queer feeling when he turned his pathetic little face upon them.

And there was one child in particular upon whom Dante longed to look. Longed, yet dared not. For Beatrice—they called her Bice—was the daughter of one of the wealthier citizens of Florence, Folco de' Portinari. One day, indeed, Dante had stolen a glance at her during a *festa*. She had golden hair and a crimson dress. Dante thought she had descended from heaven for the sole purpose of feasting his eyes. After the fleeting glimpse she was gone. They were only nine years old at the time.

Several years later it was Beatrice who looked upon Dante. "Passing through a street, she turned her eyes toward the spot where I stood greatly abashed, and with ineffable courtesy she bestowed upon me a modest smile."

Such was the beginning and the end of their romance. Dante was too well aware of the hopelessness of his passion for Beatrice. He was short, emaciated, hook-nosed, tongue-tied and obscure. Once, at a wedding, the girls mimicked his awkward gestures and his halting words. He didn't know how to talk. But he did know how to write. Someday he would write about Beatrice. He would consecrate her gentle beauty in such wise as no woman had ever been consecrated before. With Beatrice as his guide he would translate his human passion into a divine poem.

II

BEATRICE married the son of a rich banker and died shortly after her marriage. From that day on Dante lived a life of "spiritual widowhood." He entered into the political life of his city, he fought in the battle of Campaldino, he joined in the dalliance and the dances of the Florentine artistic circles and he became an ardent follower of the popular sport of falconry. But all these were surface activities. Deep down in his heart he lived for one purpose—to perpetuate in song the fleeting vision of happiness he had experienced through his brief acquaintance with Beatrice.

And this song of happiness grew gradually in a most unhappy heart. For Dante's was a turbulent spirit in a turbulent age. Florence was torn between two contending political factions— the Guelphs and the Ghibellines, representing roughly the Liberals and the Conservatives of the present age. Dante, a man of free expression and independent thought, was an adherent of neither faction. Indeed, he formed a "superior party" of his own—a party of which he was "the commander and the only soldier." For a short time he was elected to one of the magistracies of Florence, and in the interests of harmony he expelled the leaders of the quarrelsome factions. So anxious, indeed, was Dante to establish peace in Florence that he included, among those he expelled, his intimate friend, Guido Cavalcanti.

For a while there was peace in the city of Florence but not in the home of Dante. He had married Gemma Donati, a Xanthippe of conventional habits and caustic tongue. She couldn't understand her bohemian poet of a husband, with his earthly flirtations and his heavenly thoughts. And Dante couldn't tolerate his irritable spitfire of a wife, with her prurient suspicions and her commonplace mind. They had several children, but these children were not the offspring of love.

His domestic unhappiness served as a perpetual irritant upon Dante's disposition. He walked through the streets of the city with a mental chip on the shoulder. He constantly challenged people to a verbal tilt. Occasionally he engaged with his opponents in a duel of pens. One of these duels, which redounded to the credit of neither of the antagonists, was an exchange of vituperative sonnets between Dante and Donati, his political rival in Florence. Dante called Donati "not only a glutton but a lecher, not only a lecher but a thief, and not only a thief but a bastard." And Donati, in turn, accused Dante of being the "cowardly son of a cowardly father, a pauper and a parasite and a flunkey who licks the hand that smites him with the whip."

The accusations, though picturesque, were untrue—at least insofar as Dante was concerned. For Dante was anything but a coward and a flatterer. Indeed, his courage and his outspokenness were to be the cause of his greatest misfortune. Sent on a mission to Pope Boniface VIII, a man who was more interested in his temporal power than he was in his eternal salvation, Dante had the temerity to disagree with him and to tell him so to his face. The pope smiled politely—and made a mental note to keep watch over this upstart whose tongue outstripped his discretion.

[5]

Boniface was a man who never forgot. When Dante prepared to return to Florence he received word that he had been banished from that city. The charge? Embezzlement of the public funds. Dante proposed to come to the city and to face that baseless accusation, but the podesta warned him that if he set foot in Florence it would be at the peril of his life. *Igne comburatur sic quod moriatur,* he would be burned in the fire until he was dead.

And so the young poet of Florence became a homeless wanderer, silent, solitary, morose—"a pilgrim," to quote his own words, "who goes along a road where he has never been before, and who thinks that every house which he sees in the distance may be the inn, and finding it not so, turns his faith to the next one, and so from house to house until he comes to a place where he may lay down his head. . . ."

Occasionally he found shelter in the houses of the great— not, however, as an honored guest but as a despised beggar. For he was not yet known as a great poet; he was known merely as a dishonored politician condemned to death. The nobles pitied him, threw him a scrap of their meat as they would throw it to a dog and then turned away to their mistresses and their clowns. Once, when he had at last attained a measure of notice as a poet, a nobleman asked him why it was that men paid more attention to their buffoons than they did to Dante. "Because," replied Dante, "like loves like."

A restless, humiliating, bitter life. Yet Dante bore himself through it all with the pride of a master in the presence of his slaves. For, with all their material wealth, these "noblemen far from noble" were mental and spiritual paupers in Dante's eyes. His was a far more solid, far more permanent treasure than their jewels and their gold. For he possessed the treasure of an inspired mind.

III

WHILE DANTE'S MIND traveled over the infinitudes of space from hell through purgatory to heaven, his body kept longing for that little plot of Florentine soil from which he had been banished. Again and again he asked for the vindication of his rights. But the rulers of Florence refused to vindicate him; they merely offered to pardon him. Indignantly he rejected the offer. "Is this, then," he wrote, "the glorious return of Dante Alighieri to his country after nearly fifteen years of suffering and exile? Did an innocence, patent to all, merit this insult of humiliation added to the injury of persecution? Far from a man, the house-mate of philosophy, to allow himself to be offered up bound like a criminal! Far from a man, the poet of justice, to apologize to those who have oppressed him! This is not the way of returning to my country!"

But he sought other ways. Allying himself with a group of like-minded fellow exiles, he made an attempt to enter the city by force. It was a gallant but futile effort. And then he separated himself from the other exiles. His body, like his mind, must travel alone. "Through almost all parts where this language [Italian] is spoken, a wanderer, well-nigh a beggar, I have gone, unwillingly displaying to everybody the gaping wounds of my misfortune. Truly I have been a vessel without sail or rudder, driven to diverse ports, estuaries and shores by that hot blast, the breath of grievous poverty."

The report of his fame as a poet was now beginning to trickle into the various cities of Italy. But when the people beheld him they wondered whether the divine flame of genius could burn within so bedraggled a human body. "I have shown myself to the eyes of many who perhaps, through some fame of me, had imagined me in quite other guise, who upon beholding me conceived a contempt not only for my person but for my work."

His person, even under the most favorable conditions, was not such as to inspire respect. "His face," writes Boccaccio, "was long, his nose angular, his jaw large and the lower lip protruding somewhat beyond the upper as if ready for a fight. . . . His shoulders were stooped, his features dark, his eyes deep, sad and defiant." Not a pleasant companion by any means. "This Dante," observes another contemporary, Giovanni Villani, "was haughty, and shy, and disdainful, and like a philosopher almost ungracious, knew not well how to deal with unlettered folk."

And so he went alone through the world of the living. But not alone through the world of the dead. His mind conjured up a vast concourse of souls, in hell, in purgatory, in heaven—men and women and children whom he rewarded and punished, according to their deserts, with a divine judgment and a human pity. No other poet has created so many "living" characters as Dante has created in his *Divine Comedy*, the immortal epic of the dead. His characters are so vivid because Dante felt so intensely about them. Pope Boniface had threatened to destroy him by fire. The thought of fire had become seared into Dante's mind. He would avenge himself upon his enemies in accordance with the laws of Jehovah—an eye for an eye, fire unto eternity as against fire unto death. He reserved one of the most dreadful regions in hell for his enemy, Pope Boniface VIII. The pope had died in 1303, at the time when Dante was writing his *Inferno.* "Are you already standing there?" asks Dante eagerly, as he points in his vision to the pits of the simonists (men guilty of corruption in ecclesiastical matters). "Are you already there, Boniface?"

Dante places many of his enemies in the fiery and the icy caverns of hell. Yet the *Inferno* is far more than an epic of personal revenge. It is a concrete picturization of the ethical principles of the Middle Ages. Dante has been justly called "the Voice of the Silent Centuries." The human mind has always been seeking for a plan in this apparently planless world of ours. And the religious teachers of the Middle Ages tried to supply this plan. The human drama, they said, has a rational meaning and a logical plot. Virtue is rewarded and crime punished—not in this world but in the next. And Dante, with his unfettered imagination and scientific mind, gave to the "airy nothingness" of the afterworld "a local habitation and a name." He measured out the precise penalty for the precise crime. He divided his *Inferno* into twenty-four circles, each of them fitted out with its own peculiar instruments of torture for its own particular type of sinner. He visualized the geography of hell as vividly as he visualized the geography of Italy. And— so fertile was his genius—no two places and no two punishments are exactly alike.

Dante's vision of the *Inferno*, as Santayana puts it, is "the work of a sublime imagination turned sour." Yet in spite of his personal—and perfectly justified—grievances, he tried to be as impartial as it was possible for any human poet to be. He placed in hell not merely *his own* enemies but *God's* enemies, not only Boniface whom he hated but Francesca of Rimini whom he loved. He punished them for their transgressions, but he pitied them for their sufferings.

But let us briefly accompany Dante on this most exciting journey ever made by the human mind.

One day, Dante tells us, he finds himself lost in a dark wood. He is about to be attacked by a leopard, a lion and a wolf (lust, ambition and avarice), when the ancient poet, Virgil, comes to his rescue. In his famous epic, the *Aeneid*, Virgil has once taken a journey into Hades. He now offers himself as a guide for another pilgrimage into the regions of the underworld.

Together they descend into the bowels of the earth until they find themselves in the outer circles of hell. Here Dante encounters the souls of the lazy, the insignificant, those who during their lifetime were not exactly bad yet never took the trouble to be good. In hell they must pay the penalty for their indifference. Their punishment is to be constantly driven to work, without a moment's rest, "like grains of sand eddying forever in the whirlwind."

We next come into the inner regions of hell. These regions are divided into three sections: the first circle contains the hotheaded sinners; the second circle encloses the cheaters and the frauds; and the third and most terrible circle imprisons the cold-blooded assassins and the traitors and the spies.

It is a dark and horrible and hopeless place into which Dante takes us. "All hope abandon, ye who enter here." In the first circle the souls of the passionate are cleansed of their passion in burning flakes of fire upon stretches of burning sand. In the second circle the souls of the fraudulent are driven by the whips of the devils into a slimy pool whose stench offends the nostrils. These souls are steeped in disgusting physical filth in hell, just as they have been steeped in disgusting moral filth on earth. These sharpers and swindlers and forgers and thieves, "men who seemed to shed no tears for pain," are being constantly and painfully twisted into all sorts of beastly shapes. Finally, in the third circle, we behold the punishment of the stool pigeons and the stabbers-in-the-back. These are the most despicable of all the criminals in hell. The third circle, which has been especially reserved for their punishment, encloses an enormous sea of ice, to represent the icy hearts of its occupants. Their bodies stick like bits of straw into this solid sea, and even their outcries and their tears have become petrified in this horrible desolation of frost. Their hopes, like their tears, have turned into ice. For them there is no release from hell.

These, then, are the three regions of hell—fire, slime and ice. They correspond to the three types of crime—passion, trickery and brutality. Of the three, Dante tells us, brutality is the worst.

And now, having guided us through the various regions of hell, Dante conducts us to the next stage in the journey of the human soul—the Mountain of Purgatory. This is the mountain upon which the souls of the dead are to be purged for their heavenly dwelling after the completion of their punishment in hell. It is a towering stairway of rocks rising in the middle of the mysterious Atlantic—this ocean had not as yet been explored in Dante's day—and reaching up until, with the topmost boughs of its Earthly Paradise, it touches the lowest of the heavens. Long and difficult is the ascent over this Mountain of Purification to the Gates of Heaven, and it is only through the wings of longing and hope that Dante is able to surmount it. On the way Dante stops to converse with the laboring souls and to cheer them on in their upward climb. "Over the steps of sincerity, contrition and love lies the way to God."

As Dante, guided by Virgil, advances slowly to the top a

radiant music descends upon them. Faintly at first, and then more and ever more resoundingly, come the words, "Glory to God in the Highest!"

And thus they move slowly upward amidst the souls that are being purified with the sweet bitterness of repentance, until at last they arrive upon the glittering threshold of heaven. And now it is no longer Virgil who leads the way but Beatrice, the Lady of Light whom he has loved in Florence and whose death has bereft him of his earthly joy. From star to star she guides the poet, in an ever-ascending circle of rapture and glory, until they come to the Heaven of heavens, the dwelling place of God. The higher they go, the more dazzling the light and the more radiant the face of Beatrice, the Blessed Damozel of Heavenly Joy.

Altogether there are nine circles in the heavens. They rise one above the other like the terraces of some enchanted garden, each of them ablaze with a different form of light. Now the rays are molded into an immense eagle, now into a vast cross and now into a ladder of flame that towers into the infinite. These ever-changing figures are formed by the incessant movement of the souls. They range themselves into panoramas of light that may be compared to the sweeping glories of a sunset or a sunrise.

Human language, even the language of the greatest poet, observes Dante, is unable to picture the splendor of heaven, its intoxicating profusion of flowers and incense and music and light. Heaven, in a word, is Light—a light that is Beauty, a beauty that is Love. All the souls in Paradise are gathered into an infinite ocean of Light and Beauty and Love. All become One in the radiant presence of God—"One universal smile of unutterable joy."

From this height of Paradise Dante glances down upon our earth, and his face is suffused with a smile of pity at our littleness:

> O foolish vanity of mortal men!
> For statues some, and some for empty praise
> Are yearning; this man longs for heaps of gold;

> That man, by folly driv'n, aspires to rule;
> Another, yielding to the spur of greed,
> Takes joy in murdering his fellow men. . . .
> What senseless sensual joys, what bootless pride!

And then, after this fleeting glance upon the earth, the poet turns back to heaven and puts the masterly finishing stroke to his *Divine Comedy:*

> I raised my eyes aloft, and I beheld
> The scattered chapters of the Universe
> Gathered and bound into a single book
> By the austere and tender hand of God.

IV

DANTE WROTE HIS *Divine Comedy* as a compensation for his thwarted life. Exiled, hunted, despised, he created a world in which he would be welcomed, befriended and extolled. Compelled to seek for the charity of the great, he raised himself to a height from which he could judge the kings and the princes and the popes. Defeated and humiliated in the world of men, he pictured himself triumphant in the world of God. The *Divine Comedy* is a dreamworld of refuge for a stricken man—for *all* stricken men.

For the poet who had so greatly suffered had conceived a great tenderness for all suffering things. Come ye all, my unhappy brothers and sisters, into the kingdom of heaven and the gracious presence of the Lady of Light. "The purpose of this poem," wrote Dante, "is to remove mankind from their state of misery and to lead them to a state of happiness."

And with this purpose in mind he "held heartbreak at bay for twenty years" and refused to die till he had finished his work. Hunger, poverty, insults, degradations, threats, even occasional blows—all these he endured and went resolutely on with his inspired task. At last the poem was finished and there was nothing else for him to do. So he laid his head on an exile's pillow and closed his eyes.

V

WHEN Dante was alive and obscure his native city of Florence had threatened to reduce him to ashes. But now that he was famous and dead she begged for the honor of welcoming his ashes home. But in vain. He was buried in Ravenna, the city in which he died.

Five hundred years after the death of Dante, Lord Byron visited his grave. And this poet, who had never displayed his emotion in the presence of the living, knelt down and wept in the presence of the dead.

CHAUCER

Great Poems by Chaucer

Canterbury Tales.
Legend of Good Women.
Troilus and Cressida.
Book of the Duchess.

Assembly of Fowls.
House of Fame.
Anelida and Arcite.
Romance of the Rose (*translation*).

Geoffrey Chaucer

1340–1400

Aᴌᴌ London is out in force to welcome the triumphal procession. The road to Canterbury is lined with cheering crowds. For the French have been routed at Poitiers and the Black Prince has returned to England with the French king as his prisoner. Never has the national pride of Britain been so profoundly stirred. Every Englishman has covered himself with glory—the knight who has fought on horseback, the yeoman with his longbow, the merchant who has financed the expedition, the wives and the mothers who have bravely carried on with their household duties while their men have been fighting abroad.

For several days London has worked feverishly to prepare a royal welcome. And now is the great moment. The guilds have turned out all aglitter in their livery—the weavers and the dyers and the carpenters parading in their silk jackets and their silver daggers, while their wives and their doxies and their daughters are trying to outvie one another in the splendor of their colors. A few old beards are shocked by the "outrageous attire" of the maidens, and they point their fingers with scorn at the even more outrageous finery of the noble ladies as they prance by on their richly caparisoned steeds. "Ods blood, but the ladies of

London do love to overdress!" cries one of the old men to another.

But the old man's voice is drowned out in a general shout. For here comes the procession—a thousand knights of London on horseback, followed by companies of men-at-arms and archers. And now observe the Gascon nobles leading the unhappy king of France on a white charger. What gallantry! For side by side with his captive, and sitting on a modest little black horse, rides his conqueror, the Black Prince of England.

Prominent among those who watched the great spectacle were Lionel, the younger brother of the Black Prince, and his amiable wife, the Countess Elizabeth. And among her retinue of resplendent pages stood Geoffrey Chaucer, a charming little fellow dressed in red and black breeches and a short red cloak. Chaucer's young heart beat high. He was proud to be standing by his lady. He roared his approval lustily and whistled at the elegant horses in the procession. Truly this was a merry season for a lad who was page to the Countess Elizabeth. First there had been the dazzling celebration of the Feast of Saint George. On that occasion the countess had bought him a new livery for three shillings and sixpence. Then there was a round of special visits to the castles at Windsor and Woodstock and Hatfield. England was a jolly spectacle! Life was an exciting feast! He only wished he had been able to follow the parade all the way from Canterbury.

II

FRANCE was a stubborn country, refusing to live up to her treaty. Her captive king, in his eagerness to go home, had promised to cede any amount of territory exacted by England. But the council of ministers in Paris, secure in the thought that they were out of reach of the British prisons, had steadfastly refused any diminution of their kingdom. The Black Prince swore a mighty oath. Had the French, then, forgotten Poitiers? And he made preparations for an expeditionary force that would wage even more terrible warfare upon the intractable French people. Every strong-limbed Englishman was present in the vast army that assembled at Dover for the invasion.

"God and Saint George for England!" Six thousand supply carts were shipped across the Channel—handmills to grind corn, ovens to bake bread, falconers and greyhounds for the king to hunt with during the tedious months of the siege. Geoffrey Chaucer's eyes were aglow. Only two years after the grand procession in London Town, and here he was soldiering on the coast of France. Please God, his king would arrive at Rheims and be crowned monarch of France as well as of England. They were marching to Montreuil near the sea, to the south of Boulogne. Timidly he entered a grand cathedral to pray for the success of his king. It was a gigantic creature of stone with pointed locks and rose-colored eyes and tapering pilaster ribs. A truly beautiful creation of God, this Gothic cathedral. And the French whom he had sworn to murder in battle, it was they who had built this holy architecture. In the villages he had seen little children and old women looking with terror-stricken faces at the English knights and archers as they marched by at the head of their long baggage trains. He remembered especially the wide, wondering eyes of a small boy of ten. He began to feel somewhat ashamed of himself. Why had he taken so much pride in conquering a country he had never seen and a people he had scarcely known?

In the snows of winter the British arrived before Rheims and settled down to a siege. Foraging parties were sent out to plunder the outlying districts of their provisions. On one of these raids Geoffrey Chaucer was seized by the French and made prisoner within the walls of Rheims. Happily he strolled under the spell of the stained-glass windows and the granite and marble statuary of the Rheims cathedral. In England the courtly classes spoke the French language but they had failed to capture the spirit of the French art. The English had never molded such architectural phantasy as this! A young man must be a soldier and travel to other countries in order to get his full taste of beauty.

When Chaucer was finally ransomed he returned to London with his head full of Rheims. It was a strange military conquest.

III

THE Countess Elizabeth passed on from her Eden of England to another Paradise. Geoffrey Chaucer found himself released from service. But only for a while. A close friend of his youth, John of Gaunt, had inherited the tremendous Duchy of Lancaster and had become the richest man in England. With the help of this influential friend, Geoffrey became once more a member of the royal court. He had been appointed as the unofficial poet of the king. This was quite in keeping with the Chaucer tradition. For generations his ancestors had supplied the wine for the royal banquets. And now he too was called upon to enliven the festivities of the king—with the wine of his songs.

And with the spice of his diplomatic wisdom. For the king had invited him into his inner council of intrigue. Before long, Chaucer found himself an expert in the moving of the political chessmen upon the checkerboard of foreign entanglements.

The king sent him upon a diplomatic mission to Genoa. Once more he found himself on alien soil in the service of his country. And once more the poet within him peeped out from behind the mask of the man of the world. For here in Italy, amid the plots and the counterplots of the doges and the kings, he found the frescoes of Giotto and the poetry of Dante. Italy was ancient Greece come to life again. The very stars over the peninsula held within them the fires of an artistic sunrise that would outshine the political intrigues of the night.

But in his enthusiasm for Italian art the young poet-diplomat didn't neglect his political mission. Having brought it to a satisfactory conclusion, he returned to his king and received a triple reward for his services—an appointment to a customs office in the port of London, the free lease of a dwelling at

Aldgate and the daily delivery of a pitcher of wine from the royal cellars "for the refreshment of his household."

New distinctions, new distractions. He had married an extravagant young woman, Philippa, who led him a merry chase in her effort to "keep up with the nobility." He was obliged to pour all his earnings into the bottomless sieve of her desires.

Yet for all of his wife's demands upon his attention he found plenty of time to devote to his mistress—the Muse. He composed romantic tales of derring-do and read them aloud when the royal banquet tables were cleared and the red light from the torches fell upon the ermines and the velvets of the assembled company. Like a "jeweler with his hands full he poured out pearls and glass beads in profusion, sparkling diamonds and common agates, black jet and ruby roses."

And he was dissatisfied. For a poet must be always in quest of the truth. And thus far he had captured nothing but the *outward trappings* of the truth—the gaudy colors and the fantastic shapes of its garment. There was no substance to his poetry, just as there was no substance to the faery creatures of mists and rainbows that he so prettily portrayed. He was living in an unsubstantial dream.

He did much traveling on his official business, and as he spurred his horse along the roads he had much time for thought. Especially he liked to be on the highways in the month of May, when the fresh verdure of the English landscape sank into his very soul. There was something more magical in the homespun beauty of England than in all the tinsel scenes of his romances. Enough of his pretty little "books and songs and ditties in rhyme." The beauty that was England would henceforth be the burden of his song.

IV

ONE DAY Geoffrey sat at his desk upstairs in his library at Aldgate. This room was reached by a circular stairway of stone. Near by on the shelves were a hundred books in Latin and in French. He must cease dreaming and return to business. No time now for nodding his drowsy head while his brother-in-law sat talking to him across the table in a droning voice. "The old days of chivalry are no more. The era of England's glory is a thing of the past. The serfs have deserted their masters. The yeomen are streaming into the cities and swelling the guilds of the laborers . . ." Chaucer's head nodded, and the sentences came to him in mutilated fragments, as through a mist. ". . . agitators . . . outrageous demands for wages . . . freeholders gathering into a Parliament . . ." Chaucer shook himself awake for a moment. "Parliament," he whispered to himself. Parliament of the freeholders—free as the birds—Parliament of the Birds . . . "What a splendid idea for a poem!" Suppose the birds were called in conclave as in the fable? The sparrow and the peacock, the crows and the ravens and the popinjay, the cormorant "hot and full of gluttony"—all of them brought together to judge the wooing of a female eagle by three brash suitors of her species. . . . There, now, he was dreaming again as his brother-in-law continued in his monotonous voice. "Wat Tyler and his mob . . . marching to the Tower . . . rioting against the poll taxes . . . An evil time, Geoffrey . . . this fatal day." This day? Again Chaucer shook the slumber out of his head. Why, this was St Valentine's Day, and all the feathered creatures were screaming their sentiments on the great wooing of the eagle. Now the goose makes haste to rush in with a ready-made resolution. But she will be rebuffed very smartly by the sparrow hawk amidst the general uproar. . . .

But down in the street there is a real uproar. The rebellion of the dispossessed has at last broken loose. The mob has stormed against the Tower. Chaucer's terrified wife, with their child in her arms, rushes into his study. "We are lost, Geoffrey! The mob is armed!"

Riots, pillage, murder. Geoffrey's heart is torn between his sympathy for the rebels and his loyalty toward the king. He listens to the harangue of one of the leaders of the rebellion—the Kentish priest, John Wycliffe: "My good friends, things cannot go well in England, nor ever will, until everything shall be held in common—when there shall be neither vassal nor lord, and all distinctions shall be leveled . . ."

And then Chaucer's own voice speaks within him: "You owe everything to the king, Geoffrey—your livelihood, your rank, your service. You are of the ancient régime; you are its culture, its heart, its delusion. Yours is the pageantry of an age-old dream. Do not let it pass into a rude awakening."

V

THE NOBLES suppressed the rebellion, and Geoffrey remained in the service of the king. Often he rode to a tavern at Southwark after the transaction of his daily business in London. Generally he sat in a corner of the tavern by himself. For he was a man of extreme reserve, preoccupied with his own thoughts. One May evening, as he sat thus musing in his corner, a crowd of travelers poured into the tavern with a great deal of commotion. "These must be Canterbury pilgrims," thought Geoffrey, "stopping for the night on their way to the shrine of Saint Thomas à Becket." It was interesting to see so many different classes of English society mingled together on their common pilgrimage in this "merry month of May." Here were yeomen and scholars and friars and physicians and parsons and plowmen and sailors and stewards and lawyers and merchants and monks—all seated at the tavern and exchanging their stories and their banter in a spirit of comradeship to be found nowhere but in an English hostelry. Geoffrey counted twenty-nine people in the company of pilgrims. "All England" was at the Tabard Inn tonight!

The host was a merry fellow with a face "bred on port" and a hearty voice that ran like thunder across the beams of the ceiling. And as he talked he smiled upon the demure nun who had taken her seat at the table and who daintily lisped in French. A morose-looking merchant, with a forked beard and a Flanders beaver hat, spoke earnestly to his neighbor about his trading ships and his "wool stations" across the sea. At the other end of the table a doctor was recounting his successful jousts with death and held them all agape with bated breath. "I never saw such a goodly crowd of people!" roared the host. And then he turned to a stately knight who sat sipping quietly from his tankard of ale. "Have you lately returned from the battlefield?"

"I am always returning from one or another battlefield, mine host," replied the knight. "I have fought for the faith in many a Christian and a heathen land—in Alexandria, Turkey, Prussia, France, Lithuania, Spain. And now, in my hour of ease between two wars, I am embarked upon my Canterbury pilgrimage."

Chaucer looked at the knight in his fustian doublet. The old age of chivalry was breaking up before the new era of trade. Life was a rolling ocean forever stirred by the restless winds. New winds, new waves—but the same unyielding, changeless sea. Chaucer turned his attention from the knight to another of the guests—a friar whose eyes shone like the stars on a frosty evening. "I'm a gay and important fellow," sang the friar, a little the worse for his ale. "In all the orders there's none more mellow."

Chaucer smiled as he listened to the friar. "A father-confessor," he mused, "and the son of the devil."

And the friar, as if he read the silent thoughts of the poet, returned merrily: "I've been licensed by the Pope's own hand. I'll give full confession to anyone—for the proper fee."

The nun scowled at him and then became absorbed in her supper. Daintily she "wet her fingers in the sauce," careful not to let the slightest morsel of food slip from her lips. Geoffrey was amused at her mincing manners. She looked so sensitive, so timid, so gentle—as if her heart would break at the sight of a bleeding mouse.

In the meantime the other guests had been indulging in quips and pranks and jolly banter amid the clink of the brimming decanter. A miller, with a beard red as a fox, a wart on the tip of his nose and a mouth wide as a furnace, was addressing himself to a pale young fellow wrapped in a threadbare cloak.

Dante

Chaucer

"Come, come, my friend, I am sure by the looks of you that you must be a scholar."

"You are right. I am a philosopher." And then, with a wry smile, "My coffers are lined with learning, not with gold."

"And your belly, I dare say, is forever lined with hunger."

"I could feed you up, my man," volunteered a franklin whose beard shone white as a daisy against a sanguine complexion. "You need acquaintance with my larders. My home, for all its lack of textbooks, shows meat and drink aplenty."

"Stay with us," shouted the miller, "and we will turn you yet into a son of Epicurus——"

"—and give you an aching constitution to add to your metaphysical problems," interposed the doctor.

Back and forth the conversation flew, like colored balls in the hands of jugglers. And now a jolly fat woman in her middle years joined in the sport and became the center of the circle. She was dressed in scarlet stockings and a yellow mantle. On her head she wore a turban of kerchiefs that weighed "at least ten pounds." The miller had whispered something into her ear, whereupon she had blushed more scarlet than her stockings and had opened her mouth in a grin that exhibited a huge gap in her teeth. "Yes, my good folk," she said, addressing herself to the entire company rather than to the miller. "I've had five husbands since the day I was twelve. And now I'm looking for the sixth. . . . God bade us all to wax and multiply, and I have done His bidding faithfully. . . . When I speak of love I speak with complete authority. . . . With my ardent loving I have sent five men into the grave. And may the Lord have mercy on their souls. . . ."

Up spoke a flaxen-haired youth. "By Our Lady, you've been a noble preacher to me. I was about to take a wife . . ."

The night was well advanced. It was time for the pilgrims to retire, for they were eager to get an early start the following day.

As the pilgrims rose from the table the host made a suggestion. "Good friends," he said, "you have a long journey ahead of you on the morrow. And I will fashion you some sport. Let each one of you tell two tales on the way to Canterbury and two tales on the way back. And he whose tales are adjudged the best shall on his return receive free bed and board at the Tabard Inn."

With a merry chorus of assent the pilgrims went up to bed. . . .

Geoffrey Chaucer opened his eyes. He was alone. He had dozed off in his corner over his bottle of wine. The Tabard Inn and the people of his fantasy had faded away. The host of the tavern in which he had been dozing was snuffing out the lights of the candles. Chaucer rose to his feet. "I wonder," he murmured, "what sort of stories these pilgrims will be telling to one another?"

The host turned to him with a quizzical look on his face. "Were you speaking about something, sir?"

"Yes," replied Chaucer with a smile. "*The Canterbury Tales.*"

VI

WHEN *The Canterbury Tales* was published Chaucer's fame as the Father of English Literature was assured. There were times thereafter when his purse was empty, but his life had been fulfilled. He had given a new music to his native tongue and new magic to his native land. Under the enchantment of his pen the English language and the English landscape were to remain forever alive, forever "fresher than the May with flowers new."

And the people of England, too, were invested with the breath of immortal life. Such is the spell of *The Canterbury Tales*—the morning song of the modern world. . . .

As the years went on Chaucer made ready to leave the tavern of life and to start upon his pilgrimage. At times he had his misgivings, for he was not certain of the way to the holy shrine.

> A thousand times I have heard men tell
> That there is joy in heaven, and pain in hell;
> And I accord it well that it is so.
> But nevertheless I know indeed also

That there is none who in this country dwell
That have ever been to heaven or to hell.

But when the hour announced the dawn of departure he was ready to start. "Forward, Pilgrim, into the morning and unafraid!"

VILLON

Great Poems by Villon

The Little Testament.   *..dicil.*
The Great Testament: Ballade of   *Lyrics.*
Dead Ladies, Lament of the   *Ballads.*
Old Hag, The Fat Margot,   *Jobelin.*
Prayer of Villon's Mother.

François Villon

François de Montcorbier

1431–after 1463

A<small>ND NOW WE COME</small> to the strangest singer of them all—"our sad, bad, glad, mad brother," François Villon. Lean and lousy, a bundle of skin and bone and fire, sharp-featured, nervous, shifty, "dry and black as a maulkin," upper lip disfigured from the slash of a dagger, eyes twisted into a furtive squint against the sudden leap from a gendarme out of the shadows—he is the cleverest sneak thief in Paris and the greatest poet in France. At twenty he has already seduced his women; at twenty-four he has murdered a priest; at twenty-five he has become a leading member of the *Coquille*, or the Gentlemen of the Dirk—the underworld gang of sharpers, filchers, brigands, burglars, pickpockets, highwaymen, assassins and thugs who have turned the fifteenth century into an age of terror. Yet he can sing. *Mille diables*, how he can sing! And his wit is as sharp as a needle. And he knows his Latin texts, for he is a master of the liberal as well as of the lecherous arts. And his faith is deep and his devotion to his friends sincere. Few men have been guilty of fouler crimes. Few men have given voice to purer thoughts.

An amazing product of an amazing age. The city of Paris had been bled dry by the successive onslaughts of the Hundred Years' War. Students begged for their bread on the street corners. Robberies, riots and murder were the order of the day. Epidemics raged without a letup. Within a single year the bubonic plague had carried off fifty thousand victims in Paris. Wolves prowled in the suburbs, attacking and killing not only children but grownups. Day and night the streets resounded with the cry: *Hélas, je meurs de faim et de froid!* Alas, I am perishing with hunger and cold!

Such was the environment into which François de Montcorbier was born (1431). His parents were desperately poor. They brought up their unwelcome guest on "turnip tops and curses." Often he would have gone hungry had he not acquired the knack of snitching food from the neighborhood stores. Indeed, the education of François began with stealing. Reading and writing came later on.

He lost his father when he was a little child. When he reached his twelfth birthday his mother felt that she had done all she could for him. She threw him upon the mercies of a distant relative, Father Guillaume de Villon. The kindly old priest accepted the burden. He took François into his home and gave him his name.

He found the child quick of perception but deaf to all authority. Hoping nevertheless to make a cleric of him, he enrolled him (in 1443) at the University of Paris.

The professors tried their best, by the diligent application of birches to breeches, to turn the little ruffian into a gentleman. But in vain. His first years had stamped themselves too indelibly upon his oversensitive mind. He took the bachelor's and the master's degree, and he came out of the university a first-rate scholar, an inspired poet and a champion rogue. His natural inclination for roguery had brought him together with two other birds of a feather—Colin des Cayeulx and Regnier de Montigny. To his university professors who were trying to prepare him for the world Villon added these two private tutors who undertook to prepare him for the underworld. Colin des Cayeulx, the son of a locksmith, had inherited his father's mechanical skill to such a degree that he became one of the most notorious pick-locks in Paris. On September 26, 1460, his career as a master burglar came to an end on the gallows of Montfaucon. Villon's other professor in perversity, Regnier de Montigny, was a better born and more versatile scoundrel than Colin. He was a swindler, sharper, drunkard, murderer, gangster, church robber and all-round thug. His career was more daring and therefore less durable than that of his colleague. He was hanged in 1457.

With these blackguards as his extracurricular teachers, Villon annexed to his two academic titles the unacademic degree of M.C. (Master of Crime). He was now ready to launch upon his postgraduate course from the university to the penitentiary. He divided his time into three shifts: his afternoons he spent in creative writing, his nights in debauchery and thieving, and his mornings in sleeping it off. His gentle guardian, Guillaume de Villon, pleaded with him to put an end to his evil ways, but to no avail. Life in the house of the cloister was too dull for a young madcap who had fire in his veins. It was so much more exciting to sneak out at night, when the old man was asleep, and to go off a-drinking and a-wenching at the Mule Tavern, the Pine-Cone Inn or the Wooden Sword. And from there a sally into the dark with congenial hoodlums for a robbery or a rape—or, if need be, a tournament of bared knuckles and bleeding noses. Hahay, but that was the life! What if they caught you and chopped off your hand—the hand with which you wrote your poetry? You could always, at a venture, learn to write with your other hand. Indeed, all life was a venture—and the greater the risk the greater the fun.

Yet time and again, for his foster father's sake, he promised to give up his old haunts and habits. After all, what is the material advantage of your criminal ways? "You steal, you kill, you fill your bag," and what then? "Women and wine will cop your swag."

Very well, then, he would reform. It would give the old gentleman *so* much pleasure. But first he must have a final fling—just one more stolen kiss, one more drink, one more fight, one more midnight exploration into a neighbor's house.

[*33*]

And before he knew it he was plunged once more up to his neck in the slime of the Parisian sewers.

At last, however, he felt that he was really on the eve of redemption. It was the fifth of June 1455—the holy night of the Feast of Corpus Christi, *La Feste-Dieu*. The windows of Paris were aglitter with candles and the altars were redolent with incense. Processions of singing men and women and children, crowned with roses and with flaming torches in their hands, were winding over the streets. And in the midst of these processions the Body of God was carried in a blaze of light under a canopy of velvet and gold.

François Villon, sitting over his supper in the house of Father Villon, was shaping a sacred poem in his mind. For he had a devout heart in that weak-willed body of his. He had yielded himself completely to that moment of penitence, of soul searching, of peace.

It was the last moment of peace that Villon was to know for a long time. Having finished his supper, he left the table and walked out into the street. He directed his footsteps, through force of habit, toward the Mule Tavern. But he didn't go inside. Enough of that sort of debauchery. He would just sit down for a few minutes on the stone bench across the street, and then he would return home to enter a new life.

He was joined by a young woman and a priest—acquaintances he had picked up in his diversified adventures over the city. A few drowsy words about this, that and the other thing— and then suddenly an argument over the woman, a quarrel, a scuffle, and the priest lay mortally wounded of a dagger stab. Villon's own upper lip was slashed in the fight. It resulted in his disfigurement for life.

Fortunately for Villon's neck, the dying priest "remitted and forgave" him for the murder. However, Paris was not a healthy place for Villon just then. Hastily slinging a bundle of his belongings over his shoulder, he vanished by devious ways out through the city gate.

II

WE NOW FIND HIM tramping over the countryside, a full-fledged member of the *Coquille*. He is their counselor, their poet laureate, their unholy confessor. When they are hungry he contrives ways and means of stealing food for them—"Master Villon is a nursing mother to us." And when any of them are brought to the gallows' end of their journey he sends them merrily off to hell with an orison addressed to the devil and a requiem of obscene laughter.

It is a variegated and a risky life that he leads as a *Coquillard* —picking locks, selling false jewels for diamonds, cheating at the country taverns with trick cards and loaded dice, occasionally holding up a traveler in the woods or on the highways—snitching bits of paper on which to write his verses, slinking and singing his way through the hamlets, amusing the peasants and seducing their wives, and always just half a step ahead of the hangman.

Finally, thanks to the tireless efforts of his foster father, he was permitted to return to Paris. For a while he tried "an honest stunt" as the tutor of a few youngsters whose relatives were apparently unaware of his past, and then he returned to "the masters and the mistresses" of his old-time dissipations. He surrendered himself especially to the piercing eyes and the lashing tongue of Katherine de Vausselles, "my lady of the twisted nose." Villon had conceived an ardent passion for Katherine, but Katherine entertained an ardent passion for money. "She let me open my heart to her, but only to make mock of me." She deceived him with a more domineering and more prosperous lover. And, by way of adding injury to perjury, she thrashed him in front of her other lover. "I was beaten like linen in a stream, stark naked. I have no wish to conceal it. Who made me swallow this humiliation? Katherine de Vausselles. And who was the third person present? Her lover, Noel."

Villon's humiliation became the talk of the Parisian underworld. People began to titter behind his back. "You can hardly blame the bitch for the way she treats him. Look at his scarecrow body and his hangdog face." There was nothing for him to do but to leave Paris again. But first he would bequeath to the city a farewell fling of his sardonic verse. And so he wrote a burlesque will, the *Little Testament*, leaving his fame to Guillaume de Villon, his joy to his friends, his pain to his enemies and his "poor, pale and piteous heart" to the mistress who had brought him to this sorry plight—"and may God have mercy upon her soul!"

Having finished his *Little Testament*, Villon packed his belongings, paid his last round of visits to his friends, waved them all a hearty au revoir—and then abruptly changed his plans.

III

A FAREWELL SUPPER on Christmas Eve 1456. François Villon is playing host to four of his cronies at the Mule Tavern. A sudden evil inspiration seizes their drink-befuddled minds. A few minutes later five silent figures are slinking through the Christmas shadows in the direction of the College of Navarre. François has been persuaded that it is more profitable to stay and to steal in Paris than to go off adventuring on the road.

The robbery of the College of Navarre netted Villon about fifteen hundred dollars and—as we shall see later—came near to costing him his life.

But for the present the police were unable to connect Villon and his cronies with the robbery. The burglars celebrated their "good fortune" in a series of carousals, with roast goose as the main dish and rosy-cheeked girls as a spicy dessert.

And then one day the poet awoke to find himself plucked of his last stolen penny. Once more he resolved to leave Paris— and this time he kept his resolution. Slinging a peddler's pack over his shoulder, in order to forestall any suspicious questioning as to his business, he tramped off in the direction of Anjou.

It was a long road he was now compelled to travel. For five

years he sneaked in and out of various towns and villages "through the back door." Fearful of the "brass buttons" of the gendarmerie, he slept for the most part under haystacks or in deserted barns. Occasionally he would stop for a snack at a country wineshop, amusing the bumpkins with his ribald verses and picking their pockets as they gaped at him with admiration. Always he kept glancing furtively behind him, expecting at any moment to feel a heavy hand upon his shoulder. And on many occasions indeed his nimble fists and his uncontrolled temper landed him in an overnight cell. With his every arrest he feared that the old robbery at the College of Navarre would rise out of the past to carry him off to the gibbet. But as the years went on he began at last to hope that this one crime, at least, would remain in the limbo of unsolved mysteries. Thank the devil for that! Yet twice he found himself in a death cell on other charges—many a trivial crime in those days was punishable by "dangling and strangling." Fortunately he was able, through the intercession of Father Guillaume and his other friends, to escape the rope on both occasions.

And so he dragged his bleeding feet through the dust and the mud in an endless effort to escape from his fate—from his own unhappy self. A pitiable, revolting, enchanting figure, this satyr singer of the filthy stews and the starry heavens—a ribald, swearing, dreaming, dangerous, jolly, tragic creature, gaunt as a skeleton and ugly as a toad. His long stay in prison and his fear of death had reduced his already emaciated body to a tortured bundle of nerves. Again and again he had been put through the third degree. Water had been poured down his throat through a funnel until his heart and his lungs had been ready to burst. The dampness of the prison had penetrated to the very marrow of his bones. His ill-nourished health had completely broken down, and he was now a consumptive for life. He was the pathetic symbol of existence reduced to the lowest denominator—a clod of filthy human soil compounded of poverty, suffering and crime.

Yet the seed of genius had been planted in it, and it needed just this combination of poverty and suffering and crime to flower into the master poem of his life—the *Great Testament.*

IV

THE *Great Testament* is to the *Little Testament* as the sun is to the moon—a bigger, warmer, more dazzling and more painful body of light. His device in the writing of the *Little Testament* had been the words—*Je ris en pleurs*, I laugh through my tears. For the composition of the *Great Testament* he seems to have adopted the exact opposite of this device. For here he weeps through his laughter. In this poem—it is really a collection of poems—he can still jest, but there is a noble sadness in the manner of his jesting. Villon has now become thoroughly acquainted with the stupidity and the sublimity of man. He has learned through suffering. He has probed to the very bottom of misery and found there the secret of beauty. His mature imagination has discovered the bitter pathos of life and the pathetic bitterness of death.

The *Little Testament*, in spite of its occasional grandeur, is a burlesque. The *Great Testament*, in spite of its frequent vulgarities, is a grandiose hymn. He wrote the greater part of this work, it is interesting to note, while he was awaiting execution in prison. It is the final confession of one of the world's most despicable scoundrels who nevertheless possessed the grace of devotion and the gift of music in his soul.

The poem begins with an apology for his wasted life. He has supped his fill of shame, yet he believes that he has been neither altogether foolish nor altogether wise. His life has been harnessed to sorrow, with necessity holding the reins. "Necessity drives men astray, and hunger goads the wolf to leap snarling from the woods."

But what is the good of lamenting our past misfortunes? After all, there is no life without suffering. Rich man, poor man, beggarman, thief, all of us come to the selfsame grief. Every adventure is but a road to death. "Even Helen dies, and Paris;

and there is no death without pain. . . . And when death has
seized you by the throat"—Villon's mind was very much occupied with his own impending fate when he wrote these lines—
"a sweat descends upon your limbs. God, what a sweat! And
there is no one can relieve you of your agony: no child or brother
or sister who can volunteer to take your place. . . . Death makes
you shiver and go white, turns your nose into a hook, tightens
your veins, causes your neck to swell, your flesh to go soft, your
nerves and joints to stretch and dilate. . . . O body of woman,
so tender and smooth and precious and soft, must you, too, be
subjected to this terrible doom?"

And this thought leads him to sing one of the saddest, sweetest
songs that ever came from the heart of man—the *Ballade des
Dames du Temps Jadis.* Innumerable English translations have
been made of this *Ballade of Dead Ladies.* But not one of them has
caught the spirit of the original—not even the half-successful
version of Dante Gabriel Rossetti, with its haunting line, "But
where are the snows of yesteryear?" Compared to the poignant
freshness of such lines as

> Où sont-ils, où, Vierge souvraine?
> Mais où sont les neiges d'antan?

even the best of the English versions are like the desiccated
petals of a flower pressed between the pages of a musty book.

Villon follows the *Ballade* with a few other poems of a similar
trend, and then he shakes himself free of his melancholy
thoughts. For he is a poet of many moods. After the cloud
comes a burst of sunlight. Once more the air is filled with the
careless laughter of the vagabond. Since life is so short and pain
so certain, let us stop regretting the past and dreading the future.
Let us be merry today. Let us gather the grapes while the soft
ripe juice can be crushed out of them. "Take them right and
left, and spare nary a one." Tomorrow they will be wrinkled
and dry.

And then, with another sudden change of temper, Villon
cries out that the devil is in all women and that for a single

moment of joy they burden you with a lifetime of sorrow. Never put your faith in the daughters of Eve.

> They are sweet as civet in your eye,
> But trust them, and your peace is done.
> For white or brown, and low or high,
> Happy are they that deal with none.

We have now descended to a lower level in his poetry. Again he is the sardonic street gamin who thumbs his nose at fate and who greets the solemn *citoyens* of Paris with a volley of obscene catcalls. We come to the body of the *Testament*, in which he bequeaths a thousand gibes and jests and curses to all and sundry. And then, sinking still lower in his poetry—and in his soul—he paints a realistic picture of his life in a brothel. This close-up view of Villon's career at its low ebb is one of the frankest and one of the most sordid poems in any language. He is employed as waiter, janitor and general pimp at the bordel of the fat Margot. He works for her not only because she pays him well but because she intrigues him. "For her sweet sake I gird on my sword and buckler. When customers arrive I run and get a pitcher to bring them wine . . . I serve them with cheese and bread and fruit; and if they are free with their money, I urge them to visit us again whenever they are in the mood for sport. . . ."

But Villon is not always happy in this "house of joy." "When Margot comes to bed without my money I cannot bear the sight of her . . . I snatch her clothes and swear that I will sell them for my overdue pay. . . . Then she screams and calls the devil to witness that she will not let me do it. Whereupon I biff her in the face with my closed fist and leave my autograph under her nose. . . ."

An ugly trade. But what is a poor devil of a poet to do when he has no board or bed and his hopes are all in tatters? At least he has found a temporary home here, and food, and a bit of the warmth of human sympathy. "Wind, hail or frost, my bread is baked. I am a lecher, and Margot is a slut. We are two of a

kind and equally worthless." But we understand each other.
"Bad cat, bad rat. We are in love with filth, and filth is in love
with us, in this brothel where we drive our dishonorable trade."

Well, ladies and gentlemen, here you have him at his un-
adorned ugliest. Do you shut your eyes and hold your nose?
Do you feel nauseated at the offensive picture? Then turn
away, if you will, to your good and holy poets and see whether
you can find in any of them a poem that is more imperishably
tender or more passionately devout than Villon's *Ballade to the
Madonna*. This poem, which lies buried like a nugget of gold in
the muck of his indecent laughter, is a prayer to the Virgin put
into the mouth of Villon's old mother. Let us view this prayer
in the exquisite though inadequate paraphrase of J. M. Synge:

"Mother of God that's Lady of the Heavens, take myself, the
poor sinner, the way I'll be along with them that's chosen.

"Let you say to your own Son that He'd have a right to forgive my share of sins, when it's the like He'd done, many's the
day, with big and famous sinners. I'm a poor aged woman was
never at school, and is no scholar with letters, but I've seen
pictures in the chapel with Paradise on one side, and harps and
pipes in it, and the place on the other side, where sinners do
be boiled in torment; the one gave me great joy, and the other
a great fright and scaring; let me have the good place, Mother
of God, and it's in your faith I'll live always. . . .

"It's yourself that bore Jesus, that has no end or death, and
He the Lord Almighty, that took our weakness and gave Him-
self to sorrows, a young and gentle man. It's Himself is Our
Lord, surely, and it's in that faith I'll live always."

It is at such moments that the heart of Villon comes passionately close to the heart of mankind. For his *Ballade to the Madonna* is not merely the individual prayer of Villon, it is the
universal prayer of Man—

God's waif who sings his mournful magic strain,
And lives a lackey in the House of Pain.

V

VILLON concludes his *Great Testament*, one of the most amazing mixtures of sublimity and slime in all literature, with an epitaph for his own grave:

"This good-for-nothing, crackbrained outcast has returned his body to the Earth, our common Mother. The worms will not find much meat on it, for hunger has already bitten it too near the bone. . . . Rest was never his until death came and booted him out of the world. Lord of Mercy, have pity on his soul and give him eternal peace."

Pauvre François! He was to have another tilt with his restless fate before he came to his final peace. One day he got mixed up in a drunken brawl and was arrested. This in itself was nothing unusual or particularly serious. But the Parisian police were anxious to get rid of him "for good and all." Most of his cronies were already "dangling and drying" in the air. It would be a healthy thing for the city, thought the gendarmes, if they could find an excuse to string up Villon's body, too, alongside of the others. Accordingly they unearthed a number of his forgotten crimes, including the now solved robbery at the College of Navarre, and passed the death sentence upon him.

And so here he was, facing the gibbet for the third—and, he felt hopelessly certain, for the last—time. *Grand Dieu*, what an end! As he lay in the damp straw of his cell he pictured his body "swaying and swiggling at the butt of a rope . . . the way he'd be half an hour, in great anguish, getting his death." And after that his flesh would be rotting in the air, and the birds would be pecking at his eyes, and the young toughs of the gutter would be bringing their wenches to dance under the gibbet and to point with ribald gestures at his skeleton swinging in the moonlight. He covered his face with his hands to shut out the nightmare.

But he awoke from the nightmare—to a dismal dawn. His death sentence, thanks once more to the interposition of Father Guillaume, was commuted to a ten years' exile. He was allowed three days to prepare for the journey and to take leave of his friends. And then on a bleak January morning (in 1463) he dragged his lean and lonely figure out of the Gate of Saint Jacques and trudged off into the drifted snow.

And into the winter mists of oblivion. For we never hear of him again.

MILTON

Great Poems by Milton

Paradise Lost.
Paradise Regained.
Samson Agonistes.
L'Allegro.
Il Penseroso.
Comus.
Lycidas.
Hymn on the Morning of Christ's
    Nativity.
On His Blindness.
To Mr Lawrence.
To Cyriack Skinner.

To the Lady Margaret Ley.
At a Solemn Music.
Massacre in Piemont.
When the Assault Was Intended
    to the City.
Psalms.
Odes.
Sonnets.
Elegies.
Epigrams.
To the Bishop of Winchester.
Latin Poems.

John Milton

1608–1674

To BE A GREAT POET, observes Taine, you must be a great man.
Milton fulfilled that requirement. Throughout his life he was a
soldier in the forefront of the battle for human freedom.

He strove greatly and he suffered greatly. He lived in a
tragic age, and his own life was like a tragedy in three acts.
The first act (1608–39) was a period of education, of experi-
mentation, of instinctive groping toward the light. The child,
conscious of nobility within himself, grew into the man who expected nobility of everybody else. Dedicated to justice, he tried
to discover and to perfect a language that would serve as the
bugle call to justice among all men. His poetry was his religion.
He adopted literature as a priesthood. He wrote not for personal
honor but for universal honesty. In his effort to find the right
medium for the expression of his best thoughts, he tried many
different forms of poetry—the lyric, the masque, the sonnet, the
elegy, the pastoral, the ode. At first, in his eagerness to reach
the entire world, he chose Latin as the vehicle for his poetry,
since Latin was the international language of the day. But later
on, as he realized that a poet must first of all address himself to
his own people, he abandoned his Latin idiom and began to
write in his native tongue. He saw his nation suffering from its

superstitions and its oppressions, and he tried to liberate it with his songs. But he suffered from the excessive optimism of inexperience. He was a young prophet who believed too much in the intelligence of his public. As he grew older he found that it was impossible to reform politics with poetry. He needed a simpler language in order to reach the ears of the public. And so he courageously renounced his ambition to be a great poet. For more than twenty years he devoted himself almost exclusively to revolutionary manifestoes in prose.

This was the second act of the drama of his life (1640–62). From a distinguished poet he allowed himself to become a despised pamphleteer. He attacked the more covetous members of the clergy, and he called down upon himself the hatred of the bigots. He questioned the justice of the divorce laws and was repaid with the wages of derision. He denounced the tyranny of the nobility and was himself denounced as a traitor to his country. When Charles I was executed he defended the rights of the rebels who had brought the royal criminal to justice. The secret adherents of the king made a mental note of this defense of liberty and vowed vengeance against its author. For the time being, to be sure, Milton was safe from his enemies. But he was not safe from his destiny. Appointed as the foreign-language secretary to Oliver Cromwell, he worked so hard in the service of freedom that he lost the sight of his eyes. But he was not disheartened. He had lived to see his dream realized His country was free! . . . And then came the turning point of the tragedy. The republic was overthrown, and the monarchy was restored. Old, blind, disillusioned and heartbroken, Milton was cast into prison. His vision of a better world had been but a foolish mirage. His country was not yet willing to be free. Milton was but another of the rejected prophets of an ungrateful race.

The third act of the tragedy (1663–74) began upon a quiet enough note. But it was the calm before the storm. Disgusted with the foolishness of man, Milton turned to the wisdom of God. Once more he took refuge in his poetry and pictured the epic struggle between good and evil, with man as the pawn. Milton's *Paradise Lost* was an escape from himself. It was an appeal from human to divine judgment, a plea directed by the advocate of life to the supreme court of eternity. But his countrymen, in whose behalf he had braved the miseries of the earth and challenged the mysteries of the heavens, remained thankless to the end. They repaid the bread of his generosity with the stones of persecution until finally, like the defeated champion in the Old Testament, he groped his way into the temple of the Philistines and shook it down in ruins over their heads. His poem on Samson, the last of his works, was a fitting climax to the tragedy of his life—a life, to quote his own words, "dark in light" and "exposed to daily fraud, contempt, abuse and wrong." Paraphrase another passage in this poem, and you have a perfect summary of his own career:

> Milton hath quit himself
> Like Milton, and heroically hath finished
> A life heroic.

In the life of Milton the Great Dramatist of Heaven showed the little dramatists of the earth how to write a perfect tragedy.

II

MILTON has been justly called the "splendid bridge from the old world to the new." For in his genius he combined the magnificent scholarship of the Renaissance with the magnificent rebellion of the Reformation. He came of a family of scholars and rebels. His grandfather was a learned Catholic, and his father was a disinherited Protestant. Undismayed by his punishment for his adoption of the Protestant faith, his father had made a success of his life. By profession a scrivener—a man who prepared legal documents for attorneys—he devoted himself to his two favorite hobbies, music and poetry, acquired a "plentiful estate" and bought a house on Bread Street, a thoroughfare in the business heart of the city yet close enough to the countryside to be filled with the fragrance of the meadows on summer nights. It was in this house on Bread Street that the future poet of Paradise was born.

The third of six children, John Milton grew up in an atmosphere of scholarship, refinement and independence. "My father," he writes, "was distinguished by the undeviating integrity of his life; my mother, by the esteem in which she was held and the alms which she bestowed. My father destined me from a child to the pursuits of literature; and my appetite for knowledge was so voracious that, from twelve years of age, I hardly ever left my studies or went to bed before midnight. . . . My eyes were naturally weak, and I was subject to frequent headaches; which, however, could not chill the ardor of my curiosity or retard the progress of my improvement."

There were plenty of family discussions that helped to feed young Milton's insatiable "curiosity for improvement." Following the example of his father, Milton was not the youngster to keep his convictions to himself. His teachers looked upon him as a scholar of "excellent erudition and somewhat strange views." And it was only the excellence of his erudition that saved him from punishment on those frequent occasions when Dr Gill, the headmaster of St Paul's, "enjoyed one of his whipping fits."

At the University of Cambridge, which he entered at sixteen, he was regarded as an outspoken radical. He declared that it was hard for him to digest "the asinine feast of sowthistles and brambles" with which the professors stuffed the students' minds while they "persisted in starving their spirits." Milton had a scuffle with one of his tutors—an act of insubordination which resulted in his temporary dismissal from the college.

Milton was a rebel. But he was not a boor. Indeed, his handsome face and his refined bearing won for him the title of "the Cambridge Lady." Teachers and students alike, while they disapproved of his ideas, respected his character. And his intellect. When he left Cambridge he thanked "the Fellows of that College who, at my parting, after I had taken two degrees, assured me of their singular good affection toward me."

He was now a bachelor and master of arts, an expert in eight languages and a poet who could court the muse in Latin and in English with equal facility. He had decided to devote his life to literature. His father had hoped that he might combine his poetry with the priesthood, but Milton had set his mind definitely against the church as a profession. He was too good a Christian, he said, to make a business of Christianity. He preferred to serve the Lord as a prophet rather than as a priest.

With this high purpose in mind he retired to Horton, the "village of rivulets and nightingales." He remained here for five years—the happiest period of his life. Thanks to his father's industry, he was freed from the immediate burden of working for a living. He could study and dream and indulge his desire to "hear himself think in the solitude of the woodlands." He read the classics, he mastered the organ, he studied mathematics, he explored the Bible and he observed from a distance "the inquisitous and tyrannical duncery" of the oppressors of mankind.

And all these experiences he distilled into his early poems. These poems were few in number, "but all of them roses"— *L'Allegro*, *Il Penseroso*, *Comus*, *Lycidas*, a handful of other experiments every one of which was a perfect achievement in its field.

Yet Milton was not satisfied with his work. "I am letting my wings grow and preparing to fly, but my Pegasus has not yet feathers enough to soar aloft in the fields of air." He would go to Italy and there, under its soft skies, he would try to further the sunward progress of his poetry.

His Italian trip was something of a triumphal procession for a young poet of twenty-four. The leading scholars of Italy were familiar with his Latin if not with his English verses. They received him like "a traveler returned to his native land." He accepted his honors modestly, steeped himself in the poetry of Dante and of Petrarch and planned to write a leisurely epic on the exploits of King Arthur.

But suddenly there was an interruption to his pleasures and his plans. His country was threatened by a civil war. This was no time for a patriotic Englishman to be writing elegant verses in Italy. Hurriedly he packed his belongings and returned to England.

The first act of his drama was finished.

III

IN THE SECOND ACT of his drama Milton lived, instead of writing, an epic. Having found lodgings in London, he placed himself upon the firing line of the revolution, sending broadside after broadside of propaganda into the ranks of the enemy. "Inasmuch as I had so prepared myself from my youth that I could not be ignorant (as to) what is of divine and what of human right, I resolved to transfer into this struggle all my genius and all the strength of my industry." He was determined, at the sacrifice of his poetry and, if necessary, of his life, to defend the human rights of the people against the so-called "divine" rights of their oppressors. He thoroughly disliked the "turbulent, noisy sea" of religious and political controversy, but he had enlisted as a soldier in the people's cause and he would stay in the fight until the end. He refused to buy his "ease and leisure with the sweat of other men." First of all he directed his attack against the "money-changers who were polluting the temple of Christianity"—men who, "ordained to be the pastors of the flock had allowed themselves to become the wolves; and who, instead of feeding their people, were feeding *upon* them."

Milton, it must be emphasized, was not fighting against the church; he was merely fighting against its abuses. Like the prophets of the Old Testament, he "pealed forth the thunder of the Lord" against His servants who had betrayed their trust. And, too, like the prophets of the Old Testament, he knew that he courted danger and even possible death when he dared to assail the strongholds of privilege with the weapons of truth. But he never hesitated.

Not even when the Parliament passed a law against the free-dom of speech. Charged by the Public Censors (August 24, 1644) with the publication of "scandalous and seditious" pamphlets, he replied to the charge by issuing "the most scandalous and seditious pamphlet of them all." This was his famous *Areopagitica*, a timely and timeless defense of the right of free speech. It is almost as vicious to kill a good book, he points out, as it is to kill a man. "He who kills a man kills a reasonable creature, God's image; but he who destroys a good book kills reason itself, kills the image of God, as it were, in the eye. Many a man lives a burden to the earth; but a good book is the precious lifeblood of a master spirit, embalmed and treasured up on purpose to a life beyond life." He who suppresses a good book, therefore, "slays an immortality rather than a life."

In such wise did he defy the censors. But more daring even than his defiance against the censors was his opposition to the king. In the struggle between tyranny and rebellion he un-hesitatingly took the side of the rebels. And when in the winter of 1649 the head of Charles I rolled upon the scaffold Milton not only sanctioned but actually sanctified the execution. "The Lord," he wrote to his rebellious nation, "has gloriously delivered you . . . from tyranny. . . . He has endowed you with greatness of mind to be the first of mankind who, after having conquered their own king and had him delivered into their hands, have not scrupled to condemn him judicially and, pursuant to that sentence of condemnation, to put him to death."

And then Milton went on to admonish his countrymen to moderation in the midst of their victory: "After the performing of so glorious an act (the execution of Charles), you ought to do nothing that is mean and little. . . . As you have subdued your enemies in the field, so must you demonstrate that you of all mankind are best able to subdue ambition, avarice, the love of riches . . . to show as great justice and temperance in maintaining your liberty as you have shown courage in freeing yourselves from slavery."

These words, observed the hardheaded leaders of the revolution, were as impractical as they were noble. Milton had overestimated, they said, the human capacity for goodness. He believed that a new lamp had suddenly been lighted in the soul of man. But he failed to recognize the walls of mud that housed this lamp. The millennium, to Milton's great disappointment, did not arrive with the Revolution of 1649.

IV

IN THE MIDST of the national tempest Milton was now caught up in a domestic whirlpool. At the age of thirty-five he had married a girl of seventeen. It was an unfortunate match for both, since there was as much difference in their tastes as in their ages. Mary Powell was gay, lighthearted and lightheaded—hardly the companion for a man who lived perpetually in the clouds and who "carried his head like a sacrament." Moreover, Mary was a royalist, while Milton was a rebel. Mary stood just one month of Milton's rebellious austerity, and then she turned rebel herself. She left him. Milton sent letter after letter to her, but she remained stubbornly at her father's house. Whereupon Milton, always insistent upon what he considered the just cause, took the fight to the enemy. He wrote a pamphlet in favor of divorce—a veritable bombshell in those days of puritanical conventionality. But he went even further than that. Considering himself, owing to his wife's stubbornness, at least morally if not legally divorced, he began to pay court to another young lady. This final boldness on Milton's part brought Mary Powell back to her senses. One day, as he was visiting the house of a friend, he was surprised to find that Mary had come there ahead of him. Falling on her knees, she begged him with tears in her eyes to forgive her.

Milton, "as one disarmed," forgot his anger. The uncongenial marriage knot was retied—to their mutual regret. Mary took her entire family—father, mother, several brothers and sisters—into the Milton household. From that day on there was no peace either for Milton or for his wife. Milton was "constitutionally unfit to soothe and fondle," and Mary was "mentally unfit to converse and consort with." The house in which they lived, none too big even for a small and concordant family, was now a continual hurricane of discord. Milton was not made for human companionship. The Powells incessantly got on his nerves—and he on theirs. Added to the disharmony of a large family was the noisy restlessness of a poorly disciplined classroom. For Milton had opened an academy in his house. His father's fortune had been seriously impaired as a result of the civil war, and Milton had found it necessary to take in pupils for a living.

After the execution of Charles I, however, he was able to dispense with his academy. Oliver Cromwell, the dictator of the Commonwealth, appointed him "Secretary for Foreign Tongues." His duties consisted in "the preparation and translation of despatches from and to foreign governments." His pen, it was understood, was also to be at the beck and call of the new government's propaganda department.

It was a tremendous task that Milton had undertaken—so tremendous, indeed, that he lost his eyesight in its performance. His physician had warned him of his impending blindness. He had urged him to take a rest from his labors. But Milton wouldn't listen to him. "The choice lay before me," he tells us, "between dereliction of a supreme duty and loss of eyesight. In such a case I could not listen to a physician . . . I could but obey the inward monitor that spoke to me from above."

His blindness threw him into dismay but not into despair. "If my affliction is incurable, I prepare and compose myself accordingly." He found a great measure of comfort, indeed of exaltation, in the fact that he had sacrificed his eyes in behalf of his country.

> What supports me, dost thou ask?
> The conscience, friend, to have lost them overplied
> In liberty's defense, my noble task,
> Of which all Europe rings from side to side.

Now that a veil had been drawn between himself and the immediate world, he took joy in the inner vision that he entertained of a greater, newer, better world. A world of free men, in which there would be but a single compassionate master—God.

But this vision, too, was to be snatched away from him. Oliver Cromwell, whom Milton regarded as God's chosen minister in the establishment of the new order, had turned back from his original inclination "toward a generous view of things." He had gone the way of all dictators. From a protector he had become an oppressor.

And then came the death of Cromwell and the restoration of the Stuarts to the throne. Monarchy was once more in the saddle. Milton's dream of a freer world had proved to be but the sleeping vision of a blind man. The awakening was to plunge him into a poignant realization of his blindness. "Day brought back my night," he tells us bitterly in one of his sonnets.

In the night that followed the funeral of the republic many of the noblest men in England were put to death. A few were fortunate enough to escape with a prison term. Among these lesser victims of a wholesale vengeance was the blind poet. For a time he had eluded capture by hiding himself in the house of a friend. His books were burned by the public hangman, his property was confiscated and a mock funeral was held in his dishonor for the amusement of the pleasure-loving King Charles II. And then his hiding place was discovered and he was carried off to jail. To his friends who urged him to make his peace with the king he replied, "My aim is to live and die an honest man."

And thus ended the second act in the drama of his life.

V

FORTUNATELY for posterity, King Charles was too easygoing an adversary to clamor for Milton's death. He ordered the poet's release, and Milton returned to the fitful dream of his life. It

Villon

Milton

had been a life full of sadness. His first wife had died. He had married a second time and had again become a widower two years later. A third marriage had brought him further obligations but no further happiness. The prophets of the world are made for solitude. Like a radiating fire, they warm at a distance but scorch at too close a range. The members of Milton's household, even his own daughters, found his resoluteness unendurable. They were compelled against their will to serve as his secretaries. Sometimes they would be wakened in the middle of the night because he happened to be in an inspired mood and wanted to dictate his thoughts before they escaped him. One of his daughters, on hearing that he was about to be married, remarked dryly that his marriage was indifferent news to her but that his death would be *good* news. It was bitter to be afflicted with sightless eyes and a tenacious will.

Bitter—and superb. It was one of the grand spectacles of man's struggle against death—this unconquerable determination of a poet to translate his vision of heaven when his earthly vision had been lost. To the friends who occasionally came to visit him he looked like a stricken demigod. Dressed in quiet black, he sat in an armchair as on a throne. The room was hung with old green draperies. His oval face was pale but not sallow. His eyes, blue gray and clear, betrayed no hint of blindness. His light brown hair, parted in the middle, fell in long waves over his shoulders. His features were marked by a "severe composure," save for a sensitive pouting of the mouth. "The entire expression was that of English intrepidity mixed with unutterable sorrow." Such, at this period, was the poet who was writing his *Paradise Lost*—a Christian Homer calling upon the gods and the angels to come down and walk among men.

Paradise Lost, to quote Milton's own words, was an epic attempt to "justify the ways of God to Man." But, incorrigible rebel that he was, what he actually succeeded in doing was to justify the ways of Man to God. His human sympathies were with the sinners rather than with the censors. He drew even

Satan, the rebel against God, with a charitable pen. Milton's Satan is not so much a fomenter of anarchy as a fighter against authority. "Better to reign in hell," exclaims Satan, "than serve in heaven."

Milton, observed the mystic poet, William Blake, "was of the Devil's party without knowing it." Blake might have been nearer the truth, perhaps, had he said that Milton was of *Man's* party without knowing it. The blind poet's tenderest words are reserved for the moral blindness of his fellow men. He punishes Adam and he defends him. He scolds Eve and he pities her. Adam is not quite sure, because Milton was not quite sure, whether the expulsion from Paradise was not after all a good thing for Man. "Full of doubt I stand," muses Adam as the gates of Paradise close behind him,

> Whether I should repent me now of sin
> By me done and occasioned, and rejoice
> Much more, that much more good thereof shall spring.

It is better to lose and to recover our heaven than never to have felt the sadness of the loss and the joy of the recovery. Without human suffering there can be no human tenderness. And one of the tenderest scenes in *Paradise Lost*, in all poetry, is the departure of Adam and Eve from their lost Paradise:

> They, looking back, all the eastern side beheld
> Of Paradise, so late their happy seat,
> Waved over by that flaming brand; the gate
> With dreadful faces thronged and fiery arms.
> Some natural tears they dropped, but wiped them soon.
> The world was all before them, where to choose
> Their place of rest, and Providence their guide.
> They, hand in hand, with wandering steps and slow,
> Through Eden took their solitary way.

VI

MILTON, too, had lost his Paradise—the Eden of a free England. And sadly he traced his solitary way to death. His great epic poetry fell upon a heedless world. It had taken him ten years to write *Paradise Lost,* and the publishers repaid him with five pounds for his labor. He was old and sick and discouraged. His daughters had left him. His house on Bread Street had been destroyed in the Great London Fire (1666). His name was a byword of derision among the Royalists who were now entrenched in their power. It was under these circumstances that he undertook to write his last, and by some considered his greatest, poem—the tragedy of Samson. This poem is the symbolical picture of his own career. For Milton, as Edward Garnett points out, is a counterpart of Samson—"old, blind, helpless, mocked, decried, miserable in the failure of all his ideals, upheld only by his faith and his own unconquerable spirit."

But this poem is a picture not only of Milton but of the English people as well. They too, in the days of Charles II, were helpless and defeated and decried. It was bitter gall to Milton to see "this extolled and magnified nation . . . falling back, or rather creeping back, to their once abjured and detested thraldom of kingship." The English nation was an enslaved and enfeebled Samson. But the day would yet come when it would "burst its bonds and bring down ruin upon the Philistines!"

It was in this hope that he died (November 8, 1674). A mere handful of people at the time were aware of the fact that the world had lost one of its prophets. Most of the contemporary English critics ignored his death, just as they had ignored his life. One of them, however, a certain Mr Thurloe, condescended to take notice of him. And this is what he said: "John Milton was a blind old man who wrote Latin documents."

But the verdict of posterity has come closer to the heart of his genius. And this verdict is—that Milton was one of the few who were able to see in a generation of blind men.

POPE

Great Poems by Pope

An Essay on Criticism.
An Essay on Man.
The Rape of the Lock.
The Dunciad.
Translation of the *Iliad*.
Translation of (parts of) the *Odyssey*.
Translation of the *Odes* of Horace.
Ode on Solitude.
Windsor Forest.
The Dying Christian to His Soul.

Ode for Music on St Cecilia's Day.
Eloisa to Abélard.
Epistle to Dr Arbuthnot.
Epigrams.
Epitaphs.
Pastorals.
Satires.
The Balance of Europe.
Messiah.
The Challenge.
The Looking-Glass.

Alexander Pope

1688–1774

HE WAS A "crazy little carcass" of a man. He had the arms and the legs of a spider. He protruded behind and before. But he had a sound philosophy in his head. " 'Tis a pity I am so sickly," he told himself. And he looked at his hard-living, hard-drinking literary friends and added, " 'Tis a pity *they* are so healthy." He was a wit, but he had no humor—a satirist who ridiculed but rarely laughed. For to laugh, as someone has pointed out, you must have a heart full of tears—and Pope had only a head full of manners.

From childhood his ambition had been to sparkle as the chief ornament in fashionable London society. But all the demons of destiny seemed to have been arrayed against him from his birth. As a cripple, he was debarred from most of the activities of his able-bodied companions. As the son of a commoner, he was denied the privileges and the distinctions of an inherited title. And as a Catholic, he was precluded from a university training and a public career. Amidst her plentiful shower of brickbats, however, Nature had carelessly tossed him a nugget of gold. He was born with a genius for writing poetry.

And a level head. He never forgot the advice given him in his early years. "We've had great poets, Alexander, but few who were *correct*. Be elegant in your phrases, raise the topic of a dainty eyebrow to a place among the stars, transfer the drawing rooms of London to the heights of Mount Olympus, make the beauty of a duchess the theme of a conversation for the gods, and you shall be the one true monarch of this British realm."

At the age of twelve he laid down a systematic plan for a lifetime of study. He seized upon knowledge, especially *poetical* knowledge, with the rapacity of a tiger. At fourteen he perfected his style in the polished versification of the heroic rhymed couplet, made famous by the courtly pen of Dryden. At eighteen he considered himself an established poet and he commenced to frequent Will's Coffee House—the gathering place of the literary wits of the day. At twenty-three he published a cleverly conceived and elaborately executed poem on the canons of literary criticism. This work was adjudged a masterpiece by a majority of the critics. But they merely re-echoed the poet's own high estimate of himself. Long before this he had discovered a lifelong avocation. He devoted all his spare time to the pleasure of reading his verse. He was certain that "not one gentleman in sixty . . . could comprehend him." He was convinced that he was the greatest genius of the century. He expressed nothing but contempt for the rest of the world.

This pathetic and misshapen little body was suffering from a curious malady, an eternal lust for power—the power of the mind. For that was the weapon which provided him with all his protection. A playful dog could knock his body to the dust and drag it unceremoniously away. But someday all mankind would tremble before his intellect. Someday he would be privileged to see "men not afraid of God, afraid of me!"

II

MORALLY, politically and culturally the society of manners into which the poet had interloped was made to order for a satirist. It was an age "when wives locked Adam out of Eden and shut themselves up with the devil." The large number of distilleries in London, observed a contemporary historian, "is more significant than any event in the purely political or military annals of the century." Physicians recommended gambling to their patients as a form of distraction. It was no time for weaklings. Anybody who, because of a frail constitution, found himself condemned to a life of "virtuous boredom" merely "hastened his end by good living."

It was an age of political and social and literary squabbles in which gentlemen threw filth at one another. And Pope made his literary bow in the most approved fashion. With the brash impertinence of youth he wrote a review of the pastoral poems of a celebrated contemporary poet—a man who was several years his senior. This "social lion of the coffeehouses," Ambrose Phillips, had composed verses that for a long time had been titillating the second-rate ears of London society. And on the occasion of his latest volume the legion of the faithful were most audible in their praise. Pope's review, too, started off like an assenting voice in the general chorus of hosannas. In justice to Mr Phillips, he wrote, it would be well "to examine certain passages of his poetry that all the critics seem to have overlooked and which are most characteristic of his genius." And then he quoted, among other poems, a shepherd's dirge to his love:

> Ah me the while! ah me, the luckless day,
> Ah luckless lad! the rather might I say,
> Ah silly I! more silly than my sheep,
> Which on the flowery plain I once did keep.

"Surely he vies with Virgil in the stately sublimity of his poetic sensibility. The verse *Ah silly I! more silly than my sheep* is unexcelled for its expression of the poet's simple philosophy."

And then came the sudden subtle sting at the end: "How prettily Mr Phillips asks his sheep to teach him how to bleat!"

Fashionable London was aghast at this merciless unveiling of Ambrose Phillips' "bleating muse" by a youth scarcely out of his swaddling clothes. Mr Phillips himself took immediate steps "to avenge his honor." Having ascertained the name of the coffeehouse that Pope frequented, he repaired thither with a birch which he publicly swore he would apply to within an inch of Pope's life "if that little fellow ever sets foot in Button's again." Fortunately Pope got wind of the intention of his brother poet and changed the scene of his conviviality to another coffeehouse.

But he couldn't change his nose for satire. Before long he had thrust this impudent nose into another quarrel. In a poem discussing the ancient and the modern drama he made a sly and rather savage thrust at the failure of a play written by a certain Mr Dennis, the vainest if not the ablest of contemporary playwrights.

Beware of an artist wounded in his vanity. Dennis lost no time in striking back at the presumptuous upstart. And his attack took the form of personal abuse. "Who is this young, short, squab gentleman whose crooked back resembles the very bow of the god of Love?" . . . He may advocate the dramatic standards of the ancient Greeks, "but he has reason to thank the gods that *he* was born a modern." For, according to ancient custom, only those babies born sound in body were permitted to survive. "Had Mr Pope been born of Greek parents, his life would have been no longer than the fame of one of his poems— half a day."

Such was the facetious pleasantry of the times—an age of slugging below the belt and with brassbound fists. Pope recoiled from the blow. But he recovered quickly enough. So *that* was how they wanted to fight? Well, he would show them who was the better fighter! Let them just try to kill his poor little body, to throttle the feeble spark of life with which a stingy destiny had handicapped him. He had a far stronger weapon than theirs —the forked lightning of a flame-tipped tongue!

And so this mighty Jupiter of four feet sat in his study, his body propped up by pillows until his elbows barely reached the level of his writing table, and manufactured the thunderbolts of his verses. He relieved his constant headaches by inhaling cups of steamed coffee. He lived to write. Day and night he thought of nothing but ideas for dazzling and devastating rhymes—rhymes that would be the admiration and the terror of the world.

His mind had become a trick mirror of nature. It distorted the foibles of the day into hilarious travesties. An amusing episode had taken place in one of the London salons. Lord Petre, a hot-blooded young charmer of twenty-two, had applied a pair of scissors to the golden head of Miss Arabella Fermor, a noted beauty of the day, and with "one fell snip" had parted the lady from a lock of her hair.

There was a terrible scandal. The respective families of the young lord and the young lady engaged in an epic parlor warfare that reverberated over the teacups of London; and Alexander Pope, playing Homer to this modern conflict, composed a mock heroic poem on *The Rape of the Lock*. It was a jeweled pin of satirical verse that transfixed the butterfly wings of this society to eternal ridicule. Never before had the elegant inanities and the stupid preoccupations of Lady Arabella and her friends been exposed in such language of honeyed poison. "At every word a reputation dies." The fashionable world was both shocked and entranced. Once more the elfin poet's pen had proved to be a wasp. With a bound he had become the Archbishop of Satire in England—a position of equal eminence to that held by his friend Jonathan Swift, the Dean of Derision in Ireland.

For years the rhyming Ariel and the prose Puck banded together at the club and indulged in duels of words about literature and life. Pope was instinctively attracted to this man with an intellect as restive as his own but with a physical vitality far more powerful to endure the ardors of life; and Swift was torn between amusement and admiration for this pitiable, majestic little poet who strutted about laced in stiff canvas to keep his miniature body erect and who wore three pairs of stockings to swell his pin-sized legs to something approaching the normal. Perhaps it was when he sat in the company of this pompous and pathetic Lilliputian with his shiny short sword at his side that the huge and somber Gulliver first conceived of his immortal satire about a whole island of pompous and pathetic little men.

It was a strange fellowship, indeed, that held the two sad purveyors of the world's great laughter so closely bound together. As the years progressed conversation between them became impossible. For Swift was growing more and more deaf, and Pope hadn't the physical strength to shout loudly enough. And as the dwarf and the titan sat for hours observing each other before going their ways, the old dean muttered, "Look at this abortion of a man on the legs of a spider. What a freak of the body!" And the young poet chuckled, "Look at these gloomy eyes with their glint of insanity. What a freak of the mind!"

Two products of the "elegant era"—an age of intellect without a heart.

III

IT WAS perfectly correct to pretend to your friends that you despised your own poetry. Why waste your time boasting about your work when everybody else is praising it? "I write," said Pope, "when I have nothing better to do." Yet those who knew him intimately were aware of the fact that he had his writing box placed on his bed before he rose to begin the day and that his servants were frequently called in the middle of the night to supply him with pencil and paper lest he lose a random thought. He kept thousands of pages of elegantly turned phrases which he sifted and scrambled and worked into his poems when the proper occasion arose. He polished and repolished his verses until it seemed as if they would expire through surfeit of wit "as bodies perish through excess of blood."

It was in this frame of mind that he set about translating the rugged *Iliad* of Homer into the elegance of his Georgian English. It was like dressing an eagle in the feathers of a peacock. With a graceful gesture of the wand he had transformed an epic drama into a pastoral idyl. "A very pretty poem, Mr Pope," remarked an astute critic, "but you must not call it Homer." Yet it tickled the fashionable palates of the eighteenth century and brought the author, for his efforts, a sum of money unequaled in the annals of poetry. The publisher alone realized from this translation a sufficient profit to enable him to retire from business and to buy himself into the office of High Sheriff of Sussex. As for Pope, he preened his little feathers with a false assumption of modesty, invested his riches to good advantage and despised the public that had made him rich.

For he regarded himself as a god among fops. Passion with them, he said, was merely fashion; and knowledge, sheer pretense. "A little learning is a dangerous thing." While engaged in the translation of the *Iliad* he had called upon Lord Halifax, one of the pillars of English society, who fancied himself a man of letters. At his lordship's request he had read him some of the verses. During the recital the "scholarly" nobleman assumed an air of ponderous concentration and declared at its conclusion: "I beg your pardon, Mr Pope, but there is something in that passage that does not please me. Be so good as to mark the place and consider it at your leisure." Three months later the poet returned with the manuscript untouched and reread the identical passage in an altered voice. "Ah, now the verses are perfectly right!" exclaimed the lord with a beaming face. "Nothing can be better!"

With the money he had received from his translation of the *Iliad* Pope was now able to buy an estate and to surrender himself to the life of ease and splendor which he had always envisaged. He was deluged with invitations from the great. He was patronized as much for the repulsiveness of his body as for the splendor of his mind. He took his meals with members of the Cabinet and with princes of the royal blood. Once, while the Prince of Wales was discussing the art of poetry, he fell asleep and began to snore.

"Sir," his servant told him on another occasion, "a lady called to see you while you were not at home. I could not make out her name, but she swore so dreadfully she must be a lady of quality." Meeting with fashionable ladies in waiting, using the private library of Lord Oxford, commanding the center of attraction wherever he stayed and whatever he did, he acted like a sick and peevish child in complete control of the nursery. He required constant attendance. He was unable to get out of bed or to dress himself unaided. Everywhere he went he was mothered and smothered.

He doted upon female society. He paid ardent and petulant court to Martha Blount, a neighbor of his youth and a member of his religion. He declared his passion to her in that strange egocentric tone he constantly assumed when he felt ill at ease. "It is true you are not handsome," he found the audacity to write. "And you are lonely, living away from the orbit of society . . . To correspond with Mr Pope may make anyone proud who lives under a dejection of heart in the country. Everyone values Mr Pope."

Martha accepted his affection with good humor and stood by him, nursing him intermittently—out of pity if not out of love—to the end of his life.

He was not quite so fortunate in another of his *affaires de cœur*. In the society of Lord Oxford he encountered a woman who was a proper match for his wit—Lady Mary Wortley Montagu. This "unconventional leader of a conventional set" had as a mere child, it was said, consented to the inscription of her name upon a drinking cup of the taverns, so that she might "ever after pass around from lip to lip."

Pope found himself completely under the spell of Lady Montagu. She had a masculine intellect. She was delighted with his poetry. She confessed herself enchanted at his mock attentions. "I hate all other women for your sake," he had declared to her in his grandest manner. And she patted his smooth little head and treated him like an exquisite plaything. They got on famously until one day, reeling with the fumes of wine, he attempted to step out of his role as a mock courtier and to assume the part of a serious lover.

Many a lover has encountered a woman's wrath. But pity the

man who calls forth a woman's ridicule. Lady Mary made a brave attempt at anger, but the very absurdity of the situation —a hunchback manikin making love to a lady of state—overwhelmed her. Pushing him away from her, she sat back and burst into a tempest of laughter.

The great poet grew pale and rushed from the room. He never forgave Lady Mary for her mortal insult. To the end of his days he hounded her with a pen of fire and discharged volley after volley of vituperation against all her associates.

Oddly enough, out of the depths of his most scurrilous quarrels flashed some of his greatest satirical verse—like the reflection of the sun shining out of a mud puddle. One of the most dazzling of Pope's satires, whose leer was no less than its luster, was directed against Lord Harvey, an admirer of Lady Montagu's who had taken up the cudgels in her behalf:

> Yet let me flap this bug with gilded wings,
> This painted child of dirt, that stinks and stings.
>
> . . . .
>
> So well-bred spaniels civilly delight
> In mumbling of the game they dare not bite.

Another of his resplendent mockeries was the result of a grudge he had conceived against the famous essayist, Joseph Addison. And the last and most magnificent of his verbal bombardments grew out of the lifelong resentment he nursed against the entire literary world.

The name of this epic satire was *The Dunciad*.

IV

A FLOCK of literary moths had fluttered for many years around the flame of his genius. These unsuccessful suitors of the muse overwhelmed him with an avalanche of heroic dramas and epic poems which they begged him to revise and re-edit and sell for them. One of these perspired rather than inspired authors sent Pope a tragedy a week.

Pope finally conceived the idea of writing a mock epic on the ghastly deeds of these fourth-rate men of letters. His quarrel was not only with these "inoffensive fools" but especially with those who always went out of their way to offend him. Early in life he had vowed to revenge himself upon these adversaries. "Touch me to the quick even in the slightest degree," he had said, "and the man who offends, no matter how inadvertently, will be hounded and pursued by me his whole life long." He now reserved a place in his epic of dunces for all the critics and the poets and the playwrights and the booksellers from whom he had ever suffered the slightest discourtesy. One by one he picked them up, plucked them of all their pretensions and placed them for a roasting upon the spit of his invective.

Filled as it was with a thousand allusions to obscure personalities, the book might never have created a stir among the general public were it not for the publicity given the work by the "dunces" themselves, who lost their heads and roared the satire into national and perpetual notoriety. They met hastily and organized a front to do battle against the "deluge of poison" that had rained down on Grub Street. Although the book was at first published anonymously, they all knew that there was but one man in England capable of such vindictive verses. They were determined to revenge themselves upon Alexander Pope. They wrote letters to the Ministry alleging that Pope was an enemy of the government. They burned him in effigy. They threatened his very life. At night the midget satirist didn't venture upon the streets except with pistols in his pockets and a huge dog at his side.

But on the other hand his friends roared with delight at his brilliant sorties and came in droves to his estate at Twickenham, beseeching him never to lay down his satirical pen. He lapped up their adulation like a kitten, thanked them for their advice and protested that it was far from his desire to shine as a satirist. It hurt him sorely, he declared, that a harmless creature like himself, who had hoped only to spend a lifetime writing gentle pastoral verses and amorous epigrams, should have become the object of so much hatred. But, he reasoned, many of his colleagues were fanatically jealous of his genius and contemptuous of his "small physical parts." From the first the world of men had watched for an opportunity to trample him under. And he had saved himself only through the weapons of his satire. In self-defense he had been compelled to strike with all his power against the universal conspiracy.

Pope really believed in the actuality of this conspiracy. He suspected that no one was his friend, not even the chattering apes that hurried to Twickenham in order to bask in his society. Well, he had nothing to fear. He was independent of them all. He could stand on his own legs. He had made his name and his fortune the hard way. He could afford to take insults. "Gentlemen," he told his guests grandly, "I have a heart for all, a house for all, a fortune for all." And, should the provocation arise, a poisoned epigram for all.

He had prepared himself against them. He trusted no one on principle. Had he not secretly written a defamatory life of Swift, he chuckled, which he could publish as an instrument of vengeance should he ever find the necessity for it? But he was really a good fellow. He would show the people of England, lest they had any doubts, what a pure and candid and benevolent little poet he was after all. He would rewrite his private correspondence, revealing his innermost self to his best advantage. He would embellish these letters with "jewels of justice and sermons of sense." And then he would work out a stratagem whereby these letters would be published in the press during his lifetime—without his knowledge, of course. He would pretend that they had been stolen from him and offered to a bookseller against his will. . . .

And now this matter was off his chest. Time for another poem—*An Essay on Man*. It would be the crowning work of his *moral* poetry, just as *The Dunciad* had been the crowning work of his *satirical* poetry. He would dip the fingers of his fancy into a trunkful of conventional ideas about human destiny and trick out the lifeless limbs of a second-rate philosophy in a new attire of dazzling verse. "True wit is nature to advantage dressed—what oft is felt but ne'er so well expressed."

Such was the creed of this epigrammatic philosopher. He would manufacture a thousand proverbs whose tuneful nuances would be mouthed forever on the lips of posterity. He would string a necklace of glittering phrases around the swan's-down neck of truth and clasp them together with "a lifetime of thought enclosed in a couplet of gold":

> And spite of Pride, in erring Reason's spite,
> One truth is clear, *Whatever is, is right.*

V

In his fifty-seventh year the hunchback courtier of the muse was laid to rest. Just a short time before Pope's death his close friend—the playwright-satirist John Gay—had left the stage with an impudent toss of the head and a biting epitaph: "Life is a jest, and all things show it; I thought so once, and now I know it." Another intimate friend, Dean Swift, had gone mad. And now Alexander Pope, the last and the vainest survivor of this trinity of cynics, marveled on his deathbed that there should be any such thing as human vanity.

To the minds of a few Pope's death was a relief like the passing of a frightful dream. But the majority stood gallantly by his memory. For they recalled, in spite of the ephemeral imperfections of the man, the enduring lines of the poet—lines addressed to all those who would properly appraise the value of a lyric or a life:

> . . . what affects our hearts
> Is not th'exactness of peculiar parts;
> 'Tis not a lip or eye we beauty call,
> *But the joint force and full result of all.*

BURNS

Great Poems by Burns

The Twa Dogs.
The Holy Fair.
Hallowe'en.
Address to the Unco Guid.
The Cotter's Saturday Night.
Tam o' Shanter.
To a Mouse.
To a Louse.
To a Mountain Daisy.
The Jolly Beggars.
The Poet's Welcome to His Love-
    Begotten Daughter.
Holy Willie's Prayer.
To Mary in Heaven.

Green Grow the Rashes, O.
M'Pherson's Farewell.
John Anderson My Jo.
Willie Brew'd a Peck o' Maut.
Sweet Afton.
Auld Lang Syne.
Comin' thro' the Rye.
Duncan Gray.
The Young Highland Rover.
My Heart's in the Highlands.
A Red, Red Rose.
Fairest Maid on Devon Banks.
Ae Fond Kiss.

Robert Burns

1759–1796

HE ARRIVED ON EARTH in the bleakest of weather—a furious January blizzard that swept away the roof of the clay cottage which his father had built. "A novelist might perhaps have viewed the scene with satisfaction, but not so I," remarked Burns ruefully many years later. He came to a father who could barely wrest a living out of his seven stony acres of plowland but who, for all that, had within him the spirit of a "deep-seated piety"; and to a mother who was the bonniest lass in all Ayrshire, with an open eye for beauty and a heart full of song.

Starvation and toil and misery were the three fates that spun the thread of a Scotch peasant's life in the eighteenth century. When Robbie was seven his father was compelled to abandon his Ayrshire farm and to accept a tenancy at Whitsuntide. Robbie took his place at the plow and worked long hours in the fields. The work sapped his fiber, stooped his shoulders and broke down his health. When he was scarce fifteen he developed the symptoms of a rheumatic heart. Before he had really begun to live the ironic powers of heaven had prepared a warrant for his early death.

But in the meantime he was young; his senses were alive and

tingling. Always he worked with his tools in one hand and with a book in the other. Songs were his chief joy. He pored over the old Scottish lays while driving his cart or walking to the fields. He hoped that he would someday write songs like these!

And the day on which he composed his first shy words came sooner than ever he expected. It was the custom of the country for boys and girls to work together in the fields at harvesttime. And Robbie at fifteen was given a "bonnie, sweet, sonsie" miss of fourteen to help him in his labors. Under the warm autumn sun the young lad picked the nettles from the hand of his little partner, and a new feeling was born. She sang a wild folk tune, and his heartstrings vibrated to the "delicious passion." He must think of appropriate words for the lovely music. He wasn't foolish enough to believe that he could ever write anything equal to those splendid printed poems composed by the men who read Greek and Latin. But his girl had sung a tune which a country boy like himself had composed long since for another bonny lass in the harvest fields, and Robbie saw no reason why he mightn't try to fit this tune to a few simple rhymes.

Thus began his poetry—and his love.

II

THE FAMILY MOVED to a new farm on the north bank of the River Ayr. He attended a dancing school in the neighboring village to give his rustic manners "a brush." He was eighteen now—browned by many years of the sun and the wind and still occupied with his singing and his plowing and his dreaming. He had made a feeble attempt to learn a lesson or two of Latin; but all he had been able to master, as he laughingly remarked, was the motto *omnia vincit amor*—love conquers all things.

His lively imagination was bent upon more contemporary conquests than the victory of a scholar over a dead language. Nature had discovered in him a mortal weakness—an insatiable inclination toward "the adorable sex." He had gone to a schoolmaster to learn mathematics, but a "charming fillette" who lived next door upset his trigonometry. He became involved in half the love affairs of the parish. Midnight trysts, a stealthy tap on the window, a stroll through the barley under the warm harvest moon, tears, explanations, smiles, "a wee bit o' Paradise"—and then back to his toiling and his dreaming.

The intensity of his imagination exceeded anything his companions had ever known. When he selected his lassie he invested her with a multitude of charms out of the vast resources of his poetic genius. With a single magical phrase he could transform a silly country doxy into a goddess. "My passions, once lighted up, rage like so many devils," he confessed, "till they find vent in rhyme."

And he also tried to find relief in marriage. The "lady of his choice" was a maidservant at Cessnock Water. Burns paid court to her in eloquent and—he believed at the time—sincere verses:

> O Mary, canst thou wreck his peace
> Wha for thy sake would gladly dee?
> Or canst thou break that heart of his
> Whase only faut is loving thee?

But the young lady apparently felt no compunction about "breaking that heart of his." Her kitchen-nurtured mind was too practical to surrender itself to a ne'er-do-well rhymester. Baffled in his love, Burns accepted an opportunity to enter the flax-dressing business together with his stepuncle at the town of Irvine.

He was twenty now, and he looked years older. His complexion was dark and his eye luminous. His face had a thoughtful expression that amounted at times to sadness. Among his male companions he was silent and reserved. "I am not formed for the bustle of the busy nor the flutter of the gay." But in the company of his "bonny lassies" he unburdened himself of all his restraint. He lived and he loved freely. He dressed himself in elegant clothes and displayed the only "tied hair" in the parish. Indeed, he had become somewhat of a fop.

Yet for all his foppery he fell in with a crowd of adventurers who smuggled wine along the coast. He struck up a friendship with a dissolute sailor who, "where women were concerned, was even a greater fool than myself." But he failed in the flax business. He was robbed by his partner. The shop burned to the ground during a New Year's carousal. And he returned home empty-handed.

He found his father on his deathbed. A lifetime of excessive work and insufficient play had hastened his end.

"Robbie," he said, "I die in fear for your future. Promise me you will reform."

Robbie held his father's hand and promised. Not long thereafter a young girl in the parish was delivered of an illegitimate child. When the announcement of the birth was made at the kirk the young poet stepped forward and confessed that he was the father.

III

WITH tender embarrassment Burns wrote a poem of welcome to his little "love-begotten daughter."

> Gude grant that thou may ay inherit
> Thy mither's looks and gracefu' merit,
> An' thy poor, worthless daddie's spirit
> Without his failins!

He brought the wee lass back to his farm and put her in the care of his mother and his elder brother. For the nonce he was sober. Together with his brother he leased several acres of farmland at Mossgiel, near the parish of Lochlea. He felt the weight of his new duties keenly—for a time. "I read farming books, I attended markets, and, in short, in spite of the devil, the world and the flesh, I should have been a wise man." But misfortune pursued him. The rains were insufficient. His crops were poor. Within a short time his enthusiasm for farming had evaporated.

He was fearful of the violent stirrings within him. The kelpies in his heart were pushing him to music and madness. He sensed the spirits of the old Highland minstrels arising from their graves and beckoning him to join them in their wanderings. The life of a farmer was not for him. The horizons of his genius were broader than the earth. "My soul is uneasy and confined to the plow." He must sing. By the devil, he must sing!

And so he went back to his singing. With the boldness of youth under the stimulus of drink, he took to firing "random shots o' country wit" at the political and the ecclesiastical "misleaders" of the parish.

He became an outcast in the society of all but "the infidels and the wenches." His reputation for loose living had caused the parents of the community to shut their doors in his face. And now to the other charges was added the crime of impiety. It was enough to make the body of his poor old father turn in his grave.

But Robbie was unperturbed. "What if they call me an unredeemed son of Satan for hooting at the pulpit?" He gloried in his evil reputation. There wasn't a mother's daughter for fifty miles around who hadn't heard of Robbie Burns and who didn't pray for the opportunity to meet him.

One day he was out taking a walk with his dog. He espied a plump young lassie bleaching her linen on the washing green. He had met her before at a village dance. And his pup had got himself entangled between her petticoats. "I wish I could get a lass to like me as well as my dog," he had told the blushing young girl. And now as he passed her on the green she called after him: "Have you found the lass?"

From then on they got better acquainted. "You have your Meg," he wrote to a friend, "and I have my darling Jean."

Once again the village was scandalized. Jean was brought to bed and delivered of twins. Burns offered to marry the girl, went so far as to draw up a marriage contract in order to prove his sincerity to the congregation of the kirk. But the father of the young woman objected strenuously. "I'd rather have bastards for grandchildren than a blackguard for a son-in-law."

While the village church board was deliberating as to his punishment for his transgression against Jean he strolled along the sequestered banks of the Ayr—with a new Highland sweetheart. And one soft afternoon Robert Burns and Mary Campbell stood on the two sides of a small brook, holding a Bible between them, and vowed eternal love. Then they parted, never to meet again. Mary Campbell went back to her native county, fell ill and died of fever. And Burns returned to face the displeasure of his parish church for his dalliance with Jean Armour.

Her father was determined to have the young poet thrown into jail. Burns was desperate. He must fly from the parish. But where? Hastily he packed his belongings under the skylight of his tiny bedroom. Perhaps he could take passage on the next boat to Jamaica and try to get a job as a bookkeeper on one of the island plantations? But he had no money to pay for his passage. His farm was ruined, his income squandered. He must beg, borrow, steal!

"You have an odd lot of poems lying around, Robbie," suggested one of his friends. "Why don't you try to sell them?"

Burns laughed bitterly. "This is no time for joking, lad. I've got to sell something that's worth *money*."

Nevertheless the verses were collected and published—and Burns remained in Scotland and found himself famous.

IV

THE LYRICS of "his scandals and his sadness," penned hurriedly on scraps of wastepaper, swept over the country like wildfire. "Princes and peasants, old and young, high and low, grave and gay . . . were alike delighted, agitated, transported." Robbie Burns scratched his head in bewilderment. He had tried to flee from jail and he had bounced into the hands of fame. The ways of men were beyond his ken. The social leaders of Edinburgh invited him to the capital. They were curious to meet the "Ayrshire plowman who wrote such amazing songs." His friends lent him a pony on which to make the journey. He mounted and rode down to the city in a daze. As he passed through county after county his "fellow plowmen" lined the route and cheered him wildly. He was "downright struck and trembling in every nerve."

When he reached the capital the salons of the mighty were thrown open to him. Weak with excitement, he wrote home about his reception:

> This wot ye all whom it concerns,
> I, Rhymer Robin, alias Burns,
> October twenty-third,
> A ne'er to be forgotten day,
> Sae far I clambered up the brae,
> I dinner'd with a Lord!

And as if he couldn't believe it himself, he repeated: "But wi' a Lord! Stand out, my shin—a Lord, a Peer, an *Earl's Son!*"

Soon, however, he became suspicious of the gentry who made such a twitter about him. He felt his origin keenly; he was ashamed of his ill breeding. He felt that these aristocrats, who had been blessed with a better education, looked down upon him. To them he was a seven days' wonder, a curiosity to be gazed at. These fortunate children of power and plenty liked him but they did not respect him. They were astonished that so vulgar a peasant should have been endowed with so graceful a genius. They considered him a freak of nature—something to amuse them, like a magician or a clown.

He conceived an overpowering resentment against them. He had put aside his country clothes but he couldn't put off his country manners. And therefore they ridiculed him behind his back. Very well, he would answer them in kind. A fig for those fat carcasses branded with a peerage, who looked down with a lordly air upon a genius of humble rank!

He rushed to the gin-drenched taverns of Edinburgh, where he met his "brother men" again. Here at table he was king once more, crowing above the drunken roost, passing the smoking bowl and the bawdy joke to people who understood and loved him. Let them prate about decorum who had "a character to lose"!

And in the meantime, just as Burns had grown tired of the gentry, the gentry had grown tired of Burns—with his talk about cowmaids and mountain daisies and country Halloweens. The Arcadian fashion passed almost as quickly as it had arrived. One door after another turned against Burns. And he was left alone with his little book of verses and his bitter dreams. To Dr Blair, one of the kindliest and most sympathetic of the aristocratic patrons who once had made so great a fuss over him, he wrote: "I have often felt the embarrassment of my singular situation. However the meteorlike novelty of my appearance in the world might attract notice, I foresaw only too clearly the time when the tide of popularity would leave me and recede."

"You have had to stand a severe trial," Dr Blair wrote in return. "I am happy that you have stood it so well." And then he hinted delicately: "You are now, I presume, to retire to a more private walk of life. . . . You will not, I hope, neglect . . . to promote esteem by cultivating your genius. . . . At the same time, be not overeager to come forward too rapidly. . . ."

He rode away from Edinburgh a sadder and a wiser man. He passed "many miles through a wild country, among cliffs gray with eternal snows and gloomy savage glens." The intoxication of glory was not such a desirable stimulant after all. Of one thing he was certain:

> Nae treasures, nor pleasures,
>   Could make us happy lang;
> The heart aye's the part aye
>   That makes us right or wrang.

V

HE RETURNED to his native village determined to right the wrong he had committed against Jean Armour. Now that he had achieved some measure of success, her father no longer objected to the marriage. Jean was made "an honest woman," and the poet tried to settle down once more to his farming, "the proper business for an honest man." He was able to lease a plot of land through the intercession of his friends, who secured for him a part-time job, with a meager but steady salary, as the county excise officer. The plot of ground that he rented, the Ellisland farm, was more remarkable for its beauty than for its fertility. "Mr Burns," remarked a friendly neighbor, "you have made a poet's, not a farmer's, choice."

When the farm had been rendered habitable Robbie sent for his family. As soon as they arrived he ordered a servant to place the Bible upon a bowl of salt and to carry it ceremoniously into the house. Then, with his wife on his arm, he followed the servant and took formal possession. He gave a housewarming party at which all the neighbors gathered from miles around and drank lustily: "Here's luck to the rooftree of the Burns!"

He paid perfunctory attention to his farm and threw himself heartily into the adventure of his excise duties. These duties kept him on horseback surveying the county against smuggling from the coast. He rode scores of miles every day and searched the cellars of the countryfolk for illegal barrels of wine. Irony of fate, that a man with so intense a thirst for the bottle should be called upon to restrict its traffic!

However, he was none too strict in his enforcement of the law against the countryfolk. One day he came to the door of a poor old woman who was doing a little illegal business. He put his forefinger to his lips. "Kate, are you mad?" he asked with a twinkle in his eye. "Don't you know that the supervisor and I will be upon you in forty minutes?"

And the countryfolk repaid him for his thoughtfulness. Every wine barrel in the district was opened to him on his visits. And then his tongue grew eloquent, and his words flowed as freely as the wine. He spun fancy after fancy of the most amazing texture. "Some tales are lies frae end to end, and some great lies were never penn'd." Swaying with intoxication, he told them how Willie "brewed a peck o' maut," how Tam o' Shanter lost the tail of his mare, how the "dogs rejoic'd they were nae men," and how one cold night, as he "stagger'd o'er the hills," he came upon Death himself, with his "awfu' scythe o'er his shouther." And this story, Burns insisted, "is just as true as the Devil's in hell or in Dublin City." *Vive le vin! Vive la bagatelle!*

Thus he used to entertain the countryfolk through the night. And then he mounted his horse in the dawn and rode through the quiet fields, gradually sobering and realizing that the crops on his farm were failing through his neglect. If ever he would be forced to give up *this* farm, as he had been forced to give up his other farms! He shuddered in the cold. Once again he would find himself landless—and this time with a wife and wee bairns on his hands. There would be no soil for his sons, no harvest for his old age. They would be driven into the city on the miserable and precarious salary of an excise officer. . . . These forebodings would gather like clouds in his mind, only to be scattered by the sunlight of his songs.

Three years of poor harvests in the fields and rich harvests in the poet's fancy. And as each harvesting season approached he wandered gloomily on the banks of the Nith. Oftentimes he "screened himself on the lee side of a corn stack from the cutting edge of the night wind and lingered till the dawn approached and wiped the stars out one by one." Meanwhile at the farm the lasses did nothing "but bake bread" and the lads sat by the fireside "and ate it warm." Ellisland was bound to fail under a poet's management.

And it did. There finally came a day when Burns was unable to meet his rent. "Jeanie, we must pull up the stakes and wander on!" Sell the furniture, break up the home, gather the bairns and wander on—landless, beaten, despised! Well, what other end to the business would you expect of a ne'er-do-well who is always sitting over his wine cups and spinning rhymes whilst others are making hay? A professional poet? Not even that, observed the thrifty folk as they shook their heads in pity. "Robbie Burns is a professional fool!"

He sends his wife and his children to Dumfriesshire to spare them the sight of the breaking up of their home. He himself remains to see the furniture auctioned off piece by piece. The auctioneer appears with a list of the household articles and with a bottle of wine to celebrate the business. The villagers nip their brandy and shout their bids with gusto. Finally the auction is completed. The customers pour into the farmhouse in a riot of drunken debauch. Lewd jokes, boisterous dancing, spitting on the floor and mud trailing across the threshold over which the servant had once carried the Bible whilst the hopeful young poet, with his wife leaning on his arm, had followed to take possession. Now the household gods are gone, and anarchy reigns in their stead.

"To make a happy fireside clime for weans and wife"—*that* is "the pathos and sublime of human life." And Robert Burns looks on, frozen to the spot, shaking his head in horrible bewilderment.

VI

HE JOINED his weans and wife at Dumfriesshire, where he rented a humble cottage and continued his excise duties. His "reputation for evil" had preceded him. The respectable folk of the town would have nothing to do with him except in a business way. He himself couldn't understand why he was rapidly traveling down the path to ruin. He had everything to live for—a devoted wife, splendid children, the golden gift of song. And a genius for translating his songs into imperishable verse. And brains enough to bless him with prosperity if only he had the will.

He sat with his glass of wine and wondered. . . . Well, why bother his head about all this? "The best-laid plans of mice and men go crazy at the nappy. Here's to gettin' unco fu' and tipplin', sobbin' happy!" When he had the taste of wine on his tongue everything became clear as day. It was the lords and ladies that strutted over the world in their indecent avarice who were keeping lads like him down. That was it! While they were titled and toasted he was compelled to lead the life of a lackey. They were persecuting him, hounding him to hell. "What special merit do they possess that they were ushered into the world with the scepter? What is my demerit that I have been ushered into the world with a kick?"

He called it fate and kept on drinking. "Oh, to be a sturdy savage stalking in the pride of his independence!" And he was nothing but a civilized slave—a slave to his poverty, without an aim or a hope, buffeted about by the terrible intensity of his feelings. Across the channel a nation of underdogs like himself had risen to a man and had bared their strength to the world. "Lord love the people of France!" Soon there would be neither kings nor peasants in the world—only poets. Poets like himself, singing out the hymn of brotherhood and liberty. And then he'd never again feel ashamed of his failure to reap a harvest. And he would never again be bewildered. . . .

VII

THERE WAS much smuggling along the coast of Scotland. One day a strange-looking brig put into the Solway. It looked like a pirate ship. Burns was given orders to observe its movements closely. When the brig reached the shallow waters the poet drew his sword and led a band of dragoons aboard her. Smugglers! He commanded them to surrender.

The following day the ship's arms were put up at auction. Burns bought four carronades. He dispatched them to the revolutionary government in France with a message expressing his sympathy for their cause. The guns were intercepted at the Dover customs before they could cross the Channel. The British rulers had no love for the "bloody mobocracy" in Paris which had thrust the king into prison and which had uprooted the foundations of orderly society. His Majesty's government decided to investigate the radical in their midst who had dared to send ammunition to the French Terrorists. A secret agent was assigned to keep an eye on Burns.

He was half crazy—declared the burghers of Dumfriesshire—wagging that loose tongue of his and shouting his admiration

Pope

Burns

for the rebels in every tavern. A man who was earning his bread on a government job had no business to flaunt such treasonable talk against the prime minister. It was the inflaming wine that did it. Could not someone sober him up? What dangerous nonsense issued from his lips! "It's comin' yet for a' that, that man to man the world o'er shall brithers be for a' that." Good lord, those were the very sentiments of the revolutionary maniacs in Paris who daily fed their monster guillotine with the blood of the nobles. Hush him up!

But oftentimes he's quiet and more sober, as he sits at his morning fireside rocking in his chair and singing songs of the doons and the glens of Scotland. In such a mood the peace of God comes over all who hear him—all but the singer of the song. He is calmer at these moments and sadder. For always there is the question on his lips, the bewilderment in his eye, the rebellion in his soul.

> Ye banks and braes o' bonnie Doon,
>   How can ye bloom sae fresh and fair!
> How can ye chant, ye little birds,
>   And I sae weary fu' o' care!

More solitary than ever. Even the women of Dumfries have left him. All the outcast women, one by one, have abandoned the outcast man. His wife, to be sure, has remained by his side —loving, forgiving, devoted. But she is only one. His heart is a roving bee. It needs the sup of many a wildwood flower. "Robin was a rovin' lad, kissin', rovin' Robin." A rovin' lad and a sad one.

When he wasn't at the tavern he could be found at home explaining to his oldest boy passages from the great English poets. "There is not among all the stories ever penn'd so rueful a narrative as the life of a poet, my son. A life subjected to constant temptation, cruelty and scorn. Look your father in the eye, lad —singer of the sweetest rhymes in the English tongue. Look him well in the eye—a drunken, good-for-nothing, disgusting, degenerate, unhappy tramp!"

He had begun to sense the approach of death. Though he was only thirty-seven, he felt "old as Methuselah and weak as a woman's tear." His heart was almost done. He prepared himself for the end. He offered as souvenirs to his friends the pistols he had carried with him on his customs business. "Take them," he said. "I have found them an honor to their maker, which is more than I can say of their user."

And one winter night he sat down as usual with his companions in the tavern. "My friends," he said, "I am going to die." A fiddler jerked himself out of his doze and stared at him. A soldier lounging by the side of his hizzie was all eyes. A half-bloated songstress stopped her tune.

The devil lurked in the poet's eye. "At last, my braw lads and lassies, I've found my aim in life. I know where I'm heading. I've received an invitation from death." He held a hand over his heart. "What say you, Merry Andrew and Poosie Nancy? Don't you ken He who made my heart will bear with me and give me the fairest sort of trial before His judgment seat?" And then, with a sad smile: "Farewell, you cuckolds and you budgets, you ragged members of the wandering train, farewell."

He started homeward. His head was sleepy. Strange fumes and tunes were mingling in his brain. "We'll take a cup o' kindness yet for auld lang syne. . . ." The wind lashed the snow against his face. The air was filled with the dance of swirling ghosts. Gradually his eyes grew heavy and a delicious numbness descended upon his arms and his legs. And now listen to that exquisite music! Millions of voices the whole world over, voices husky with emotions and memories, have joined in a mighty chorus, singing the song of the swirling snow.

He sank to the ground wrapped in the mantle of his dreams. . . . "And here's a hand, my trusty fiere, and gie's a hand o' thine; we'll take a cup o' kindness yet 'r auld lang syne. . . ."

When he awoke it was still and cold and daylight. He dragged himself to his feet and walked on. But his footsteps to the end of the journey were few. He had accepted the invitation of death.

WORDSWORTH

Great Poems by Wordsworth

Ode on Immortality.
The Excursion.
The Prelude.
Lines on Tintern Abbey.
Ode to Duty.
The Happy Warrior.
My Heart Leaps Up.
The Borderers.
The Solitary Reaper.
To a Highland Girl.
Yarrow Visited.
Yarrow Revisited.
To a Distant Friend.
A Lesson.
The Idiot Boy.
Peter Bell.

We Are Seven.
The Thorn.
She Was a Phantom of Delight.
The Lost Love.
The Education of Nature.
Desideria.
England and Switzerland.
The Affliction of Margaret.
The Reverie of Poor Susan.
Goody Blake and Harry Gill.
Simon Lee, the Old Huntsman.
Lucy Gray, or Solitude.
Ruth.
Michael.
Alice Fell, or Poverty.

William Wordsworth

1770–1850

HE CAME from a family that had been established in England before the Norman Conquest. He had in him the blood of the Norse and of the Vikings. He possessed the fundamental seriousness, the enduring tenacity and the rigorous asceticism which are characteristics of the Northern races. And above all he possessed an instinctive pride in the majestic dignity assigned to him as a human being. He spent many of his boyhood hours in roaming over the mountains and boating on the lakes, and as he grew intimate with the vast horizons of the Cumberland countryside he developed a muscular pride and a freedom and rebelliousness against opposition of any kind.

He was a headstrong young man when he left the Cumberland County for his university training at Cambridge. He had clung by his finger tips to the fissures on a crag over a raven's nest. He had seen a suicide drawn from the water "with his ghastly face upright." He had piloted his boat dizzily until the mountains appeared to take monster strides after him. And on one of his rambles over the Cumberland moors he had come across a gibbet upon which murderers had been hanged in the past. He had been brought up with an intimate knowledge of the terrible grandeur of nature.

[*93*]

In the academic seclusion of his college days, however, his genius underwent a period of apparent decay, like a planted seed, before it "came to a soul in grass and flowers." The poetry he wrote at Cambridge was trivial and weak. His career seemed to be assuming the shape of consistent mediocrity. But then something stupendous happened.

II

IT WAS on a trip to Paris that he found himself caught up in the maelstrom of the Revolution. His guardian uncle—he had lost his parents in his childhood—had been urging him to study for the ministry. Wordsworth, in a spurt of rebellion, had decided otherwise. Upon receiving his college degree he had sailed for France to study the language in order to obtain a position as the traveling companion of a nobleman while he prepared himself at the same time for a career in journalism.

He remained in France for sixteen months—a period in which the entire world seemed to be turning topsy-turvy. Louis XVI had been dethroned. Society had been transformed into a welter of licentiousness. With the fall of the constitution the "rule of restraint" had given way to the "misrule of freedom." Decency was thrown into the sewers. Men had relapsed into a state of primitive barbarism.

Into this corrosive atmosphere of the Reign of Terror came the young poet sprung from English merchants and landowners. His delicate ear had thus far been startled by nothing more discordant than the hooting of the screech owl in the woodlands. Until now he had encountered every phase of nature but human nature. And with the eager susceptibility of untried youth he enjoyed his new experience. At Orleans he met a Republican officer who plied him with the freethinking and free-living philosophy of Godwin, of Paine and of Rousseau. Wordsworth became an ardent apostle of the "new order" in France.

And—for a short period—he became an ardent disciple of Venus. For at Orleans he met a young Frenchwoman, Annette

Vallon, who was well equipped to initiate him into the mysteries of this pagan goddess of love. At first Annette was merely his teacher of French; then she became his mistress and, finally, the mother of his child.

Finding himself thus unexpectedly burdened with a serious responsibility, Wordsworth returned to England with the intention of securing a position and sending for Annette. He had no idea that France and England would be at war within a few weeks. When the war broke out he was agonized at the thought that he must now remain separated from his mistress and his child. But as the days lengthened into months and the months into years the anguish of the lover gradually became mellowed into the fantasy of the poet. Out of his personal suffering he had learned to draw the universal qualities of his art. His passion had become crystallized into a quiet emotion recollected from the past, and finally it was transmuted into the cold sacredness of a shrine built upon the dust of a tender experience and shaded by the yews of a lingering sentimentality.

Annette was dead to him. She now represented no individual emotion, no personal force, no poignant memories. She had become blended with all the elements that "roll'd round in earth's diurnal course, with rocks, and stones, and trees." In 1802 he married a conventional young English girl, Mary Hutchinson. Shortly before the marriage he had paid a final visit to France where, coldly and civilly, he met his anonymous child of love and the woman who had inspired him with a man's and a poet's passion.

There, in France, remained the birthplace of his poetic impulse. In the arms of Annette he had read the first syllables of life's mysterious epic. Life is an energy exercised in pain and translated into art.

III

DURING the troubled days before his marriage he had turned for salvation to his sister Dorothy—a vigorous young woman of ardent sensibility who was blessed with a fair proportion of his own great genius. With her "love and sympathy and daily care" she had nursed him back to a robust mental health. In her company he had begun to live "his second life." They had settled at Racedown, in Dorsetshire, seven miles from the Channel. Here, through the generosity of a friend, they had secured a cottage rent free, and here they had found a blessed trinity of congenial literary spirits—Charles Lamb, the gentle essayist; William Hazlitt, the severe critic; and Samuel Taylor Coleridge, the bewildered poet.

The literary bond between Wordsworth and Coleridge had developed into an intimate friendship. Wordsworth had given up his Dorsetshire cottage and moved to Alfoxden in order to be physically as well as intellectually closer to "the magic spinner of rhyme." Together with Shelley he might have said to the skylark genius of Coleridge, "Teach me half the gladness that thy brain must know. . . ." But Coleridge was a critic rather than a teacher to Wordsworth—a tuning fork for the vibrant and now fully awakened emotions of his fellow poet.

For Wordsworth was no longer a pupil in the school of song. Having made a pilgrimage to other shores in search of reality, he had returned to find reality in his own country, in the childhood scenes of his native hillsides and rivers and forests. Here in England, as everywhere else, lay the truth ready to be revealed to all those who had eyes to see—not through "the mean and vulgar works of man," but through "the passions that build up our human soul . . . with high objects, with eternal things."

The truth is engraved upon the leaves of the trees, the petals of the flowers, the mountain crags inscribed with their ancient hieroglyphics by the primeval pen of the glaciers, the islands in the seas, the stars in the heavens. It is written upon every page of the infinite book of nature. The objects of nature are but the letters of the alphabet in this immortal epic of the Great Poet. And the passions of men are the rhythmic cadences with which they read, each in his blind, blundering, individual way, the ultimate meaning of this great epic.

Wordsworth came to Coleridge with this philosophy well

learned. His passion for Annette had taught him the value of all passion. And little by little his emotions had been fused into harmony by his thought. His senses were no less keen than ever. The fires were still smoldering in his eyes above a strongly arched nose and a voluptuous mouth. But his sensuous appetites had become transformed into the hunger of the mind—the experience of excitements "recollected in tranquillity," refined through the filter of reason and touched with the fire of living words. He had become an essentially "interior" man. "Of moral strength and intellectual power, of joy in widest commonalty spread, of the individual mind that keeps her own inviolate retirement, subject there to Conscience only, and the law supreme of that Intelligence which governs all—of these I sing."

Wordsworth had undergone a profound sublimation, an emotional ablution, a religious conversion in the highest artistic sense. It was an individual and a personal revival, like that of a saint or a prophet who finds God in the wilderness. Wordsworth had found Him in the lakeside regions of England. "Anyone living in the English countryside may look upon the glassy waters of a lake and feel his imagination carried into recesses of feeling otherwise impenetrable." The very heavens are brought into its depths, and the world looks up to the spectator in a new light through this purified medium. "Not a breath of air, no restlessness of insects, and not a moving object perceptible," except the clouds gliding in the depths of the water or a traveler passing along and reflecting his inverted image. The very motion of this reflected landscape "seems governed by the quiet" of a timeless, spaceless world. And it may happen that a heron crosses the horizon "silently in the liquid depths," while from above the lake the voice of the real bird awakens in the spectator "the recollection of appetites and instincts, pursuits and occupations that deform and agitate the world of men" yet have no power to disturb the serenity of nature. This looking glass of nature through which the world may see its perfect lineaments, caught as it were in an arrested moment of time and unruffled by the slightest stirring of the breeze, is an exact condition of the mind of the poet which catches the rays of the ideal world dwelling in "the light of setting suns" and transforms them into the image of eternity for all men to behold. "Be still my heart, that I may see the mirror'd skies of Galilee." The ripples of spiritual tumult that all too frequently ruffle the serenity of the human soul are set at rest under the peaceful tranquillity of the poet's faith. The clear eye must never be deceived by the temporary ruffles. It must steadfastly keep in mind the essential unity under the apparent diversity of things. The World is One. It appears to be broken into disunited fragments only when the wind disturbs the reflecting surface of the lake. Let us learn—declares Wordsworth—to see parts not as parts but with a feeling for the whole. "Tumult and peace and darkness and light are all alike the workings of one mind, the features of the same face"—the face of mankind, which is but a troubled and imperfect image of the face of God.

IV

AT ALFOXDEN Wordsworth planned with Coleridge to issue a volume of verse that would exemplify the "union of deep feeling with profound thought." Wordsworth instinctively rebelled against the tradition of Pope and of Dryden, who had clothed the simple muse with a pompous dress of "gaudy and inane phraseology." He would show in his poetry that an object may be beautiful in itself without the trickery of stylistic ornamentation. He would show the glory of common things. He would deal not with the kings of romance but with the rustic people of his own Lake Country. "Poetry sheds no tears such as angels weep, but natural and human tears; she can boast of no celestial Ichor."

And the poet is simply "a man speaking to men"—an individual who is endowed, it is true, with a keener than average sensitivity and with a superior knowledge of human nature, but who weeps and loves and prays and plans and hopes like all other men. This is what he would show in his poetry. He would sing of the charities that soothe and heal and bless, "like flowers scattered at the feet of men." He would celebrate the existence sanctified by suffering, the faith that looks through death, the strength in what remains behind when all the joys have passed, "the clouds that gather round the setting sun." Above all he planned to give utterance to the humble country-folk whose thoughts lay often beyond the reach of their "few words of English speech."

They were familiar characters all, the heroes and the heroines of his simple poems. In every English village you could find the men and the women so sadly neglected by the poets of the past— old huntsmen like Simon Lee, the sole survivor of a merry company, left friendless now with his vanished hopes and his battered memories; young girls like Ruth, betrayed and abandoned by the youth from over the seas; Johnny, the idiot boy, who sits mooning in the meadows under the silver stars; the solitary singing highland lass who fills the vale to overflowing with her song; and Mother Marget, who for seven long years has received no tidings of her only child. "And that is true. I've wet my path with tears like dew, weeping for him when no one knew." What a wealth of beauty is to be found in these homely annals of the poor! The best stories have not as yet been written. They are the simplest stories, dealing with the lives of the humblest folk.

> O reader, had you in your mind
> Such stores as silent thought can bring,
> O gentle reader, you would find
> A tale in everything.

Into the mind of man looked Wordsworth. This was the "haunt and main region of his song." The young intellectuals of the scientific age, the men and the women who had discarded the orthodoxies of the old religions and the mythologies of the old gods, were now delighted to discover in Wordsworth's poetry a medicine for their moral and intellectual confusion. Here was a doctrine worthy of the intelligence and the dignity of man. Here was a true religion of the soul—an "eternity" of thought which, in a calm grandeur of spirit, fertilized all it surveyed and gave to all forms and images an "everlasting motion." Here in the simple music of Isaiah spoke another prophet of the common destiny of all mankind, of the "hope that can never die" and "of something evermore about to be."

Wordsworth's book of *Lyrical Ballads* was a document of social revolution. For underneath the quiet dignity of the sage smoldered the fires of the impassioned rebel who once had pitched "a vagrant tent among the unfenced regions" of the French Revolution. And now, in that perfect moment when the mind of man embraces the heart, he called in ringing tones to his fellow Englishmen: "We who speak the tongue which Shakespeare spoke, the faith and morals hold which Milton held," *must die or else be free!*

V

WORDSWORTH moved to Grasmere in the Lake Country and lived there with little interruption to the end of his life. But the "perfect moment" of his inspiration had passed. When he reached the age of thirty-seven the "golden years" of his harvest were over. The prophet had become silent forevermore. He had won his fame as the spokesman for liberalism. But as his fame advanced his liberalism retrogressed. When he assumed the post of poet laureate he had become "the most conventional singer in England." He had withdrawn into the bosom of nature and had lost complete contact with the realities of life. The romantic environment of the lakes and the mountains, the incredible ease of his existence and the increasing succession of his honors had rendered him smug and unimpressionable and cold. He had himself become a rock-rooted mountain, towering above the clouds and impervious to the cries of the mortals who toiled in the valleys below. There is only one thing more fatal to inspiration than complete failure—and that is complete success. One of the most pathetic chapters in the history of literature is the degradation of the artists who start their lives in the flame of rebellion and end it in the ashes of complacency.

The cooling of Wordsworth's republican ardor had commenced years earlier, during the excesses of the French Revolution. "Where will it end," he had demanded of the extremists, "when you have set an example of this kind?" As he grew older he blamed his own youthful indiscretions—especially that hasty alliance with Annette—upon "the general debasement of that revolutionary epoch." He was thankful that he had forgotten those hotheaded passions of his youth and that everybody else in England had forgotten them too. Fortunately for his present "respectability," he had possessed the discreet foresight to destroy in his letters and papers every shred of evidence pointing to that not so very "respectable" episode with the French girl.

Indeed, no one outside of his immediate family knew anything about this episode, and so well did they keep the secret that it was not unearthed until the research scholars of the twentieth century launched upon their diligent prospecting into the mining fields of biography.

But to return to our story. "No moralist is so severe as a reformed rake." Overwhelmed with his "sense of honor," Wordsworth lost his sense of humor. He passed judgment on the drug habits of his friend Coleridge and broke up their lifelong attachment. When De Quincey, who had several love children, eventually married the mother and invited Wordsworth to pay him a visit the poet drew his moral skirts about him and declined the invitation.

He had become reactionary not only morally but politically as well. In the morning of his youthful enthusiasm he had declared his disapproval of "monarchical and aristocratical governments." But now he allied himself with the Tories and bitterly opposed the passage of a bill to broaden the popular vote. Once he had upheld the gospel of a nation's right to fight for its independence and had urged his government to all possible aid for Spain in her struggle against Napoleonism. But in his later years he remained silent and unconcerned when the

Spanish people rose up against the tyranny of their own government. Nor did he show any concern when the Italians took part
in the gallant *Risorgimento* to overthrow the yoke of Austria.

The liberal poet of the old generation was dead. It was merely
his ghost that was now walking over the earth. And one of the
liberal poets of the new generation—Robert Browning—wrote
a fitting epitaph for "the man who had sold his soul for the
poet laureateship of England."

> Just for a handful of silver he left us,
> Just for a ribbon to stick in his coat . . .

He was the "lost leader" of the nineteenth century. He had
outlived the fire of his genius. The poetry of his late years was
but a caricature of his former art. Sometimes his pen lapsed
"into sheer idiocy," and often his sentiments provoked nothing
but derision from those who had formerly loved him. And even
when at times the sunbeams of a happy expression tinted the
landscape of his poetic mind the clouds quickly gathered and a
chill stillness descended like the night.

And yet he was mercifully spared the greatest torture destiny
can inflict on a man who has once been great. He failed to
realize his own decay. To the very end he retained complete
faith in his intellectual power. He had not the slightest doubt
of his nobility. Carlyle, describing him in his advanced years,
called him "a veteran of the wars of poetry" who talked well
and firmly in his own cause, "as a wise tradesman would talk
of his tools and workshop—as no one unwise could" . . . a man
well adapted for "much silence or many words" . . . a poet who
lived in a world where no one had ever dared to cross or contra-
dict his slightest whim.

Although he had written his greatest poetry in his youth, he
spent his final years continually revising his work as if loath
to part company with his immortal thoughts. He put the final
touches to *The Prelude*—an autobiographical poem dealing with
the growth of a poet's mind—at a time when most men are
ready to write their epilogues. And occasionally, as he hovered

around the harvest of his memories, the old days returned upon him in a lightning flash and once more his eye caught a glimpse of the hidden bowers of man's "unconquerable mind."

One by one, in the prolonged autumn of his age, the friends and relatives of his spring and summer had dropped like tired leaves from the tree of life. Yet he remained untouched by physical decay. His passing, in the "pleasant season" of his eightieth year, was as peaceful as his writing. His presence "faded like the air," leaving to the memory the fragrance of his verse and the burning caverns of light in his eye—

> The light that never was on sea or land,
> The consecration, and the Poet's dream.

COLERIDGE

Great Poems by Coleridge

Rime of the Ancient Mariner.
Kubla Khan.
Christabel.
Love.
Youth and Age.
Hymn before Sunrise.
The Three Graves.
Melancholy.

Dejection: an Ode.
Remorse.
Zapolya: a Christmas Tale.
The Piccolomini.
The Fall of Robespierre.
Ode to Tranquillity.
Ode to the Departing Year.

Samuel Taylor Coleridge

1772–1834

As a child he was morbidly imaginative. He played alone. He was forever acting out the books he had read, fancying himself as King Arthur or Hamlet or Robinson Crusoe or one of the "Seven Champions of Christendom." He was fretful and passionate—despised by the other boys and adored by the fussy old women. By the time he was eight he was a *character*.

At the death of his father, the vicar of Ottery St Mary at Devon, he was sent to London to live with his uncle. He entered Christ's Hospital, the famous charity school of the "bluecoat scholars." The discipline was harsh, the learning strict, the food scanty and poor. "Every morning, a bit of dry bread and some bad small beer. Every evening, a larger piece of bread, and cheese or butter. . . . Excepting on Wednesdays, I never had a belly full. Our appetites were damped, never satisfied; we had no vegetables."

At frequent intervals the boys were given a day's vacation. Those who had families and friends in the city were glad to take advantage of the "furlough." But those who were friendless and homeless went through a day of torture when the gates were closed from morning until sunset. On such days Coleridge was left largely to his own resources. When the weather was favorable he spent the long hours swimming in the New River and sunning himself on its banks. But whenever a fog hung over London and a chill gripped the air the youngster would tramp through the dismal streets or stand desolately in the market place waiting for the hours to pass. At such periods he keenly felt the loss of his father.

As a general thing, however, his spirits were high. For he lived in a world of fancy an infinity of miles away from the pinch of reality. One day, as he was walking through the streets of London, he imagined himself to be the mighty Leander swimming the Hellespont. He thrashed his arms about him in the air, accidentally clutching the coattails of a man who was passing by. "Help!" cried the gentleman. "My pockets are being picked!" Tearfully Coleridge explained that he was no pickpocket but only a young poet. The gentleman, who happened to possess a sense of humor as well as a fondness for books, presented Coleridge with a subscription card to the circulating library at Cheapside. Thereafter Coleridge read two volumes a day.

He devoured Blanchard's *Medical Dictionary* (in Latin) and decided that he would become apprenticed to a surgeon. But then he turned to the works of Voltaire and transferred his affections from medicine to metaphysics. He was now certain that he wanted to be an atheistic philosopher. One day the master of his school informed him that he was planning to send him to Cambridge, where Coleridge was to study theology with a view to taking holy orders. But the boy shook his head. "Please, sir," he ventured timidly, "I am an infidel."

By the time he was seventeen, however, his master had flogged his infidelity out of his system. His ear had become once more attuned to the siren voice of the Muse, and it was to her that he was now determined to devote his entire life.

At eighteen he entered Cambridge University—only to launch upon another phase of his indecisive restlessness. His appearance, like his mind, was a picture of paradoxes. His large luminous eyes and thoughtful brow were in striking contrast with his flabby cheeks and his heavy lips. His breeches were unbuttoned at the knees; his shoes were down at the heels.

But all this was in keeping with the restless spirit that was sweeping into disorder the dress and the ideas of the European students. The French Revolution had just begun. The professors and the preachers of Cambridge were severe in the disciplining of their "lunatic fringe." They had placed on trial a young undergraduate for the "crime" of advancing a unitarian doctrine. During the remarks of the defense a student was heard to clap loudly. Instantly a proctor pounced upon a scholar who sat next to him and accused him of the outburst.

"Would, sir, that I had the power," replied the student mournfully. And he held up the stump of an arm.

"It was I who clapped," confessed Coleridge after the trial was over. The proctor looked at Coleridge and smiled wryly. "I was well aware of the fact. You have had a narrow escape."

His life at Cambridge was a series of "narrow escapes." When he had taken possession of his college room an upholsterer visited him and offered to supply the furnishings. "How would you like the interior done?" asked the upholsterer.

The unworldly young man, believing that the upholsterer was offering him a university service at no expense, answered gaily, "Just as you please, sir." He always spent recklessly the money that he never possessed.

And he was reckless about everything else. In his second year at Cambridge he stole away from the college and enlisted in a regiment of dragoons, giving his name as Silas Titus Comberbach. He turned out to be the most awkward horseman in the entire regiment. He was unable to keep astride his saddle. He couldn't clean his horse properly. He failed to keep track of his equipment, and his carbine grew rusty. But he was a great favorite with his messmates for his brilliant stories and his spontaneous verses.

And it was this very brilliance that put an end to his military career. One day, while scrubbing his horse in the stable, he took a piece of chalk and wrote a Latin inscription on the wall.

An officer who chanced upon the writing, elated to find a man of culture in his ranks, appointed Coleridge as his orderly. It was the young soldier-poet's duty to walk behind his officer in the streets. On one of these promenades he was recognized by a fellow student who reported the incident to the university. Within a few days Coleridge found himself back with his books.

II

DURING these hectic student days Coleridge met Robert Southey, who was two years his senior. Southey, expelled from Westminster for an article he had written against flogging, had been refused admission to Christ's College because of his heterodox theology and his republican politics. Balliol College, however, had displayed a greater measure of liberality and had enrolled him as a student. Immediately upon his matriculation he created a furore by appearing at dinner in an unpowdered wig— an unheard-of impertinence within the sacred precincts of Oxford.

It was on a visit to Oxford that Coleridge first became acquainted with Southey. Shortly thereafter, when Southey introduced him to his fiancée, Coleridge promptly fell in love with her sister.

The Misses Fricker were the daughters of a manufacturer who had died bankrupt. Prim, penniless and devout, they offered a triple challenge to the two poets—a chivalrous desire to "liberate them from their priggishness, their poverty and their prayers." The impetuous Southey had selected Edith, the younger and more stubborn of the sisters, who went promptly ahead to convert her converter. She transformed Southey "from a poet into a gentleman." Coleridge undertook the task of conquering the heart and the mind of the more pliable sister, Sarah, a not unattractive girl of twenty-three.

And now that they had found their fiancées the two young poets were obliged to look after their finances. With true poetical impracticality they hit upon what they regarded as a simple device. They would take ship for America and buy a tract of wilderness—far from the wickedness of society, unhampered by governments and taxes and wars. And here they would build a Plato's Republic "for the entire human race."

But first there was the "little matter" of chartering a ship to take them to America. And after that they must have enough money to purchase a tract of land and the implements with which to cultivate this land. Two thousand pounds, they believed, would be sufficient to make everything "perfectly delightful."

With this dream in their minds they set about recruiting men and money for their American utopia. They got plenty of men, for every penniless youngster was eager to secure "a little plot in Paradise"—at other people's expense. But those other people were never found to supply the expense. Southey had depended upon a wealthy aunt, or rather upon her colored manservant, Shadrach, to solve their problem for them. Shadrach had been converted to their utopian dream and had promised to intercede with the "old lady" in Southey's behalf. But when the old lady learned about the project she turned both Southey and her servant out of her house into the rain. With the supreme generosity of one who has nothing to give, Southey wrote to Coleridge: "Shad goes with us. He is my brother!"

There was one final hope for the raising of the necessary funds. Coleridge was publishing his first volume of poetry. This book, he confidently believed, would carry them all into the Promised Land.

When the book was published it brought Coleridge $150. With this sum, pitiable for his stupendous dream but fabulous for his personal needs, he left college, married Sarah Fricker and took a cottage in Bristol.

As for Southey, he married Sarah's sister, accepted a business offer from a wealthy uncle and settled down in Lisbon.

And utopia remained in the hands of the American Indians.

III

COLERIDGE had chosen to carve out a career for himself by the point of his pen. With the help of a number of advance subscriptions he launched a political journal entitled *The Watchman* and dedicated it to the principle *that all might know the truth and that the truth might make us free.*

But the life of *The Watchman* was brief. For Coleridge had failed in the first requisite of successful journalism—to give the public not what the editor wills but what the public expects. One of the subscribers complained that he wasn't getting enough book reviews for his money; another, that his son was being corrupted by the editor's politics; still another, that his wife was being bored by the editor's poetry. After ten issues *The Watchman* passed into oblivion.

In his pursuit of "bread and cheese" the poet had begun to toy with the idea of preaching in a Unitarian pulpit. To test out his oratorical skill he had preached a sermon to an audience of seventeen at the town of Bath. When he had scarcely begun one of the seventeen stole quietly out of the chapel. A few minutes later another of the audience followed suit; then another and still another. When the sermon was over there was no one left in the audience but an old lady. She was sound asleep.

In the meantime his wife had given birth to a son. The problem of rent and rations had become more urgent than ever. Fortunately a fellow poet by the name of Thomas Poole secured for him a comfortable cottage in Somersetshire at the modest rental of seven pounds a year. Another "angel in disguise," a gentleman of Birmingham who had been attracted by Coleridge's articles and poems, offered to send his son to him as a student lodger and to pay him an adequate monthly wage for the boy's education.

Coleridge seized the twofold opportunity with the greatest enthusiasm. For the time being he was freed from financial worries and able to give voice to his poetical dreams. Only three miles away from his Somersetshire cottage another young dreamer—William Wordsworth—had settled down at the hamlet of Alfoxden. The two poets were constantly in each other's company. They wandered together over the countryside, discussed each other's "views and visions" and "saw into the very soul of things."

At times they continued their solitary rambles until late at night. As a result of these rambles strange rumors had begun to fly around the neighboring villages. People whispered that they were smugglers receiving shipments from the harbor. Some took oath that they were operating an illegal still. A few were even convinced that they were spies plotting an outrage against the government. A censorious old busybody of the neighborhood went in alarm to the British Home Office and demanded that a secret agent be sent down to watch these two men. Along came the secret agent. For three weeks he shadowed Wordsworth and Coleridge. He hid himself for hours behind a bank at the seaside, where they discussed Spinoza (pronouncing the philosopher's name *Spy-noza*); and when he caught the sound of "spy" in their conversation he was certain of their sinister designs. Had they not prowled over the channel coast with books and papers in their hands, taking charts and maps of the countryside? He summoned witnesses. "Please, sir, we have heard . . . We don't wish to say ill of anybody—but . . ."

"Speak out!" barked the secret agent. "Don't be afraid. You are doing your duty to your king and country. What have you heard?"

"Why, folks do say, your honor," replied one of the witnesses, "as how they are poets and they are going to put Somersetshire in print."

The "dangerous revolutionaries" were plotting nothing less than a book of poems! Together they had drawn up the plan for a volume of verse that would challenge the accepted poetical standards of England. Dryden and Pope had laid down the creed of adherence to the ancient classics. Dryden had maintained that poetry must deal only with lofty subjects artificially dressed in pompous phraseology. And Pope had declared that all poetry, whether serious or witty, must have the mechanical sparkle of the polished gem. But Wordsworth believed that the best of English poetry, of *all* poetry, was the simple expression of the homely lives and the honest thoughts of the common people. The most artless folklore is the most artistic of poetry. Coleridge, while he subscribed to the theory of Wordsworth, insisted that poetry had one other function to perform. It must not only be simple, it must also be magical. The poet must delve down into the deep cisterns of his subconscious and send bubbling into the healthy sunshine of the world of normal experience the crystal rivers of his fancy reflecting the landscape of a *supernatural* as well as of a *natural* world.

To illustrate this second "cardinal" function of the Muse, Coleridge planned to write a poem in the style of the ancient ballad. He looked thoughtfully over the waters of the Bristol channel from a ruined port. The scene of his narrative would be the sea—the symbol of, and the setting for, the pilgrimage of the human soul. His protagonist would be an ancient mariner, adrift in a demon-ridden vessel and condemned to a terrible punishment for the killing of a living thing.

When *The Rime of the Ancient Mariner* appeared in print it startled many people out of their senses. For here was an imagery that could have been engendered in no normal mind. It was like the flickering of the fantastic shadows cast by the fires of a witches' caldron on Walpurgisnacht. "Here," remarked one of the critics, "is a nightmare known only to a man in a fainting fit when the blood turns cold and the sweat melts silently from the limbs."

Moreover, many of the readers found it difficult to understand the meaning of this most eccentric poem. In one issue of the *Morning Post* the following anonymous stanza was addressed to the author:

> Your poem must eternal be,
> Dear sir! It cannot fail,

For 'tis incomprehensible,
And without head or tail.

"Who the devil could have sent this in?" an indignant friend
asked Coleridge.

"I did," replied Coleridge.

IV

It was no surprise to anybody when a poet of such fantastic
visions succumbed to the opium habit. All his life he had suffered from rheumatism. He had ransacked the medical journals
for remedies to relieve his pain. And one day he had found the
"infallible" remedy. It worked like a miracle. The pains vanished instantly. He carried the opium about on his person
wherever he went—at first in all innocence. He was alive again.
Nothing could exceed his triumph. For the opium had brought
him not only blessed relief but glorious dreams. On one occasion he fell asleep in his chair under the influence of the drug.
When he awoke three hours later he reached instantly for pen
and ink and paper to write down all he had seen in his sleep.
The palace of Kubla Khan!

> In Xanadu did Kubla Khan
> A stately pleasure-dome decree;
> Where Alph, the sacred river, ran
> Through caverns measureless to man
> Down to a sunless sea. . . .

And he went on to describe the gardens and the fountains,
the incense-bearing trees, the ancient forests. The scenery, the
colors, the very words came to him exactly as he had seen them
in his vision.

But suddenly he was obliged to lay aside his pen. A visitor
had come to see him. When he returned to his study after an
hour's conversation the spell was over, the magic forgotten, the
vision gone. He looked sadly at the fragment of the great poem
he had dreamed. The rest would be forever lost to the world.

And yet perhaps by a simple device he might recapture the spell. . . .

And so he went back to his opium. Like Faust, he was eager to explore the haunts of forbidden experience. And, like Faust, he was ready to pay for this with his soul. He left his family and his friends and took a boat for the island of Malta. He told them that the Mediterranean trip was vital for his health. What he actually wanted was to be away from all restraining influence. He desired to be left alone with his drug.

For a while he communicated with his family. And then he stopped his correspondence. How could he write to his wife in that old familiar term of endearment, *my darling Sarah*, and to his son, *my blessed Hartley*, realizing as he did to what depths his soul was gradually descending? If they learned the truth, would they not turn from him in disgust?

For two years he remained away from England and left all letters unanswered. The well of his manhood had run dry.

V

Finally his friends prevailed upon him to return to England. His brother-in-law, Southey, had turned back to his muse and was already achieving distinction as a popular poet. Wordsworth was at the height of his creative genius. These old comrades of his were now working with tireless energy. They read him their poems in the first flush of their inspiration. But his own pen was idle. His innermost feelings were lacerated. He couldn't go on like this—an object of pity to his friends and of disgust to his family.

There was but one thing left for him to do, he felt. He must once again relieve his family of the burden of his presence. He fled to London and took rooms above a printing shop where the roaring of the presses drowned out the voices of self-pity that were torturing his soul. For support he secured occasional assignments in journalism.

And then, when his life seemed at its darkest, he was blessed with a sudden flash of good fortune. An influential member of the Royal Institution obtained for him a commission to deliver a series of lectures on the fine arts. This time he was an instantaneous success as a lecturer. For blocks the streets leading to the lecture hall were crowded with the carriages of the London intelligentsia, who came not only to listen to the brilliant speeches but to gaze upon the eccentric speaker. And Coleridge at this period was really something to behold—eyes ablaze with inspiration, lips black with fever and hand all atremble as it reached out for the glass of water. The audience looked on with horrified fascination at this prematurely old poet in his middle thirties, at the rapid silvering of his hair, at his almost paralytic inability to move his lower from his upper jaw. "Intellectually," remarked one of his listeners, "he seems like the one grown man in a race of children. But as for his moral strength, the most charitable comment is—silence." *A god in ruins*—such was the term applied to him by another of his listeners.

Yet the ruined god made one more attempt to reinstate himself. He returned to his family, and for a time he seemed to have achieved a measure of peace. "I have been enabled to reduce the dose (of opium) to one-sixth part of what I formerly took," he jotted down in his notes, "and my general health and mental activity are greater than I have known them for years past." For five months he remained at home. And then once more, without a word, he fled to London.

VI

He came in all humility to the office of the *Courier* and begged for a clerk's job on the paper. Old friends who once would have been honored to brush the dust off his boots were now patronizing enough to take him up as a charity case and to treat him like an office boy.

And then another flash of good fortune. Lord Byron had discovered a drama which Coleridge had written some years back. The play was produced and scored a success. Once more he was

flooded with invitations to give lectures. But his illness inter-
vened. That old and torturing rheumatism again.

And opium was such a blessed relief to his suffering! Yet this
time he was determined, at whatever torture, to break himself
of the habit. He had engaged a man to follow him at all times
and to prevent him, forcibly if necessary, from entering a
chemist's shop whenever he felt the overwhelming impulse to
purchase opium. But the sleepless nights that followed—the
long dark hours of ceaseless agony—almost robbed him of his
reason.

Finally he put himself under the care of Dr Gillman, a friendly
physician, and took up his residence at this man's house for the
remainder of his life. During the greater part of this period he
existed in a state of almost complete lethargy, failing even to
open the letters that he received from his family. Occasionally,
however, he would shake himself out of his deep sleep and
reawaken in his friends the memories of his former greatness.
At such moments he appeared superb in his broken grandeur,
like the wreckage of an ancient temple lighted up by the rays
of the setting sun. "No one who has ever heard him can forget
him." Yet few could explain what there was about his flabby
and irresolute face and the plaintive singsong of his voice that
so profoundly impressed them. Perhaps it was the tragedy of
the eyes, "the confused pain that looked mildly from them
as in a kind of astonishment." Perhaps it was the cadence of his
words that charmed and horrified and transfixed them—a
music that pealed in a great cathedral of intellect sagging
under the tempest of a terrible decay.

Very often it was impossible for anyone to jot down or even
to recall substantial parts of Coleridge's conversations. There
was no more method to his talk than to his life. He touched upon
an amazing variety of incongruous details with a rapidity that
robbed the mind of its breath. He leaped from one subject to
another until he became helplessly lost in a forest of metaphysics and his listeners were overpowered with a tragic sense of
wasted strength. Once, after Coleridge had talked for hours

in his brilliant, incoherent manner, Wordsworth and another friend left the house and walked down the street in silence. Finally Wordsworth's companion turned to him and remarked, "I was a great deal impressed with his speech. I am dazzled by his tremendous wealth of knowledge." And then he added shyly, "I didn't altogether understand the latter part of what he said."

"I didn't understand any part of it," replied Wordsworth.

"Neither did I," confessed the other.

VII

COLERIDGE enjoyed one final period of lucidity not long after he had taken up his residence with Dr Gillman. He published his *Christabel*, a poem of subtle images and sounds which he had written in the years of his unimpaired intellectual activity. But the ears of the critics were not attuned to the new music. They condemned it as "the most notable piece of impertinence of which the press has lately been guilty." The following year Coleridge published a record of his table talks and random jottings—spun together on a bare thread of autobiography—*Biographia Literaria*. This treasure house of criticism on life and literature and philosophy and art was condemned by the critics as the "wild raving of a lunatic." Finally Coleridge issued a volume of his collected verse. This too met with a similar icy blast of condemnation. "Coleridge's poetry is nothing but a quack advertisement for his insane egotism." His literary career had ended in absolute failure. Coleridge was bankrupt.

To provide a little money for the residence of his son Hartley at Oxford, he returned to his old newspaper haunts. With hat in hand he begged for work as a hack writer. And before long he had descended to the revising of school texts and the ghost-writing of sermons for indolent ministers. Once in happier days he had written, "To have lived in vain must be a painful thought to any man!" And now, at sixty, he understood the full meaning of these words. He expressed the tragedy of his failure in one of his later poems:

> All nature seems at work. Slugs leave their lair—
> The bees are stirring—birds are on the wing—
> And Winter, slumbering in the open air,
> Wears on his smiling face a dream of Spring!
> And I the while, the sole unbusy thing,
> Nor honey make, nor pair, nor build, nor sing.

Time was slipping from his grasp. And few were the intervals that illumined the meaning of his existence. Yet these were the only precious moments of his life. One such moment had come to him as he was walking in a lane near Highgate. A "loose, slack, not-well-dressed" young man stepped up and said to him, "Let me carry away the memory, Mr Coleridge, of having pressed your hand." Coleridge had inquired after his impulsive admirer. "This young man," he was told, "is John Keats." Another such golden moment had visited him when they brought him the message from Shelley, whom he had never met—a message which that "wanderer in the night and seeker for the light" had uttered shortly before his death: "Coleridge is the only man alive who can resolve the doubts and the anxieties on the great eternal questions that are crowding my brain."

And Coleridge smiled in his heart on occasions such as these. Who were those self-appointed moralists that gazed down upon him from the galleries of gossip and moaned unctuously over the "failure" of his life? What if he *had* written a pitifully meager amount of poetry? What if he *had* neglected to build a mighty memorial to his genius? What if he *had* garnered a harvest worthy only of a smaller man? So too had the ancient prophets, those dreamers of the infinite whom he so ardently admired. They too had scorned to record the most precious of their gifts in writing. Utterly careless of self-interest, they had scattered the random seeds of their gospel for the ears and the hearts of all. How could anyone measure the sum total of a poet's gift

Wordsworth

Coleridge

to humanity? They called him "a mere idle spectacle of wasted power," a stupendous do-nothing, a crude, shabby curiosity. So they had called Jeremiah. So they had called Socrates.

"By what I have effected am I to be judged by my fellow men; what I could have done is a question for my own conscience." He composed himself for his release to a world of fairer justice, more abundant mercy. He approached the end in the knowledge that he had at last broken himself from the habit of opium. He died at half-past six of a morning in mid-July. A moment later a myrtle which stood in the attic near his bed "burst into bloom and filled the chamber with its fragrance."

George Gordon Byron

1788–1824

He was still in his petticoats when he got into his first fight. His nurse had scolded him for soiling his new frock. Flying into a fury, he seized the frock with his little fists and rent it from top to bottom. Then he charged at his nurse and pummeled and kicked and scratched away at her until she was compelled to call for help. Altogether he had seven fights in his childhood. He won six of them.

He inherited his uncontrollable temper from both sides of the family. His great-uncle had killed a man in a tavern brawl. His father had eloped *with* and then *from* his first wife, had drunk away the property of his second wife and had then deserted her and gone off to die abroad. This second wife, Byron's mother, was a tigress in her own right. In her moments of fury she tore her bonnets and her dresses. When Byron was up to mischief she threw vases and fire shovels at his head and called him a "lame brat." This insult always made Byron blind with rage. For he felt extremely sensitive about his club-foot. One day when his mother hurled this distasteful epithet at him he raised a knife to his throat, and it was only with difficulty that they saved him from slashing himself. In the course of another quarrel the mother and the son threatened each other's life, and each of them went privately to the apothecary's to ascertain whether the other had been there to purchase poison.

The violent whelp of a turbulent family jungle—this is how their neighbors looked upon the youthful Lord Byron. In a somewhat softer strain Byron later described himself in his childhood as

> A little curly-headed, good-for-nothing
> And mischief-making monkey from his birth.

A mischief-making monkey—with a generous heart. One day when he was a student at Harrow a big boy was punishing a little fellow for "insubordination." The punishment consisted in a number of blows administered against "the inner fleshy side" of the little victim's arm. Byron, too small to fight the bully, asked him how many stripes he intended to inflict.

"Why do you want to know?" asked the big fellow contemptuously.

"Because, if you please," said Byron, holding out his arm, "I would take half."

II

THE LIFE OF A MAN with so varied a cluster of passions was bound to be stormy. "If I was born, as the nurses say, with a silver spoon in my mouth, it has stuck in my throat and spoiled my palate, so that nothing put into it is swallowed with much relish—unless it be cayenne." Always he craved for the burning spices of life. At eight he experienced his first love affair. "My misery, my love for that girl were so violent that I sometimes doubt if I have ever been really attached since. When I heard of her being married it nearly threw me into convulsions." At twelve he fell in love again—this time with his cousin, Margaret Parker. She died of tuberculosis, and her death came near to being the end of his own life.

He couldn't bear mental anguish. Yet in the face of physical suffering he was courageous with the courage of the stoic. While he was taking his Latin lesson at school his lame foot was stretched in a wooden contrivance in an effort to straighten it out. His teacher expressed his sympathy at the boy's suffering. "Never mind the suffering, Mr Rogers," said Byron. "If *you* can stand it, *I* can."

As a compensation for his lame foot he hardened the rest of his body with a rigorous course of physical exercise. He rode, boxed, wrestled, fenced, fired pistols and swam. Indeed, he grew up to be one of the best swimmers in England. And one of its handsomest men. With his skin of "moonlight paleness," his dark blue eyes, his dark brown hair, his aristocratic nose, voluptuous lips and sensitive smile, he was part god, part child and—he added cynically—mostly devil. "You see," he said, pointing to his physical defect, "this isn't a *club* foot, it's a *cloven* foot."

He resented his infirmity and gloried in his beauty. Anxious to retain the supple slenderness of his body, he would "nearly let himself die of hunger for days at a time . . . eating only a few biscuits and chewing mastic (to appease his appetite)." And then after a long period of fasting he would succumb to his appetite and plunge into an orgy of feasting. "Yesterday," he tells us in his journal, "I dined tête-à-tête at the Cocoa with Scope Davies—from six till midnight. . . . Drank between us one bottle of champagne and six of claret. . . ."

And thus the restlessness and the pride and the passion of his character swept him along like a consuming fire through the early years of his life. It consumed his vitality and gave wings to his imagination. His poetry was as inevitable as his passion. It was the natural outburst of a madman gifted with a divine pen. In the maddest, divinest and most diabolical of his poems, *Don Juan*, he tells us about the mood in which he gives birth to some of his inspirations:

> . . . I write this reeling,
> Having got drunk exceedingly today
> So that I seem to stand upon the ceiling.

III

AT NINETEEN, when Byron was a student at Trinity College, he published his first collection of poetry, *Hours of Idleness*. The book was caustically though not unjustly reviewed as an immature and amateurish work. This "inability" of the literary critics "to recognize his genius" threw Byron into a paroxysm of rage. He took the unfavorable reviews as a personal insult, and he avenged himself upon his "tormentors" in a satirical lampoon, *English Bards and Scotch Reviewers.*

> Prepare for rhyme—I'll publish, right or wrong:
> Fools are my theme, let satire be my song.

And then, having excoriated the "fools" with his satirical song, he shook the dust of England from his feet. He was sick of a society, he said, which "made phrases and killed men."

He arrived on the Continent, and his passions descended upon it like a hurricane. He committed every sort of folly and confessed to a good many follies which he did not commit. It delighted him to be painted, and even to paint himself, much blacker than he actually was. "Hobhouse told me an odd report—that I am a veritable Corsair, and that part of my travels are supposed to have passed in privacy. Um! People sometimes hit near the truth. . . ." One day he remarked that he would like to experience the only sensation that he had missed thus far—the sensation of being a murderer. "Vice," remarked Sir Walter Scott, referring to Byron's exaggerated self-flagellations, "ought to be a little more modest."

But modesty was the least of Byron's virtues. He was anxious to astonish the world both with the brimstone of his actions and with the brilliance of his thoughts. And he succeeded. Within three years after the completion of his *Satire*—he had now returned to England—he published *Childe Harold*, a poetical (and fictitious) version of his travels. "The effect," writes his biographer, Tom Moore, "was electric." And Byron himself summarized this sudden spontaneous acclamation of his genius in the following terse memorandum: "I awoke one morning and found myself famous." Here was an experience which Byron enjoyed to the full—to be adored by the multitude whom he despised.

And then another surprise to the public and, observed Byron cynically, even to himself. He married.

But the unhappiness that followed this marriage was no surprise to anybody. Byron was not the kind to settle down. And his wife, being the average Englishwoman of her day, was not the kind either to commit or to condone a fault. The very beginning of their honeymoon was inauspicious. As he got into the carriage after the ceremony the poet said to his bride: "Now you are my wife, and that is enough to make me hate you. But if you were somebody else's wife, that would be enough to make me love you." This sort of cynical humor didn't appeal to the matter-of-fact mind of Lady Byron. She was struck with the suspicion that Byron was mad—a suspicion which grew so steadily upon her that she had him examined by a doctor. When the doctor assured her of his mental soundness she retorted: "He may be mentally sound, but he is morally crazy."

She left him, and Byron found himself "standing alone on his hearth, with his household gods shivering around him." And then, "in the very dregs of all this bitter business," an avalanche of public denunciation swept down upon him. Not because of his infidelity but because of his frankness. To sin, believed the Englishmen of the day, was a human necessity; but to *talk* about your sin was a devilish vulgarity. Whenever he entered a ballroom all the men commanded their women to leave it. But this was not enough. The very atmosphere of England, insisted the hypocritical aristocracy, was vitiated so long as this "monster" was permitted to breathe it. Once more he was compelled to leave England—this time never to return.

His departure from England was a public event. As he walked up the gangway to his ship at Dover he was obliged to pass through a huge throng of spectators. Aristocratic ladies had put on the dresses of their chambermaids in order that they might not be observed in the crowd. The whole city seemed to have turned out. The men had come to have a last look at the rascal whom they execrated and admired. And as for the women, they prayed to be the means of his conversion—and the instruments of his diversion.

As the ship sailed into the Channel a squall blew up. "This," laughed Byron, "is my doing. . . . My grandfather, you know, was an admiral. They called him 'Foul-weather Jack,' because wherever he sailed there was commotion."

The squall developed into a tempest. The ship was being driven against the rocks. The passengers kissed their rosaries and prepared themselves for death. The only one who preserved his composure was Byron. "We're all born to die," he said. "As for me, I shall go with regret, but certainly not with fear."

But it was not yet time for him to go. The ship outrode the storm and reached Calais safely. A few days later Byron arrived in Geneva. When he registered at the Hôtel d'Angleterre he wrote opposite the word *age*—"a hundred."

Everybody at the hotel was agog to see this young-old devil of an Englishman—so young in years, so old in experience. But Byron had no time for his admirers. For he had a rendezvous with a lover—Claire Godwin, the sister-in-law of Shelley. He had never met Claire. She had written him a letter, asking him for an assignation. "An utter stranger takes the liberty of addressing you. . . . It may seem a strange assertion, but it is no less true that I place my happiness in your hands. . . . I know that you have the reputation of being mad, bad and dangerous, but nevertheless you hold my destiny. . . ."

At first Byron had refused her request. But finally he had yielded. Geneva was to be the meeting place.

He met her, despised her, loved her and then cast her off. "Now don't scold," wrote Byron to his sister. "A foolish girl, in spite of all I could say or do, would come after me, or rather went before—for I found her here. . . . I could not exactly play the Stoic with a woman who had scrambled eight hundred miles to unphilosophize me. . . ."

There was a child born of this ill-fated passion—Clara Allegra. She was put into a convent, where she drooped like an ill-tended plant and died at the age of five. Byron wanted to have her buried in the church at Harrow, but the churchwardens refused his request. An illegitimate child, they said, had no right to be buried among Christians. And so she was placed away from the society of the dead, just as her father was compelled to stay away from the society of the living.

With his usual bravado he failed to make a public display of his grief at his child's death. But he betrayed it in one of the more tender scenes of *Don Juan*—the description of the father and the dying child:

> And o'er him bent his sire, and never raised
> His eyes from off his face, but wiped the foam
> From his pale lips, and ever on him gazed.
>
> .   .   .   .
>
> The boy expired—the father held the clay
> And looked upon it long . . . .
> Then he himself sunk down all dumb and shivering,
> And gave no signs of life, save his limbs quivering.

A soul too gentle for sorrow in a body too eager for pleasure— this was the tragical paradox of Byron's personality. And in Geneva he met that other poet who, like himself, was a paradox. But Shelley was a paradox of a different type. His was a soul that had lost its way from the splendor of the mountains to the shadows of the valley. He was groping for light and gasping for breath in a world in which he found himself a stranger. And, like Byron, an *unwelcome* stranger. The two men became ardent friends. Byron admired Shelley and pitied him for his simplicity. And Shelley adored Byron and pitied him for his perversity.

For Shelley realized the fact that much of Byron's bravado was a pose—a carnival mask to conceal a sensitive face. He noticed that, in spite of Byron's cynicism, music made him weep. And poetry too, although he insisted that he was "a poet

by avocation and a pirate by vocation." Byron flouted the conventions, just as Shelley did, not out of impiety but out of
generosity. He hated oppression and coercion of any kind. He
was always fighting for the underdog, plotting revolutions, aim-
ing to overthrow tyrants and to emancipate, even against their
will, "the race of inborn slaves who wage war for their chains."

Byron and Shelley—two rebels arrayed against the world.
But while Shelley was a beacon of light, Byron was a whirlpool
of passion. He could never escape from his restlessness, from his
uncontrollable temper, from his consuming hunger for experience. "I could not tame my nature down," he confesses in his
Manfred. He was forever in search of new excitements, new
scenes, new seductions, new mistresses, new dangers. His chief
amusement was to "go a-gleaning in the conjugal gardens of
aristocracy." One after another he aimed at the forbidden
fruits of love—the Countess of Oxford, Lady Frances Webster,
Lady Caroline Lamb, Marianna Segati, La Fornarina, matrons,
maidens and trollops alike—and one by one they fell ripe and
willing into his eager hands. Life, to be endurable, must be
turned into an orgy of forgetfulness. And so—

> Let us have wine and women, mirth and laughter,
> Sermons and soda water the day after.

A brief and stormy carousal—this was Byron's idea of the
least unsatisfactory of worlds. "I will work the mine of my
youth to the last vein of ore, and then—good night."

And the last vein of ore came to him in the person of the
Countess Guiccioli. Byron, together with the Shelleys, had gone
to live in Venice—another stage in their helpless journey to
escape from themselves. And it was at one of the Venetian
receptions that he met the golden-headed countess who was
married to the gray-headed count. As he took leave from La
Guiccioli, Byron managed to slip a note into her hand. It was a
request for a secret rendezvous. She granted the request.

A few weeks later, when the Guicciolis had gone to Ravenna,
they invited Byron to visit them. He came as a guest and re-

mained as a member of the household. The count kept his eyes and his mouth discreetly shut while Byron established himself gradually as the lord of his palace and the lover of his wife.

At last it seemed to Byron that he had found the happiness for which he had been seeking all his life. The young countess was magnificent, munificent and stupid—the three characteristics, he said, which turn a woman into a perfect lover. And the palace in which they lived was as strange as it was splendid. The perfect setting for a romantic love affair. Crimson carpets, marble fountains, "sofas 'twas half a sin to sit upon, so costly were they," tapestries, pictures, vases, and in the center of the hall a marble staircase with all sorts of animals living together in animation if not in harmony—eight dogs mixing it up with five cats, three monkeys, an eagle, a parrot and a falcon. "How human, how excitingly human," remarked Byron one day as he watched a fight among the animals.

And always there was for Byron the added excitement of danger. Not from Count Guiccioli but from the police. For they knew that he was plotting to liberate Italy. They watched the palace, they threatened him with arrest, they even hinted at assassination. But all this turbulence only added spice to the banquet of his life at Ravenna. He was not afraid of death. "We Byrons die young. But while we live our cry is, *onward.* . . . What signifies self? . . . It is not one man nor a million, but the spirit of liberty which counts. . . ."

His days and his nights were as irregular as they were exciting. He got up at midday, breakfasted at two, spent the rest of the afternoon riding or pistol shooting or composing poetry, dined at eight and consumed the rest of the night talking to Shelley or meeting with his fellow conspirators and outlining his plans for the liberation of mankind. As a rule he didn't go to bed until six o'clock in the morning.

He wrote, as he lived, with a passionate and breathless rapidity. He rarely corrected his work. "I can never recast anything. I am like the tiger. If I miss the first spring, I go grumbling back to my jungle again; but if I do it, it is crushing."

And generally he succeeded in doing it, and it *was* crushing. He crushed the conventions of the public, he lunged at their prejudices and their superstitions and he shocked them into buying his books and blushing at their contents and then buying them for their friends. Within a single day the public demand exhausted thirty thousand copies of *The Corsair*. It had taken Byron only ten days to write this poem. His other books were equally spontaneous and equally popular. But perhaps the most popular, certainly the most Byronesque, book of them all was *Don Juan*, a satirical epic which he wrote during his stormy days at Palazzo Guiccioli.

Don Juan, like most of his other books, is a poetical and fictitious story of Byron's physical and mental adventures. It is a mixture of sophomoric witticisms and sublime wisdom— "a necklace of oriental pearls," to quote Taine, "in spite of the occasional intrusion of unnecessary beads of glass." The hero of this poem, like Byron himself, strives desperately against overwhelming odds—hatred, injustice, tyranny, oppression, war. Don Juan possesses two main virtues—the ultra-Puritans, observed Byron, might call them vices—a beautiful form and an impressionable heart. Can you blame beauty for being beautiful and generosity for being generous? Don Juan's aberrations are the result of a too-lavish tenderness. He yields too readily to the blandishments of love. But he yields just as readily to the appeals of distress. Far from being a rogue, Don Juan—Byron himself—is set against roguery of every kind, the roguery of malice, intolerance, barbarity, conquest, kingship and cant. Byron's main purpose in writing *Don Juan*, his main purpose in writing most of his other poems, was to shock the world out of complacency into thought. Skeptical about everything else, he was an ardent believer in the power of the word.

> For words are things; and a small drop of ink
> Falling, like dew, upon a thought, produces
> That which makes thousands, perhaps millions, think.

The word shall make you think, and thought shall make you free.

BYRON

IV

THE PASSION FOR FREEDOM was the dominant note in Byron's personality. Ever restless, ever seeking for the new adventure, the new cause, he threw himself passionately into the Greek struggle for independence. It was an unequal struggle, this resistance of the Greeks against the might of the Sultan—the fight of a small child against a powerful bully. But it was just the sort of fight that aroused all the better instincts in Byron. "How many stripes do you intend to inflict upon this little fellow?" he had once asked when he was a schoolboy at Harrow. Why do you want to know? "Because, if you please, I would take half."

He donated fifty thousand dollars to the Greeks, and then he offered to them the greatest gift in his power—his life. He enlisted in the Greek army at the beginning of 1824. Three months later he lay dead at Missolonghi, the last of the Greek strongholds. He was only thirty-six at the time.

Byron had taken half of the blows. And though he didn't live to see the end of the fight, his sacrifice proved to be enough. For the nations of Europe were electrified by his example. Money and men—from England, from France, from Russia—began to pour into the struggling country, and three years after the death of Byron the Greeks won their victory and their independence.

Percy Bysshe Shelley

1792–1822

Wᴜᴛʜ his dazzling blue eyes, his dark brown hair and his ethereal complexion, he looked like an elfin creature from another world. One day at Eton he was standing in the middle of a circle which he had drawn upon the ground. A group of his fellow pupils were looking on with wide-eyed amazement as he set fire to some alcohol in a saucer and stood enveloped in the bluish flame. Out of the flame came a shrill, piercing voice: "Demons of the air, the water and the fire, I call upon you . . ."

Suddenly one of the teachers appeared. "Shelley, what in the world are you doing there?"

"Please, sir, I'm raising the devil. . . ."

II

Eᴠᴇʀʏʙᴏᴅʏ in the school, teachers and pupils alike, had decided to ostracize this quiet but rebellious little Merlin who on occasion could "raise the devil." The slightest coercion would throw him into a passion of fury. His will was unbreakable. The regulations of the school were, to his supersensitive mind, nothing less than scourges of oppression. He walked over the campus unhappy, defiant, alone. His collar was open at the throat, and his long, uncovered hair was the plaything of the winds. They called him "the mad Shelley" and they organized a "Shelley-baiting society." Whenever he sat down on the riverbank to read his Shakespeare or his Voltaire his schoolfellows would descend upon him like a pack of hunting dogs, chase their quarry over the meadows and finally corner him into a helpless fight against overwhelming odds. Human society, he concluded, was a horde of barbarians with a veneer of culture.

And the leader of this horde of barbarians was Dr Keate, the headmaster of Eton. At the conclusion of one of his sermons Dr Keate had admonished his students to be pure in heart. "And if you're not, I'll flog purity into you through your hides."

A close second to the cruel Dr Keate, thought Shelley, was his father, Mr Timothy Shelley. Uneducated himself, Mr Timothy was passionately insistent upon giving his son a thorough education. He heartily approved of Dr Keate's nostrum to apply learning with the lash. Persuaded by Dr Keate's reports that his son was an ill-natured rebel, he turned Shelley's vacations from school into "periodical journeys into hell."

As for Shelley's mother, a pretty little pepperbox of a lady, she despised her effeminate youngster who preferred to go into the woods with a book instead of a gun.

Yet there were six members of the family who idolized Shelley—his four sisters, his younger brother and his grand-father, Sir Bysshe. His sisters and his brother looked upon him as an enchanter whose nimble fingers could conjure up all sorts of fantastic shapes and colors out of bottles and crucibles. For he was constantly experimenting with chemical substances and electrical contraptions. But even more interesting than his magical fingers was his magical tongue. He could tell the strangest tales and invent the oddest characters—witches and giants and goblins and ghosts, snake-men who lived in the underworld and who at night, when everybody was asleep, squirmed and twisted their way into the Shelley garden, and white-bearded silent skeletons who swung their scythes like lightning in the night and whose king was Father Time. "And if you wake up in the middle of the night and look out of the window, you can see these terrible creatures—yes, every single one of them!"

Sometimes, when he told these stories to the children, his grandfather would listen with a patronizing smile. Sir Bysshe, the head of the Shelley family, prided himself on the fact that he was "as rich as a prince and as rowdy as a pirate." Six feet tall, with a cynical twinkle in his blue eyes and a contemptuous smile on his handsome lips, he had a forthright humor that scandalized the slow-witted mentality of Horsham, the provincial town in which he lived. He saved his money like a miser, for he was anxious to leave his estate intact—not for the sake of his son Timothy, whom he despised, but for the sake of his grandson Percy, whom he adored. For this distinction Percy was duly grateful, although he protested that he would have no use for his grandfather's estate.

Sir Bysshe, believed Shelley, was a nobleman in an ignoble world. In this world, as Shelley had learned to know it in his adolescent years, there was one other nobleman—William Godwin. Shelley had never met Godwin, but he had read his *Political Justice*. Indeed, he had taken this book to his heart like a new Gospel. What a simple and ideal world we should have been born into, thought Shelley, if only Godwin had been God! Laborers would work but two hours a day. Conventionality would be thrown to the winds. Religion would be abolished and philosophy would take its place. The slavery of marriage would give way to the independence of free love. Men would no longer aspire to heaven, for heaven would be brought down to earth. He must be a great man, this Godwin, the *greatest* of men. Someday Shelley must make it his business to sit humbly at the feet of this master.

But for the present it was impossible. For his father had constrained Shelley to enter the university at Oxford.

III

WHEN Shelley entered Oxford (in 1810) he was an anarchist in appearance, habits and thoughts. His tall, lank and fragile figure was dressed in expensive but crumpled clothes. His hair and his boots were generally unbrushed. His face was tense. His gestures were animated, restless, impatient of control. Yet it was the impatience of an otherworldly creature chafing at the patient stupidity of his earth-bound friends.

His room, like his person, was a welter of disorder. Papers, books, buttons, shirts, pistols, poems, chemicals and crucibles lay scattered over the couches, tables and chairs. In the midst of the rubbish lay his electrical machine—a magical instrument with which he loved to startle his new acquaintances when they came into his room. Turning the handle of the machine until the sparks began to shoot into the air, he would suddenly leap upon a glass-legged stool and recite an outlandish incantation as his long dark hair crackled and stood on end. "Shelley is not raising the devil," remarked a student who had heard of his alcohol experiment at Eton. "Shelley *is* the devil."

And this, too, was what his professors said when he astounded them with an essay on *The Necessity of Atheism*. They expelled him from Oxford. Shelley went home in disgrace, only to discover new flames added to the fire of his misfortunes. His father had disinherited him.

He celebrated his attainment of the "blessed state of pennilessness" by eloping with Harriet Westbrook, the daughter of a tavern keeper. It was a marriage not of love but of sympathy. Harriet had aroused his indignation and pity by telling him that her father was trying to tyrannize over her. Among his other atrocities, she informed him, he was compelling her to go to school against her will! Shelley, who wished "no living thing to suffer pain," gave her the protection of his name and removed her from what he regarded as the pernicious influence of her family.

[*142*]

Apparently Harriet's father was not the ogre that she had pictured him to be. Or else he was flattered to see his daughter married to a young man who was the grandson and heir of a baronet. He presented the newly married couple with an allowance of two hundred pounds a year and sent them on their way rejoicing.

They went to Ireland, where Shelley, a stripling of nineteen who looked not older than fifteen, threw himself into the cause of Irish freedom. His generosity proved to be greater than his judgment. One evening, as he was addressing an audience of the Friends of Catholic Emancipation, he declared that it was vicious to refuse employment to an Irishman because of his religion. "One religion," he said, "is as good as another religion." Whereupon a fiery little Irishman in the back of the hall jumped to his feet and cried: "You're a liar, me lad. There's no religion as good as the Catholic!"

Undismayed by his rebuffs, Shelley published and distributed at his own expense an *Address to the Irish People*, urging them to free themselves from "avarice, drunkenness, injustice, folly, superstition and fear." But the Irish looked upon Shelley as a busybody and a madman. The only thing from which they were anxious to free themselves was the domination of the British. Politely but insistently they requested him to abandon his crusade and to leave them alone.

Accordingly the two young crusaders packed their clothes and their pamphlets and took the next boat back to England.

IV

THEY RENTED A COTTAGE in Lynmouth—Shelley, Harriet and their evil spirit in the form of Harriet's mustached and sourtempered maiden sister, Eliza. Harriet misunderstood Shelley, Eliza tormented him and the world anathematized him. But Shelley found a refuge from all this in the world of his poetry—a fairy-tale world of iridescent fancies and soap-bubble texture, a never-never land of splendor and wisdom and mercy and justice and love, an impossible utopia where life is untouched with the disharmony of sorrow, "an isle 'twixt heaven, air, earth and sea, cradled and hung in clear tranquillity."

And he tried to fashion this gossamer dream of his poetry after the pattern of Godwin's philosophy. He had written a letter to Godwin—a daring petition from a mere mortal who aspired to come face to face with his divinity. "You will be surprised," he wrote, "to receive a letter from a stranger. But ... the name of Godwin has been used to excite in me feelings of reverence and admiration. I have been accustomed to consider him a luminary too dazzling for the darkness which surrounds him. . . ." And then he concluded the letter with a hint —he didn't as yet dare to put it in the form of a request—that Godwin might vouchsafe him an interview.

Godwin was only too flattered to receive the homage of this unknown stranger whose pen dripped with fire. He granted the interview, and Shelley took the coach to London.

He found Godwin a rather bedraggled little divinity with a potbelly, harassed by a wife "who wore green spectacles and possessed a nasty temper and a mendacious tongue" and overburdened with poverty and a conglomeration of children by various marriages. One of his children by his first marriage was the seventeen-year-old Mary Wollstonecraft, a young girl with golden hair, a charming face and a brilliant mind—a rare compound, thought Shelley, in a world where physical and mental beauty rarely go together.

He fell in love with Mary and eloped with her. As for his desertion of Harriet, he felt no moral compunction about it. He had married her out of chivalrous pity and not out of love. Their family life had been made unbearable by the presence of that female drill sergeant, Eliza Westbrook. In addition to the nagging of Eliza, Shelley had been obliged to put up with another source of vexation—the secret unfaithfulness of Harriet. Shelley had no objection to free love openly avowed—indeed, he was heartily in favor of it. He expected people to be lavish with their love, just as he expected them to be charitable with their money. But he objected strenuously to clandestine—or, as he called it, stolen—love. He considered it no less reprehensible than stolen money.

And so, by his own standard of morality, he felt justified in leaving Harriet. He had told her frankly that he was going away with another woman, and this open avowal of his intention was to him tantamount to a moral if not a legal divorce. Such was the code of ethics in the immaterial dreamworld of his poetry.

But not in the commonplace, material world of his everyday life. When he left Harriet he tried to get the custody of their only child, Ianthe, on the ground that her mother had neglected her and was at any rate too irresponsible a woman to be entrusted with her care. But the courts refused his petition. More than that, society sided with the courts and compelled Shelley and Mary Wollstonecraft to free England of their "contaminating" presence.

Shortly after his separation from Harriet, Shelley set aside for her maintenance the greater proportion of his own income, such as it was. Moreover, Harriet had entered into an open alliance with one of her former secret lovers, and Shelley felt relieved from any further obligation toward her.

Nevertheless he was prostrated when he heard, two years later, that Harriet had committed suicide. Not that he felt in any way to blame for her tragedy. But the suffering of any living creature, especially of a woman with whom he had lived in intimacy for some time, was unendurable to his acutely emotional soul.

Shelley had now experienced enough of life to bring him to a mature understanding of it. But he was not full grown as yet. Indeed, he never grew up. To the end of his days he retained the illusions and the dreams and the irresponsibilities of a child.

V

ARRIVING upon the Continent, the Shelleys began a gypsy life that lasted for ten years. Their income—Shelley's grandfather had, after all his promises, left the bulk of his estate to Timothy and not to Percy—was scarcely enough to meet the many demands upon his generosity. He supported Leigh Hunt, the poet who had five children, a scolding wife, a rich imagination and an empty purse. He donated a hundred pounds a year to Peacock, the novelist who needed "bread, butter and leisure from worry" in order to give his imagination full play. He provided Charles Clairmont, a mere acquaintance, with enough money to marry a homely and penniless old woman with whom he had fallen in love. ("Love," wrote Shelley, "is the sole principle which should govern the world.") And he poured an endless stream of money into the bottomless sieve of Godwin's poverty. This apostle of the New Freedom, to Shelley's disappointment, had turned out to be a rather sorry product of the Old Slavery. He kept constantly denouncing Shelley for his "criminal depravity" and constantly begging him for more and more money. Occasionally Shelley resented this double-faced hypocrisy of his "illegitimate father-in-law." With sarcastic courtesy he informed Godwin that it was rather undignified for a man to accept his daughter's seducer as his own benefactor. Whereupon Godwin made the philosophic retort that it was rather courageous for a man to castigate his own benefactor as his daughter's seducer. His poverty, he said, demanded money but his morality demanded justice. So exaggerated, indeed, was his sense of justice that he returned all the checks which Shelley had made out to his name. "I will not allow the names of Shelley and of Godwin to appear on the same document," he said. And then he added: "If you make the checks payable to a third person with instructions to transfer them to me, I may consent to cash them." And Shelley, out of the goodness of his heart, always yielded to Godwin's demands.

SHELLEY

He couldn't bear the sight of suffering. Yet he was destined to suffer all his life. His days were like a procession of farewells. For many of those whom he most devotedly pitied or most dearly loved, died. First it was Harriet. The next victim was Fanny, Mary's half sister, who worshiped Shelley from a distance and who, unable to win his worship in return, followed Harriet to a suicide's grave. Next came the tragedy of Shelley's and Mary's first child, a pathetic little creature born before its time and dying within a few weeks. And after that the death of their two other children: Baby Clara—it was raining when they buried her at Lido—and Willie. This last was the hardest blow of them all. Willie—they called him "Willmouse"—was Shelley's favorite. He was an affectionate, intelligent and sensitive child, a little poet like his father. He had his father's blue eyes and his mother's golden hair. And it was a blue-and-golden day when he died. They buried him in Rome.

Restless gypsies, leaving a trail of sorrow in their wake. And wherever they went Shelley wrote his poems—those rainbow-tinted bubble worlds with which he tried to conquer the squalid world of his sorrow. To quote his own words, "he learned in suffering what he taught in song."

And there were days when he threw himself so completely into his songs that he forgot to eat his meals. Mary was in the habit of sending his food into the room where he studied, but frequently he left his plate untouched upon the bookshelf until the end of the day when, calling to his wife, he would ask, "Mary, have I dined?"

Completely absorbed in his dreamworld, he walked like a stranger in the world of men. Indeed, he generally avoided the society of men. He felt more at home among the objects of nature. He spent most of his life in the woods, among the mountains, in his boat. The rivers spoke to him, the sea waves rippled with laughter, the trees shook an intelligible music out of their leaves, the clouds flew over his head like a flock of living birds, the wind came sweeping down like a titan from the mountains, snatching the hailstones out of the pouch that had been slung over his shoulder and laughing uproariously as he scattered them over the fields.

Shelley cared little for the petty gymnastics of mortals. He preferred to watch the sunrise as it leaped upon a cloud and hurtled over the horizon; or "that orbed maiden, with white fires laden, whom mortals call the moon," as she danced daintily over the midnight floor of the heavens. The stars were a flock of golden bees. He heard their divine humming and translated it into music that mortal ears could understand. His fancy seemed suspended between heaven and earth. On the one side lay infinity gemmed with stars; on the other side sailed the earth-barque of green and gold and silver into which his body had been cast for a temporary cruise. And he noticed that a single universal law guides the course of the stars in the heavens and the destinies of men on earth. This universal law is beauty—a term which, translated into politics, means justice and, paraphrased into poetry, signifies love.

It was the aim of Shelley to abolish every injustice and "to flush the world with love." He wanted to liberate mankind from the tyranny of man. Like the divine rebel in his *Prometheus Unbound*, he was eager to wipe out "all the oppressions that are done under the sun," to bring about "the dethronement of the tyrants" and the "unveiling of the threats and the frauds" by which the human race has been deluded into submission. He would have a world without aggression, without hatred or vice, without despotism or famine or strife. He would attune the heart to the poem of pity and regenerate the soul with the religion of love.

And—it was over a hundred years ago that he wrote these prophetic words—"the world waits only the news of a revolution in Germany . . . to see the tyrants precipitated into the ruin from which they shall never arise. . . . For the defeat of the tyrants is the beginning of justice."

VI

SHELLEY was still a wandering exile, but he was no longer lonely. For he had found congenial friends—the Williamses, Lord Byron and Trelawny. The Williamses, Edward and Jane, were a charming couple. Edward, a former officer of the British Dragoons, was gay, frank and fearless. And Jane was unconventional and pretty. She had a voice "smooth and soft like the petal of a flower," and when she sang Shelley lost himself like a child in forgetful dreams.

The company of the Williamses was a soothing contrast to that of Byron, the apostle of the religion of laughter. Byron considered Shelley "the most gentle, the most amiable and least worldly-minded person" he had ever met; and Shelley, although he was not blind to Byron's moral imperfections, nevertheless found a vein of golden sincerity under the surface of his cynical indifference. These two men, the devil and the archangel in the rebellious forces of the nineteenth century, became deeply attached to each other. They spent their days in sailing upon the Italian lakes and their nights in conversing about the blunders of the gods and the sufferings of men.

Quite different from the Williamses and Byron, but equally congenial to Shelley, was Trelawny. This wild-faced, dark-mustached and dark-eyed young adventurer was a strange mixture of the poet and the pirate. Having traveled all over the world and encountered all sorts of manners and men, he was at last delighted to have made the acquaintance of the "two most interesting men of his generation"—Byron and Shelley. Trelawny's first encounter with Shelley was through Shelley's eyes. "Tre," as he was known to his friends, was paying a visit to the Williamses. He was engaged in animated conversation with them when he suddenly became aware of two flames staring at him out of the dark passage near the open door. Jane noticed Trelawny's startled look. "It's only Shelley," she laughingly observed. And then, going to the doorway, she said,

"Come in, Shelley, and meet our friend Tre who has just returned from one of his piratical expeditions."

Shelley always had the strangest way of meeting people. One day a shipbuilder by the name of Captain Roberts had come to see him about an order for a boat which Shelley wanted the captain to build for him. When the visitor arrived Shelley had disappeared. Mary invited the captain to remain for luncheon. As they sat down to table Mary cried out in amazement, "Why, Percy, how dare you!" Captain Roberts looked up and saw Shelley walking across the room stark naked. He had the appearance of a young god as he advanced toward the table, his body glittering with moisture and his hair tangled with seaweed.

"Didn't know you had a visitor, Mary," he said by way of explanation. And then, turning to the captain, he observed with a disarming smile, "I was just taking a little sea bath, sir, when I suddenly realized I might be late for luncheon."

VII

SHELLEY was passionately fond of the sea but he didn't know how to swim. Swimming, he said, was a foolish precaution against death. As for himself, he needed no such precaution. For he was more afraid of life than he was of death. Life, he observed, is the Great Mystery and death is the key to its solution. "In our present gross material state (while we are alive) our faculties are clouded. But when death removes our clay coverings the mystery will be solved." One day as he was bathing in the Arno, together with his friend Trelawny, he accidentally plunged into deep water and "lay stretched out at the bottom," writes Trelawny, "like a conger eel, not making the least effort to save himself." When rescued by Trelawny he remarked somewhat whimsically, "I always seek the bottom of the well, for they say Truth lies there. In another minute I should have found it. . . . Death is the veil which those who live call life; they sleep, and it is lifted."

And it was not long before the veil was lifted. He was but twenty-nine when he died. Yet he had lived long enough to contribute his chapter to the Bible of the religion of love. His end was like that of an ancient prophet. Together with his friend Williams he was sailing in his new boat over the Bay of Spezia. Suddenly a storm arose. It lasted only twenty minutes. When the sun came out again the boat had disappeared. Shelley had been snatched by the whirlwind out of the world whose mystery he had tried so hard to fathom.

Several days later they found his body and burned it on a funeral pyre. As the flames rose into the air Byron broke down. Turning away from the scene, he stripped and swam out into the ocean. But Trelawny remained behind to watch the body melting into the flames. At the end of three hours the heart alone remained unconsumed. And then Trelawny rescued it from the fire, burning his hand painfully as he did so.

They buried it in the Protestant cemetery of the Eternal City —this heart out of which had sprung the poetry of eternal love.

John Keats

1795–1821

He was born of undistinguished parents. His grandfather kept a livery stable. His father was the top stableman who married the daughter of his employer.

John was the first of their children. He went to school at Enfield where, like the other sons of the moderately well to do, he labored over his Latin and took his recreation in the lake. But he was more sensitive than his schoolmates; his teachers referred to him as a "creature of passion." During his early weeks at Enfield he suffered from homesickness. When he tumbled into bed at night he stuffed the blankets into his mouth so that no one would hear him sobbing. Pale, thin, scarcely above five feet, he was nevertheless a born fighter with the courage of a terrier. And upon the slightest provocation he was ready to give a good account of his fists. But he was more interested in his books than he was in his fists. Whenever he opened a book he plunged into a "positive debauch of reading."

He lost his parents before he was fifteen. His father was killed by a fall from a horse, and his mother died of consumption. The young "fighter-poet" was placed under the guardianship of Mr Abbey of Walthamstow, and the boyhood years whose excitement had been "like the reading of an ever-changing tale" came abruptly to a halt. For there was an immediate duty to be faced—he must make a definite decision as to his future career. His guardian apprenticed him to a surgeon in Edmonton. But Keats had no fondness for this sort of work. He had made up his mind to accomplish great things—but not in surgery. His well-meaning friends were rather sorry to see the direction of his thoughts when he called on one of them and requested a loan of Spenser's *Faery Queene*. He romped through the scenes of the poetic romance "like a young colt turned loose in a spring meadow." He had caught the poet's fever. There was no turning him aside.

For a while he continued his surgical apprenticeship and received his certificate as a "dresser" of wounds. Then he went back to his poetry with the excuse that he dreaded "doing mischief" in his surgical work.

He was a stubborn young man, intoxicated with a madness for beauty. No one dared argue his decision. When aroused he was a whirlwind of fury. As a child of five, in a fit of ungovernable temper, he had snatched up his sword and placed himself before the door of his mother's bedroom with the declaration that nobody must enter or leave the house. People were amazed at the intensity of his emotion. He lived his life with his entire being. "He could feel joy and sorrow with his hands."

II

HE WAS TWENTY-TWO, a young man committed to a "foolhardy" profession and devoted to a group of dreamers like himself. He drew a small income from his father's property, and he lived in Hampstead with his brother Tom, next to the Green Man Tavern. Another of his brothers, George, had married and taken his wife to America. His young sister Fanny was a girl in her teens, still living under the roof of her guardian, Mr Abbey.

John Keats was a happy young man. He was at work on a full-length poem. He had found a publisher. He deeply relished the society of his friends—the essayist Leigh Hunt, his old school chum Cowden Clarke and that delightful Falstaff of over-guzzling and overbubbling rotundity, Charles Armitage Brown.

But suddenly, and unannounced, tragedy stepped into the life of John Keats. His brother Tom was stricken with the family disease—consumption. For months the doctors, in their ignorance, bled him and starved him and reduced him to a specter. John nursed him tenderly and hour by hour watched him slip away. In order to get a much-needed rest for himself he went on a walking tour, together with Charles Brown, over the Lake Country and the Western Highlands. But a sudden cold and sore throat forced him to interrupt the trip and return to London.

He came back just in time to see his brother go. Tom was scarcely twenty at the time of his death.

In his despair John Keats plunged into the whirl of society. He sought the presence of young and attractive women. For above all he was a poet and a lover of beauty. Though bashful by nature, he had once remarked jocosely that at the sight of a beautiful woman he was "too much occupied in admiring to be awkward or in a tremble. I forget myself entirely, because I live in her." And so he feasted himself upon the conversation of the "lovely London ladies whose lips were a banquet." And among these "London ladies" was Fanny Brawne—not beautiful like the others, but lively and exciting and young. She was only eighteen when he met her for the first time. He mentioned her "somewhat casually" in a letter to his brother in America. "Shall I give you a sketch of Miss Brawne? She is about my height. . . . She wants sentiment in every feature. . . . Her mouth is bad, and good; her profile is better than her full face. . . . Her arms are good, her hands bad-ish, her feet tolerable. . . . But she is ignorant, monstrous in her behavior, flying out in all directions; calling people such names that I was forced lately to make use of the term *minx*." Such an attempt to throw dust in his brother's eye was of no avail. He had fallen madly in love with her.

III

HE LONGED for an early marriage to Fanny Brawne and for a short pleasure voyage to Rome. But such was merely a poet's dream. There would be no early marriage. He was a young man of limited means, with no regular occupation save that of writing verse. And this verse, he soon learned to his bitterness, was an object of ridicule almost everywhere. When he published his first poem, *Endymion*, beginning with the immortal line, "A thing of beauty is a joy forever," the brash young critics pounced upon him for what they termed his "cockney poetry" and referred to him as an individual "who had left a decent calling for this melancholy trade. . . . We do most solemnly assure our readers," they continued facetiously, "that this poem, containing 4074 lines, is printed on very nice hot-pressed paper and is sold for nine shillings by a very respectable London bookseller. . . . We think it necessary to add that it is all written in rhyme and for the most part (when there are syllables enough) in the heroic couplets." They concluded by advising Keats to return to his surgery or to his father's stables.

But Keats, for all his disappointment, was little daunted. He had stubbornly made up his mind to persist in his craft. Only a mediocre talent would be stopped in its development by a scurrilous attack. Many of his friends, Percy Shelley among them, declared that they had found passages of genuine poetic beauty in *Endymion*. But Keats was not to be deceived. There wasn't an atom of affectation about him. The critics were absolutely correct in regard to the "slipshod" totality of *Endymion*. "That is no fault of mine. . . . It is as good as I had the power to make it—by myself. . . . Had I been nervous about its being a perfect piece, and with that view asked advice, and trembled over every page, it would not have been written. . . . I was never afraid of failure; *for I would sooner fail than not be among the greatest.*"

The genius of poetry, he felt, must be self-taught. It must struggle through its own pitfalls to its own ultimate salvation.

IV

His FINANCIAL CONDITION had become more serious. His inheritance had been "frozen" in an interminable lawsuit. His
brother George had returned from America to collect his portion of the legacy upon the death of Tom. He had taken not
only his own share but a substantial part of John's money,
which he promised to remit as soon as he sold some property.
But John never received this remittance. In the golden dawn
of his love he scorned to deal with the minted gold of the money-
changers. Carried away by the ecstasy of his passion, he wrote
an ode to Saint Agnes—the Roman virgin of Christian faith
who had been martyred in the persecutions of Diocletian. According to the ancient legend the parents of Agnes, having come
to pray at her tomb, were dazzled at the vision of their daughter
transfigured with a crown of light and surrounded by a host of
angels. Throughout the Middle Ages the martyred Saint Agnes
had become the symbol of virgin purity who took the sinless
young maidens under her protection. Once a year, on the eve of
her name day, she blessed them with a dream in which they
beheld their future husbands. But those who wished to be
favored with this vision must first perform certain necessary
rites. They must fast all day and go to bed without a morsel of
food. They must refrain from kissing any man, woman or child
until the breaking of the fast with the husband of their dreams.
Inspired by this legend, Keats sang of one such maiden, Madeleine, who had found her true lover, Porphyro, in the moonlit
chamber of an ancient Gothic castle. And from that day on,
young lovers and maidens the world over have thrilled to the
enchantment of his song. *The Eve of St Agnes* is the first adequate
expression of the poet's genius.

And the more discerning of the critics were not slow to recognize it as such. A member of the firm which published *The Eve
of St Agnes* confided in a letter to his cousin that if this poem of
John Keats were to be compared to the poetry of Shakespeare

written at approximately the same age, the work of Keats "would be found to contain more beauties, more inspiration (and that of a higher order), less conceit and bad taste and, in a word, much more promise of excellence than are to be found in Shakespeare's work. This is a deliberate opinion, nor is it merely my own. . . ."

But Keats was not carried away by this praise. He knew that he still had much to learn before he could attain perfection. In the eagerness of his youth he was forevermore experimenting with the music of his words, with the psychology of his imagery and with the magic of his color. And he was creating effects that had never been achieved before him. He fashioned phrases that appealed not only to the outer physical senses but to the inner senses of the mind. Nor did he point a moral in his art. His art *was* his moral. He suggested rather than expounded his experience. Like the German poet Goethe, he felt that beauty was the only pathway to truth. The light of art, he believed, held more revelation than the laws of science. The genuine realities of existence were invisible to the eye of reason. They were manifest only to the poet's soul in its most sublime moments.

And in his quest to discover the realities of life he wandered through the cathedrals, companioned only by his dreams. The sun, sifted through the stained-glass windows, gave a mystical magic to the lofty silent ceilings, the channels of buttresses, the aisles of pilasters, the vast vaulted forests of the Gothic architecture. Here he could fancy himself into the past and invest it once more with the breath and the color of life. He wrote a poem in ancient ballad form, *La Belle Dame Sans Merci* (The Beautiful Lady without Mercy)—as perfect a rose of genius as ever breathed in the fragrant gardens of medieval chivalry. And then, having resurrected the romance of the Middle Ages, his restless fancy journeyed into the more distant past. He wrote an *Ode on a Grecian Urn*, a poem of pagan grandeur. He knew not a syllable of the Greek language, yet with the magic key of his genius he opened the monuments of the ancient dead and there walked forth a world of living men. But, forever restless, he immediately left this ancient world and journeyed down the corridors of his imagination back to the casements that opened upon the glowing horizons of the present.

His genius had now arrived at its modest maturity. "I am three and twenty," he remarked. "In the height of enthusiasm I have been cheated into some fine passages." This was a marvel of understatement for a poet who had already written some of the greatest lines in the English language.

In many respects, however, he was still an immature boy. If he had succeeded in echoing the sensuous pipings of Pan, he was still groping humbly for the wisdom of Plato. Only through the patient years of growth would he gradually attain to the philosopher's understanding of this life which he so gloriously felt in every fiber of his poet's being. In spite of his immortal songs his love for Fanny Brawne had all the fallibility of a youthful mortal. He loved her with a passion that demanded an outlet in a marriageable union. But due to his financial inadequacy this was impossible. He wrote her letters stamped with a great yearning and sealed in pain. During separations he accused her of unfaithfulness. For she ached with an overripeness of sociability and, for want of her lover's company, she sought the companionship of others. She was young and overbubbling with spirits. She had fallen short of his ideal because she was so charmingly human. It was the beating of her little heart for pleasure that provided her with the tempo of her life. As a lover of beauty in abstraction, Keats was a perfect poet; as an anguished young man who was insanely jealous of his sweetheart, Keats was the imperfection—of a lover. "Extreme sensibility was struggling in him with a great understanding." What was the answer to the eternal riddle?

Destiny was soon to supply the answer. On a February day in his twenty-fifth year he caught one of his frequent chills while riding in the stagecoach. He returned home with a fever and prepared to lie down. But before his head had reached the pillow he coughed and called for a candle. "That was blood from my mouth. Let me look at it." He gazed at the stain for some moments with the eye of the medical student and then turned to Charles Brown who happened to be in the room at the time. "I know the color of that blood. It is the color of consumption." And then, with an expression Brown would never erase from his mind, "That drop of blood is my death warrant."

V

THE DISEASE had taken John's mother in her prime. It had carried away his brother Tom at twenty. And now it was preparing to claim its third victim in the family—at twenty-five. So *that* was the reason for his continual susceptibility to sore throats and frequent fatigue, declared his friends. And that was the reason for the soft melancholy of his verse. He had always written with the tenderness of a dying man.

Yet even now he hoped against hope and refused to believe the worst. The physicians maintained that he had been stricken with nothing more than a cold in the lungs. For months, however, he was confined to the routine of an invalid. And from time to time, as he corrected the proofs of his poetry, the blood rushed to his lungs with such violence that he nearly suffocated.

And now the volume of his poems came off the press. But it was left far in the shadow by the glaring sunlight of glory that streamed over a contemporary volume of verse—*Poems Descriptive of Rural Life and Scenery*—written by a young peasant, John Clare, and devoured by the public in a sensational orgy of reading. John Clare lived to see his poetry die. John Keats was to die before he knew that his poetry would live.

And now the doctors told him that he must desist not only from writing but even from reading poetry. Was this, then, to be the end of all his striving? In that case he had nothing left but his love. Like a drowning man he clutched at his passion for Fanny Brawne. She was now his sole protection, his religion, his hope. If he could not have her as a wife, he wanted her as a mother. He felt like a tired child longing to be pillowed to sleep upon his mother's breast, to feel the rise and fall of her soft breath. "And so live ever—or else swoon to death." And Fanny Brawne responded admirably. She nursed him and smoothed away his dark anxieties and realized in her heart that there was no future for them, not a single hope.

When spring came and warmed the English landscape with its radiance of colors Keats was the only icy thing alive. For a time his health had rallied, but then he had again ruptured a blood vessel and had fallen into a languor. As his spirits revived they wheeled him to a window where he might observe the stirrings of the outer world. Beyond the curtain he saw all that passed. The people of reality merged with the people of his fancy—old women with bobbins and red cloaks, gypsies with hareskins and silver spoons, and a stately fellow carrying under his arm a wooden clock. He shivered as he fancied that this clock was striking out the seconds of his allotted time.

And yet the creator of so much beauty in poetry refused to believe that he had been abandoned by the Creator of so much beauty in the world. His physicians had advised him to seek a warm climate for the approaching winter, and Keats wrote cheerfully to Fanny: "'Tis not yet consumption, I believe; but it would be, were I to remain in this climate all winter." He braced himself for a journey to Italy. After a winter of sunshine he would spend an English summer close to Fanny. Perhaps, he reasoned, it was on his beloved's account that he had been imagining his sickness to be more serious than it really was. How terrible had been the thought of slipping into the ground instead of rushing into her arms! "The difference is amazing, love." Death must come to everyone at last, but before that fateful hour he would fain try the pleasures so sweet a beloved could give him. "Take care of yourself, dear, that we may both be well in the summer." What matter if he seemed to be rapidly wasting away and his sputum gave rise to alarming conclusions? Life at best was bodily decay, slow or rapid as the fates would have it. And all men sooner or later wasted away. But the genuine truth lay not in these evanescent and ugly appearances; the truth lay far beyond, in man's abiding faith in the ultimate beautiful setting of each and every destiny. For beauty is truth— truth, beauty. That is all we know on earth and all we *need* to know. . . .

Strong in the faith that truth is beauty and that beauty is immortal, he prepared to leave for Italy. He wrote to Fanny about his hope and his faith and his love. "My angel Fanny . . . I will be as patient in illness and as believing in love as I am able. . . . I shall never . . . bid you an entire farewell. . . ."

On a bleak and frozen dawn in late September the poet rode to the London docks. His friends had arranged for a young man to accompany him—an artist by the name of Joseph Severn. Together they boarded the *Maria Crowther*, and after a stormy passage down the Atlantic they sailed into the Mediterranean waters that cradled the beams of the tropical sun. Keats stood fascinated in the grip of his thoughts. Beyond lay Italy in the blinding embrace of the high noon. Life, beauty, truth, poetry—and then twilight and the night. He knew now that he faced the early setting of his own sun. But he was unafraid. The light of the morning includes in its cycle the evening star. And a poet must never fear the vespers of life.

He arrived in Naples none the better for his voyage. He coughed much blood. Somehow, as he viewed the splendid scenery, he felt himself completely detached from it. If he had been well there was enough beauty in the harbor of Naples to fill a quire of letters to Fanny. Everyone who could row a boat and walk briskly and live heartily was a different being from himself. And at times he looked even upon himself with a philosophic objectivity. He was a man, he said, walking through a strange dream of suffering.

Percy Shelley, who was residing in Naples, sent him an invitation to spend the winter with him. But Keats declined the offer and continued in the direction of Rome. Once, referring to Shelley's poetry, he had remarked: "Does Shelley go on telling strange stories of the deaths of kings? Tell him there are strange stories of the deaths of poets. Some have died before they were conceived."

He arrived in Rome "a man without lungs." His suffering was beyond description. When the doctor came to see him the poet murmured, "How long will my posthumous life last?" His companion, Joseph Severn, had snatched from him during the journey a bottle of laudanum that the poet had concealed with the purpose of taking his life, if necessary, to spare himself the misery of an extended illness. "But for me," Severn wrote home, "he would have swallowed this draught on the ship." The dying man charged Severn with keeping him alive by his cruelty. "And for this cruelty no name, no treatment, no privations can be too great for him," raged the poet. Yet Severn was a good fellow after all. What a burden he had taken upon his shoulders when he had offered to accompany a consumptive to Italy! They would probably burn the beds and the sheets and the curtains and scrape the walls when he passed on, and Severn would receive the bill. The poor devil would have to pay a good price to watch a poet die. If only he had realized when he embarked for Italy that he was traveling with a corpse on its last journey. What a bitter jest of the fates! "Well, we must be firm, Severn. You shall return to England, and I shall be laid to rest in the quiet grave." And then he added, "Thank God for the quiet. It will be the first I have ever known."

As the night came down he remembered some of the lines he had written in the brief day of his health to the great poets of the past: "Bards of passion and of mirth, who have left your souls on earth . . . you have souls in heaven, too, double-lived in regions new. . . ."

The tempest in his mind subsided like a charm. "Lift me up, Severn," he mumbled finally, in the accents of a child drifting into a pleasant sleep. "I am dying . . . I shall die easy." And when he saw the terror-flooded eyes of the artist: "Don't be frightened. Thank God it has come."

BROWNING

Great Poems by Browning

The Ring and the Book.
Paracelsus.
Sordello.
Stafford.
Pippa Passes.
A Blot on the 'Scutcheon.
My Last Duchess.
Fra Lippo Lippi.
Andrea del Sarto.
The Bishop Orders His Tomb.
Pauline.
Youth and Art.
The Pied Piper of Hamelin.
How They Brought the Good News.

Incident of the French Camp.
Home Thoughts from Abroad.
Up at a Villa—Down in the City.
Abt Vogler.
Prospice.
Rabbi Ben Ezra.
Saul.
Cavalier Tunes.
Hervé Riel.
In a Balcony.
The Lost Leader.
Love Among the Ruins.
The Heretic's Tragedy.

Robert Browning

1812–1889

As a child he kept a menagerie. What owls and snakes and monkeys and parrots he had! And there was room for an eagle, too, and for hedgehogs and toads and lizards. Lizards were his favorite creatures. Golden lizards. He knew the tune to lure them into the sunshine; he never lost that secret. . . . And next to his lizards he liked his frogs. When his stomach was upset and his mother brought him his disagreeable medicine she must promise to catch him a frog before he would swallow a spoonful.

His mother was so understanding. She was a remarkable and beautiful woman. Lovely eyes and skin and a passion for music. Blessed mother, playing wild cadences on the pianoforte! He stood silently by the oaken bookcase in the soft blue twilight, and with wistful eyes that worshiped he watched her carry the melody to her fingers as the night fell aslant on the bookshelves. And the tears ripened as the little figure stood half afraid and indistinct until she turned around and saw him. And then he ran to her and threw his arms around her. "Mother, play, play!" Sobbing at what he knew not. Plunged into a paroxysm of emotion at the music.

When he grew older he heard that she had come from the Indies, this adorable beautiful mother with the olive skin, and that she had the wild poetry of the Creoles in her blood. And he felt her sunburned passion in his own blood too. Walked around and around the dining-room table, which was just on a level with his head, reciting verses and making music. Turned the simple odes of Horace into English meter some five years before his voice changed. Fell madly and desperately in love with a married woman fifteen years his senior. And he was scarcely ten. Such, he lamented, was the way of women! For she had failed to notice him. And the passionate little poet wrote bitter sonnets to the unfaithfulness of his mistress. He yearned for dark eyes and caresses, for "wastes of ocean and illimitable sands." His father packed him off to Mr Ready's Boys' School at Peckham where he might cool his heels and await his manhood.

II

THE ELDER BROWNING had feathered a comfortable nest on his salary as a bank officer. He was a painter of talent and a scholar —big and kindly and sympathetic and firm. And amazingly courageous. When he neared the point of death—he was past eighty at the time—his cheerfulness alarmed even the doctor who attended him. "Does the old gentleman know he is dying?" the doctor inquired of his daughter in a low voice. The father overheard him and smiled. "Death is no enemy in my eyes."

Robert inherited from his father his robust optimism and his superb physique. He received a thorough preliminary training in the languages and the fine arts; and then, dispensing with a formal university education, he set out from England to travel over the continent and to acquire the less academic but more realistic degree of B.E.—Bachelor of Experience. He had decided on a literary career. And he was brimming with creative energy. He wanted to project himself into the thoughts of other people, to poetize unexplored ideals, to capture the features of the landscape that looms in the semidarkness of man's subconscious. Let others continue to mirror the morning dews. He would explore the souls of men. And this exploration, he hoped, might bring him closer to the secret of life—perhaps to the very threshold of immortality. He wanted to be the poet of life, of joyousness, of aspiration, of hope. He scoffed at the idea that the poet must be a man of melancholy moods—that he must hold a gun to his temple before he can find self-expression in his verse. Why the sighing and the crying over the transiency of things? "Have you found your life distasteful? My life did and does smack sweet."

Yet at the outset he failed in his self-appointed task. He had formed a poem—*Pauline*—out of the rose's blush when he had tried to fashion it like a flameflower that blossoms out of the hammered iron. To be sure, the poem appealed to the critics and even to some of his fellow poets. Dante Gabriel Rossetti, for example, had been "captivated by its charm." But this praise neither flattered nor satisfied Browning. He would soon try again—and then he would write such music as would frighten the spirit of repose out of all the fashionable ears!

At present, however, he was known to only a few as a poet. He was recognized rather as an artist and musician who had studied in Italy—one of a myriad of esthetes who buzzed off to Venice in order to bring home a taste of the "sweet culture" from the honeycomb of the Renaissance. How many of those who studied in Italy were genuine about their affection for her? People moistened their lips and told fantastic stories of her wonders and wrote enthusiastic letters wet with sentiment. But Browning was silent when he returned to England. If they asked him questions, what could he reply? "Italy was my university." Picking up a scrap of wastepaper and holding it carefully over a burning candle, he moved it back and forth across the smoke that rose from the flame until the paper was clouded over in spots. And then he took his pen and transformed the clouded blots into definite shapes. "These are the clouds, the canals, the buildings, the lights and the shadows of Venice. This is Italy." When he died they might dig his heart from the rest of his body and find Italy graven there.

But for the present he must return to his writing. God gave

[*171*]

man the English language so he might turn it into perfect verse. He gave man the clay for the potter's wheel. Now let it spin. Browning was a young poet of strong moods. It would be his business to describe minutely each one of these moods. He enjoyed strolling at night through Dulwich Forest, "where the stars meet and wrestle overhead." He would write a drama of the stars, scattering and flinging them across the yawning gulf of the darkness. And it would be up to the understanding reader to gather them and string them into a constellation of meaning. Oh, the wild joy of living and writing! Back in his father's library he had read about a man—no, a star—Paracelsus, the ingenious scientist-philosopher of the Middle Ages. Philippus Aureolus Theophrastus Bombastus ab Hohenheim was his Christian name. A mastermind of medievalism, a dark, long, twisting circuit of an intelligence, a superevil, superknowing power of destruction was this Paracelsus, the man who had given mankind the deadly laudanum and who had explored the mysteries of demonology. The man of science who aspired to supreme knowledge—and lacked a heart. He had studied the underground energy of the earth that bubbles up into molten fires and heaves the mountains into valleys and scoops out the beds of the oceans and heats the sap of life in the veins of flowers and beasts and men. And he had mastered his medicine and hoarded his knowledge and heaped his facts and classified his data and labeled everything—except love. He dissected the body and neglected the soul. If only some poetic impulse could stir his frozen science with the breath of April! If only the power of love could break the chrysalis of his slumbering soul! "There is no good of life but love—but love!"

Browning created quite a stir with his poem about Paracelsus. At last he had succeeded in molding the clay of his thought on the potter's wheel of his fancy. "This young poet shows genius. . . . Another Chaucer on the horizon. . . . More brightness to your plumage, more height aloft the breeze. . . . The siren waits you singing." Toasts at dinners to the young poet. Felicitations by his fellow poets, Wordsworth and Landor.

Adoration by the tragedian, Macready. "Will you write a dramatic piece for the stage? Something after *Othello*." "Macready," Browning had once remarked, "*bit* me by his performance of *Othello*."

But the occasions that "bit" Browning were few and far between. His life at London was very prosaic for a poet. He studied daily in the library of the British Museum. He took rooms near the Strand where he could keep in continual touch with the theater. He paid routine visits to the National Gallery. A monotonous life in a humdrum world.

But one day in Dulwich Forest he saw a storm crowned by a double rainbow—a bridge of color over which his fancy passed upward from earth into heaven. And in that momentary flash of inspiration he realized that this is the universal roadway of life and that everybody's passage over this road is a magnificent event, no matter how great and lordly a man may be or how obscure and small. For "God's in His Heaven" and "all's right with the world." And, fired with this inspiration, he wrote a poem, *Pippa Passes*. In this poem he tells the story of a simple mill girl, apparently too insignificant to leave any permanent traces of her passing as she strolls through the village with a song on her lips. Yet the strains of her song are carried to the ears—and to the hearts—of various groups of people who have come to a crisis in their lives. And all those who hear this song—though Pippa is unaware of her influence—are inspired with new strength, new beauty, new hope. God chooses the humblest of His creatures for His messengers. And through His chosen messengers He redeems the race. All service ranks the same with God. All people within range of all songs reflect something of the light of this universal truth. We are His puppets, best and worst. In life "there is no last nor first."

And Browning continued on his leisurely stroll until he passed into the thickest part of the forest of life. Here the intertwining branches caught the light of day in their nets and held it for ransom away from the eyes of men. And Browning, trying to pierce through the darkness, wrote another work about the mystery of the human soul. The critics called this work "a derelict upon the ocean of poetry—the most obscure verse of the century." When a friend just recovering from an illness opened a copy of *Sordello* he was thrown into a state of alarm after he had read the first few lines. "Sentence after sentence brought no consecutive thought to my brain. At last the idea occurred to me that my mental faculties had been wrecked in my illness." The perspiration rolled from his forehead, and, smiting his head, he sank back on the sofa, crying, "O God, I *am* an idiot!" He called his wife and his sister, thrust the book into their hands and asked them what they thought of it. As they commenced to read he watched their faces intently for any glimmer of understanding. Finally his wife replied, "I don't know what this man means; it is gibberish." Her husband sighed with relief. He was not an idiot after all! Lord Tennyson read the poem and remarked bitterly, "There are only two lines in it that I understand, and they are both lies." These are the opening and the closing lines of the poem: "Who will may hear Sordello's story told" and "Who would has heard Sordello's story told." Carlyle, with even greater bluntness, remarked: "My wife has read through the poem without being able to make out whether Sordello was a man or a city or a book." To all this criticism Browning replied calmly that he had "little use for the external markings of a story or the signposts of outward events." He preferred to stress "the incidents in the development of the human soul in all its obscurity."

III

As THE WHEEL of his genius kept on rotating the shape of his thought became less and less obscure. He was twenty-seven now, and he had learned to understand life because he had come to know love. One day he had opened a book of poems that touched him like an electric shock upon the first reading. "I love your verses with all my heart, dear Miss Barrett," he wrote to the authoress, "and I love you too." He made inquiries about her among his friends and discovered that she was an invalid confined to a gloom-ridden house on Wimpole Street and allowed to receive only a select circle of friends. Might he be fortunate enough for an invitation? Miss Barrett answered his letter with a kindred enthusiasm. She was overwhelmed that her poetry had brought a note of praise from Mr Browning of *Paracelsus* and *Pippa Passes*. In her weakness she was irresistibly attracted to this strongest of contemporary poets. She had admired the vitality of his verse and the serenity of his philosophy long before she had heard from him. "You are masculine to the height—and I, as a woman, have studied some of your gestures of language and intonation wistfully, as a thing beyond me far!"

Their correspondence grew. She was "headlong." She was adventurous. But she was the eldest daughter of a tyrannical father who kept her jealously under watch. For eighteen months she wouldn't allow Browning to visit her and to formalize a friendship that had grown extremely intimate in their letters. Why strengthen the links of an already irresistible attraction when there was nothing she could teach him—except grief? They were at the opposite poles of experience, he and she. Browning was a man of the world. What possible advantage could he find in a union with the sick chamber? Perhaps he was temporarily sated with all he had experienced and was looking forward to seeing her as an idealization of his quieter dreams? But would he not be instantly disillusioned when he came into the actual presence of "her emaciation and her sorrow"?

Finally, however, she gave him permission to call on her. There was no witness to their first meeting except her dog Flush. As she heard his step in the hallway and the brisk knock on the door the tears started from her eyes. She couldn't fathom the reason for these tears. Nor for the love he bore her. But as he opened the door he brought the sunlight into her room. And as his visits increased she found new strength in her limbs, a new desire to rise from her covers and to walk by his side. She laughed at the wind and looked forward to the coming of spring. He held out before her the vision of Italy and her complete physical recovery and the fulfillment of a strong and mutual love. And breathlessly she gave herself to the great adventure.

They eloped from the dusty dungeon of Wimpole Street, and they were married in a simple church ceremony. Together they left for the Continent. She had found the miracle of health when they arrived at Vaucluse, sacred with the memories of that other great pair of lovers—Petrarch and Laura. He took his wife into his arms, carried her across the waters of a stream and enthroned her on a rock as the newest Queen of Love. From southern France they traveled to Pisa and took rooms within sight of the Leaning Tower. Here, as the wind whispered from Carrara and played counterpoint to the rippling of the river Arno along the quays, the wife showed her husband the first shy sonnets she had written to him—a cycle of poems that pictured the course of her love. And now for the first time he knew the workings of a woman's heart.

And thus they traveled through the summer-deluged and welcome-laden heart of Italy. But back in England all society was agog over the news of their elopement. When Wordsworth heard of it he shook his head dubiously. "Well, I hope they may understand each other—nobody else could!"

IV

HE SAT AT THE PIANO and struck a dominant chord—a solemnity in keeping with the subdued splendor of the study. And then he launched into the cleverness of a Baldassaro toccata, tapping the keys blindly and rapidly until it seemed as if a smile of applause came from Lord Tennyson's medallion gazing down at him from the wall. And as he played the velvet-green figures on the carpet sparkled and whirled around and mated with one another in the dance. The maidens of old Venice, with their passions restrained under their masks, came suddenly into life again, three centuries after they had danced and drooped to dust. He was a subtle performer. As he touched the keys a wealth of poetical imagery rippled from his fingers— Lady Venice with her necklace of palaces and her veined canals, that happy mystery of grandees and ladies who lived at the pace of a thrust of the sword and a stolen embrace. He would write a poem about this. What had become of this Venice of a bygone day? Whither had her people gone? Surely not into the oblivion of death. For they were an intimate part of life—the life of the Renaissance. They were the ripe red wine of passion and longing and fulfillment. Not theirs the heartless scientific knowledge of Paracelsus. These were the men and the women of ancient Venice—unashamed of their paganism. Their knowledge was of the naked senses and of the pungent apples that grew out of the seeds in Eden. They were the blood of the Titians, the bones of the Michelangelos. And the poet-musician phrased the themes of old Italy on the keyboard as he phrased in his mind the theme of his poetical credo:

> . . . This world's no blot for us,
> Nor blank; it means intensely, and means good:
> To find its meaning is my meat and drink.

To find the sublime purpose of life under its grotesque face. Browning, too, was a mixture of the grotesque and the sublime. A man may be ever so healthy, he maintained, and yet artistically morbid. It is only the hearty lover of life who can appreciate its insanity. And heartily he gazed into the minds of his fellow men as they walked beside him. His interest lay not in the external wrappings of their manners and of their social conversation, not in the tinsels of the package and of the butcher's price. His concern was with the meat of the inner personality, "the unroasted joints of the human soul." He took this for his portion and roasted it to his fancy and browned it to his taste. He ate of life with a ravenous appetite. And he was unashamed.

He reveled in the life of Italy—in the ruins of past grandeur and the grandeur of living men, in the scaffoldings of unfinished churches and the blueprints of unfinished dreams. The jewel of the Mediterranean, the garden of the singing rivers, the land of the singing soul. There's a trembling tear called Italy hanging in startled wonder from the eyelash of God.

And he caught up this wonder and wove it into the golden texture of his poetry. He watched a line of monks filing like austere statues to their prayers. They held lighted tapers in their hands. But he could see the lighted tapers within their hearts—the smoldering wicks of their consuming secret passions. And he wrote a poem about one of them—*Fra Lippo*—a man whose life was a struggle between the priest and the artist within him, a poet who painted the glories of the heavens and who hungered after the pleasures of the earth. In another of his poems he depicted a more worldly type of churchman—an earth-bound bishop who miscalled himself a man of God. Liveried in greed and dying in a debauch of unwholesome memories, this paradox of a "priestly libertine" cared not for his immortal soul but for his mortal tomb—a spacious and splendid palace for the banquet of the worms.

And then, turning his eyes away from the monasteries and the graveyards, Browning looked into the homes of the people—the habitations of the twisted gargoyles of destiny. Window to window lived a man and a girl who, but for the willfulness of the fates, might have loved each other. The man sculpturing—and starving; the girl singing—and starving. They took no notice of each other but dreamed and suffered alone. And then the girl married a lord, and the man met royalty and received a knighthood. And thus they continued to dream and to suffer alone. "Each life's unfulfilled, you see." The world called the man *lucky* and the woman *clever*. Yet love "could but have happened once, and we missed it—lost it forever."

They all file by, these mismated men and women, each life unfulfilled—like a half-painted sun on the heavens. "Look you at the men and the women. God made them all—for what?" The poet-musician at the window must know, as he sits at the piano playing his favorite Baldassaro. He cannot channel his impulses into the dainty blue veins of his wife's pallid verse. Men call him befuddled and shout "obscure." Well, well, you cannot be dainty when there is so much bloodletting to be done. . . .

And so many mysteries to be unraveled. The mystery of human suffering, for example. After her summer radiance of good health that followed their marriage his wife had relapsed into her former illness. She sat in her room filled with plaster casts and portraits and fashioned her exquisite rhythms and read Italian poetry to her child Pen—and waited patiently for her death.

It was fifteen years now since their immortal marriage, a match consecrated by the ring of eternity. This ring of gold glittered against the ever-whitening skin of her finger. It will outlive the hand that wrote the *Portuguese Sonnets* and that beautiful novel in verse—*Aurora Leigh*. And when she is laid to rest her husband will slip it upon his own finger—this circle of solid gold, this precious ring of undying love.

Elizabeth looked into the face of her son and parted the fringe of his curly hair. It was remarkable that she, who before her marriage had been wasting away on Wimpole Street, should have finally acquired the strength to give her man a son. That was her special triumph of fulfillment. . . .

The thunderclouds flocked into the valley under the whiplash of the northeast wind. A sudden flash of lightning. And then the rain. When the skies were clear again Elizabeth was asleep. Her spirit had passed on beyond the thunder and the storm.

V

BROWNING stood by the bookstall in the Piazza San Lorenzo. He rummaged among the secondhand books and came across a worn and yellow pamphlet dated 1698. It contained the curious record of an old murder trial, the story of a certain Lord Guido who had ended the life of his child wife Pompilia for alleged adultery with a priest. The bare facts of the record stirred the imagination of the poet. Now that his wife had passed on and bequeathed him the ring, the symbol of immortality, he must consecrate it with the creation of an immortal book. And here, in this ancient pamphlet, was the subject matter for this book. "Each life's unfulfilled, you see." Elizabeth, "his lyric angel," lost in her prime; and here, on the faded parchment, the child wife at Rome assassinated in the very April of her youth. Guilty or innocent? Such a girlish beauty too. Before she died she swore her innocence. Beyond that the record tells nothing. But he will take this record and shape it into a meaning and round it off into a golden ring of immortal beauty.

And so he returned to England and sat down to write his masterpiece, *The Ring and the Book*. This poem is a story compounded of several stories. One by one the poet takes up the various characters involved in the murder, delves into their innermost souls, analyzes their secret motives and welds them together into a unit of hoping, loving, striving, fearing, hating, avenging and suffering human life. And it is not until the story has run its course and the cycle of characters has been completed that the meaning of each becomes manifest in the comprehensiveness of the whole. Such is the molten metal of his art.

For "Art remains the one way possible of speaking the truth." The cycle of life is but the artistic summation of our individual lives. Browning felt that a cycle of his own life had now been completed. He had broken away from Florence and returned to England. He plunged into the "grim attractions of London" and lost himself in the city smoke, he who had been born for the smokeless air. He moved to Warwick Crescent and filled his garden with pheasants and lizards and toads as of old. All this for Pen, the son and apple of his eye. "But somehow his garden was lifeless and bare in the cold and unmagical London air." Lizards must be bathed in the golden sun and luxuriate on a screen of orange leaves. This was not the old garden, alive with fragrance and music in the Florentine night. Open the heart of the poet and you will find Italy graven there.

Italy had meant Elizabeth. With her he had spent his happiest years in that country. And now he was returned to England, to write the epitaph for his own life. Well, he would compose this epitaph in large simple print—no Latin inscriptions, but words of English fire: *One who never turned his back but marched breast forward*—never doubted clouds would break, never dreamed, though right were worsted, wrong would triumph. . . . "Held, we fall to rise, are baffled, to fight better . . . sleep to wake . . ." What though he had striven so much to attain so little? "What I aspired to be and was not comforts me." What though so few of his hopes had been fulfilled?

> Ah, but a man's reach should exceed his grasp,
> Or what's a heaven for?

He walked through the streets thinking of his poetry, and people smiled as they saw him pass. For he had a peculiar optical characteristic. Each of his eyes had a different focus. One was nearsighted, for his reading; the other farsighted, "for his dreaming." When he went outdoors he was obliged to squint with his eyes in order to adjust his vision. And now, as the people smiled at his comical squint, his own face expanded into a whimsical smile. For it occurred to him that his mental vision, like his physical, had a double focus. At times he looked upon life with a too-bitter cynicism; at others, with a too-robust optimism. He must adjust himself to a normal vision in his old age—complete the cycle of his thought.

Yet with Browning nothing was ever complete. No philosophy was ever able to pronounce the final word. That ring on his finger was not the ultimate signet, to be held forever sacred because the stuff was gold. You've got to surpass this copy, this imitation of a better ring that exists—somewhere.

Or take that figure of the potter's wheel, the instrument that shapes the clay of our thoughts. One series of figures rounded off, start another—never mind what comes after, whether you've got enough clay to finish. Only begin . . . *that's* the important thing.

And where do you suppose some children found this young poet of sixty-six at the beginning of his next cycle of thought?

Strolling among his old haunts in the little town of Asolo, where first he had brought his wife at the beginning of another life seventeen years ago. Here he whistled in the chambers of the old Italian castle all over again, cocking his ear for the echo in his own favorite corner from a secret angle where he had learned to get a special sound—all over again, as if nothing had been finished, no poetry written, no problems solved. "Listen, children," he chuckles merrily, "it's no use trying to catch the echo of my voice. You must ferret out the secret angle which I alone know and listen to the sound of your own voice.

"But perhaps the mighty secret will die with me. . . ."

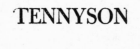

TENNYSON

Great Poems by Tennyson

Idyls of the King.
In Memoriam.
Maud.
Enoch Arden.
Locksley Hall.
The Lotos Eaters.
The Princess.
The Lady of Shalott.
Morte d'Arthur.
Ulysses.
Becket.
The Falcon.
The First Quarrel.
The Hesperides.
The Day Dream.

The Brook.
The Charge of the Light Brigade.
Ode on the Death of the Duke of
*   Wellington.*
Oenone.
The Palace of Art.
Queen Mary.
Rizpah.
Break, Break, Break.
Harold.
The Miller's Daughter.
The Sisters.
Hero to Leander.
Nothing Will Die.

Tennyson

Swinburne

Alfred Tennyson

1809–1892

THE LITTLE VILLAGE of Somersby lay cupped in the fields of green. Gray-towered churches stood guard in the mist and pealed a discourse of bells that rose like incense over the village. And beyond rolled the sounding sea.

Dr Tennyson was the rector of Somersby—a man of great physical and mental stature who raised his children and cultivated his ideas in an atmosphere of quiet refinement far removed from the distractions of the world. The Lord had blessed this goodly vicar with a family of twelve as if He had designed them to return a jury verdict on the happiness of domestic life. And Alfred, the ablest of the children, was the foreman of this jury—an experiment in the syllabus of the gods to bring to birth the soul of a genius under the best of possible conditions. Might not the superman emerge as a result of this experiment? And if the test should fail, the fault would lie in the intrinsic worthlessness of man and not in the capriciousness of the gods.

Thus was the stage set for the noble play.

II

FROM HIS INFANCY Alfred possessed a resplendent imagination. He invested the surrounding landscapes with the personifications of his fancy. Once, when a mad March wind was sweeping along the garden, the little boy of five rushed headlong at the elements, waving his hands and screaming, "I hear a voice that's speaking in the storm!" The phrase "far, far away" would always throw an uncanny spell over him. Even as a child he responded passionately to the stimulus of music and to the cadence of a well-turned verse. At fifteen the news of the death of Byron came like a terrible catastrophe to darken the joyous morning of his life. On a rock near his house he carved an epitaph underlined with emotion—*Byron is dead.*

Inwardly he was a seething volcano of passion. Outwardly he had developed the refinement of restraint and the manners of an aristocrat. He had been brought up in the atmosphere of the drawing room where graciousness and propriety were the household gods and where the instincts of rebellion were as taboo as "the skeletons in the family closet."

In such an environment personal inclination may stray at times into the byways along the road of conventionalism, but it will never take a different direction. The farthest that Tennyson ever departed from the bounds of convention was in his mild rebuke of his teachers at Cambridge. "They teach us nothing, feeding not the heart." But that was the poet protesting against the drabness of scholasticism and not the rebel fighting against the smugness of the professorial mind.

At twenty he was a physical demigod—tall commanding presence, noble face and forehead, powerful chest, long limbs and the bearing of a king. He rarely spoke in company but maintained a quizzical silence that made him out to be a very oracle of wisdom. Only when called upon to read his verse would he break his silence. And then in the most melodious of tones he charmed all those who came under his spell.

"It is not fair, Alfred," remarked one of his friends in admiration, "that you should be Apollo as well as Hercules."

His departure from Cambridge was as gracious as his residence. He danced his final quadrille in the light of a thousand smiling eyes and then, bidding his friends farewell, he clambered into a carriage on Trumpington Street and started smilingly down the highway of the years.

III

BUT THERE WAS a sudden interruption to the pleasant routine of his life. Only a month after his return from the university he stepped into his father's study—and found him dead. For several nights following the funeral Tennyson occupied his father's bed in the morbid hope of "seeing his ghost. But no ghost came." Death was an adventure that disturbed and at the same time intrigued him. It came not as a discord but as a new mysterious harmony into the symphony of his emotions. It had taken away a beloved presence, but it had left in its place a sacred peacefulness—a silent thoughtful pause in the eternal song of life.

During these days Alfred discussed the mystery of death with his close friend and schoolmate and fellow poet, Arthur Hallam. Arthur was betrothed to Tennyson's dark-eyed sister Emily and to Tennyson's questing soul. Together the two young poets would smoke far into the night as they delved into the "secrets of the gods." Sometimes Emily joined them and played her harp as her brother rested deep in his thoughts and her lover fed on her face with his hungry eyes.

Once, when the notes of the music fell away, Alfred spoke to his friend of his own intellectual despair: "Other poets are braving the mystery of life, while I am only playing with its echoes." Arthur, he pointed out, was able to see more clearly into the eternal mystery that gives great art to living and great life to art. "You have been groping steadfastly toward a definite faith. And in God's time you will arrive. I can see that by your poetry."

Arthur went on a brief vacation to Vienna. He wrote Tennyson glowing letters about the art galleries of that city—its Giorgiones, its Raphaels, its Titians. And one day there came no letter from Arthur. Instead there was a brief note from

Arthur's father. "Your friend, sir, Arthur Hallam, is . . . no more."

Tennyson was sitting at the dinner table when the letter arrived. He left his meal untouched. But through the tears that welled to his eyes he sensed the pathetic mistruth of the writing. How can one say, *no more?* "God's finger touched him, and he slept."

IV

THE POET must now continue on the quest alone. The complacency of his life had been leavened by an ample admixture of grief. Two of those he most ardently loved, his father and his friend, had been taken from him. The adage, "gently comes the world to those that are cast in gentle mold," had been proved untrue. For gentleness is but the reverse side of the coin of suffering. And wisdom is the daughter of sorrow. As the man in Tennyson grew more unhappy the poet within him became more sublime. He had been brought face to face with that masked and mysterious giant called Human Destiny. He had been challenged to wrestle with him and to unmask him if he could. Many had entered the lists before Tennyson to do battle with the Unknown Warrior. And they had fought bravely and with an energy that seemed at moments to promise them victory in the end. But so far they had all been vanquished.

Tennyson meant to succeed. In quiet meditation and not in the turmoil of the madding crowd would he wrestle with the mystery of life and death. Together with his mother and the rest of the family he moved to a stately house in Epping Forest. Here, in the midst of a park with a private pond, he settled down to explore the silent recesses of his thought.

Yet he did not confine his days to his mental exercise alone. With his superb physique, he was passionately fond of the outdoors. In the summer he took long rambles through the woods, and in the winter he skated on the pond while his long blue coat curved out behind him. And always, whether outdoors or in, he kept planning the thoughts and the cadences of his verse.

The words of the poet must perform a threefold function. They must supply color to the inner eye, music to the inner ear and hope to innermost heart.

In his earlier poetry he had fallen short of this ideal. He had expressed himself in an exuberance of style which mirrored an immaturity of experience. And the critics had sensed this defect in his poetry. But now his emotions had been sobered by his grief. Grimly he phrased the motto for his future poetry: "Every tiger madness muzzled, every serpent passion killed."

And now when he spoke he found a steady response from "a thousand deep-hearted readers." He was thirty-three when he published the collection of verse that included *Ulysses, Morte d'Arthur, Launcelot and Guinevere* and *The Lady of Shalott*—poem legends of a revitalized past, that far-off world which seemed "nearer than the present . . . a good solid planet, rolling around its green hills and paradises to the harmony of more steadfast laws." Carlyle, FitzGerald, Spedding—indeed, all his critics and his friends—were amazed at his poetic development. And Emerson in America remarked without hesitation, "There is no finer ear, no greater command of the keys of language, than Tennyson's." At the suggestion of various people of influence the court granted him an annual pension. Tennyson had experienced the sunrise of his fame.

He now plunged into a discussion of one of the leading questions of the day—the moral and intellectual status of women in civilized society. In Victorian England the "weaker sex" was regarded as a minor before the law and very often as a chattel in the husband's home. Tennyson wrote *The Princess*, a poem in which he anticipated the *Doll's House* of Henrik Ibsen and in which he advocated the spiritual and intellectual independence of the wife in the marriage partnership. Princess Ida and her maidens "rebel" from the conventions of the day, pursue a liberal course of education at an academy and prepare to enter upon a life of freedom from the restraints of love and marriage and domesticity. However, when an appeal is made to their maternal instincts, they return to the fold. For any other ending would never be tolerated by the poet's audience.

And then the poet plunged into the religious problems of the day. Often he had visited Arthur Hallam's grave close to where the sea was breaking "on the cold gray stones." And here, in the music of the waves and under the infinitude of the sky, he heard the "soft sweet echoes" of an elegy. He began to write down the words of this elegy—*In Memoriam*—"for Arthur's sake, just as he would have liked me to do them." From time to time, as the work progressed, he read the lines to a friend. And then his voice would tremble with emotion and the tears would run down his face.

Gradually the work progressed from an expression of personal grief to a universal philosophy of life. "This poem," he was able to say when it was finished, "is rather the cry of the whole human race than mine." It was the cry of a helpless creature in the clutch of a ruthless fate. Yet it was also an answer to the cry. For it was inconceivable to Tennyson that any personality with the gleam of intellect and the spark of life could suddenly vanish into oblivion and "be no more." Rather, the personality of him who had departed from the flesh took on a new and solemn grandeur—none the less real for its transformation. The soul became one with the elements of nature and laughed in the sun and spoke its language in the moaning of the wind. To be sure, there were those who doubted the survival of this spiritual presence in the soul of man. There were those who were excessively influenced by the latest scientific manuals and despaired of any immortality. "In this age of material wealth men are skeptics; in this age of evolution even the most sincere are troubled with doubts."

And yet all of us, however skeptical we may be, abhor death and yearn for eternal life. And "if God allows this strong instinct and universal yearning for another life, surely that is in a measure a presumption of its truth. We cannot give up the mighty hopes that make us men."

> Thou wilt not leave us in the dust:
> Thou madest man, he knows not why,

> He thinks he was not made to die;
> And thou hast made him: thou art just.

Then what about those who link the human race to the lowest forms of matter and speak of man as the final culmination of the beast?

> Let him, the wiser man who springs
> Hereafter, up from childhood shape
> His action like the greater ape,
> But I was *born* to other things.

Evolution? Of course! Man is forever evolving into Superman, and Life is forever merging into Immortality.

> I held it truth, with him who sings
> To one clear harp in diverse tones,
> That men may rise on steppingstones
> Of their dead selves to higher things.

As for those of us who have loved and lost, let us be consoled with the thought that "nothing walks with aimless feet . . . not one life shall be destroyed, or cast as rubbish to the void, when God hath made the pile complete."

No human being ever dies—not the son whom the aged mother has lost at sea, nor the young bride sleeping her eternal sleep under the elm, nor the stillborn child, nor the father killed in the distant wars.

> Thy voice is on the rolling air;
> I hear thee where the waters run;
> Thou standest in the rising sun,
> And in the setting thou art fair.

We who have been left behind to our sorrows, and whose understanding is that of an infant groping in the night, must never be ashamed to say to ourselves: "We need not understand; we love." And through our love we live in God—

> That God which ever lives and loves,
> One God, one law, one element,
> And one far-off divine event,
> To which the whole creation moves.

In Memoriam descended upon the people of England like a high noon of radiant beauty. It contained, in the opinion of many of the leading thinkers, "the most satisfactory things that have ever been said on the future state." To the innumerable host of the simple folk the poem served as a rallying standard in the uphill struggle of their hearts and hopes. A copy of *In Memoriam* came into the hands of Queen Victoria in the midst of her grief at the loss of her prince consort, and her tears fell upon many a line of this volume in the intimate watches of the night.

In her undying gratitude to the author of this poem the Little Lady of Windsor appointed him poet laureate and raised him to a peerage. Tennyson accepted these titles neither with a sense of elation nor in a spirit of condescension. He merely smiled and observed, "Why should I be selfish and not suffer an honor to be done to literature in my name?"

V

FOURTEEN YEARS before the publication of *In Memoriam*, while he was still serving his apprenticeship as a poet, Tennyson had attended the wedding of his brother Charles. Right after the ceremony he had bent over one of the bridesmaids, the dainty and gracious Miss Emily Sellwood, and whispered to her timidly, "Oh, happy bridesmaid, make a happy bride."

And now that his fame and his fortune were assured he turned his fourteen-year-old prayer into a reality. He married Emily and settled down as the high priest of a universal cult of worshipers. He became the voice of England's glory and the fire of England's inspiration. He wrote stirring verses to hearten England's sons in battle and stately odes to commemorate her honored dead. Though still in the prime of life, he was already acclaimed by his countrymen as a classic. The students at Oxford kept a volume of Tennyson between an annotated text of Euripides and a manual of scholastic philosophy. Young ladies found him among their wedding presents. Military officers recited the thundering verses of the *Charge of the Light Brigade* to their soldiers. A volume of his poetry, thrust hastily into a captain's breast pocket as he rushed into battle, stopped a bullet and saved the man's life. He received gifts of pipes and tobacco regularly from all corners of the world. He was showered with letters from blushing young schoolgirls who wrote rapturously about his poetry. At the death of the Duke of Wellington he wrote the funeral ode in which he went into mourning and "like a correct gentleman, with brand new gloves, wiped away his tears with a cambric handkerchief."

He paid a dear price for his fame, for the "pleasure of hearing himself talked of up and down the street." In his poetry as well as in his person he had become a slave to his nobility. Always elegant, always formal, always dressed to fit the occasion, he had trained himself to enter "any style of poetry and the feelings of any age." He was "like those musicians who use their bow in the service of all masters." And some of the more discerning spirits in England recognized the failure of his too-great success. Swinburne, for example, accused him of "too much craft and too little sincerity." As poem after poem poured from Tennyson's pen he cried, "Why, this stuff is not the Muse, it's Musery. The man has got hold of the Muse's clothesline and hung it with jewelry!"

But the few dissenting voices were lost in the general acclaim. For at his best he could fashion a music such as no other poet of his generation, not even Swinburne, was able to match.

VI

SUCH was the outcome of this experiment of the gods—to nurture the genius of a poet, under the best possible conditions. Tennyson had mastered all his worldly problems. But had he succeeded in his quest for the truth? Had he vanquished the Unknown Warrior? At times he was certain that he had pierced the mask. But he had his hours of despondency when he realized the frailty of his genius in the face of its gigantic task. In a lifetime of effort he had caught at most but a momentary reflection of the truth, hidden forever under its impenetrable veil. All the rest of his life he had groped in the darkness.

> O slender lily waving there,
>   And laughing back the light,
> In vain you tell me earth is fair
>   When all is dark as night.

Often after dinner, when the dessert was cleared, he would lay aside his pipe, pick up the manuscript of his verses and read them aloud to the assembled guests in his great "organ tones" of range and power. Such a reading had brought "glory to the eyes of Mr Gladstone and reduced George Eliot to tears." He was reassured by the glory and the tears. After all, if he had failed to see the face of truth, he had at least caught the music of her voice.

As he climbed the weary mountain of the years the power of his great body showed no signs of abating. At seventy-four he remarked proudly that "the better heart" of him was stronger than ever it had been at eighteen. At eighty-two he challenged his friends to perform after him the feat of getting up "twenty times quickly from a low chair without touching it with their hands." The "better heart" of him beat ever strongly for the woman who had blessed him with forty years of happiness as his wife.

In the summer of his eighty-third year he and Emily celebrated their anniversary. The poet gave his "bride" a gift of rosemary and roses. They were as merry as if it were their wedding day. However, as the lovers strolled around their estate, amid the scenery that had been familiar to them for half a century, a feeling of sadness descended upon the poet. For he knew that before long he must say farewell.

As the weeks passed it became apparent that his steps were beginning to falter at last. Soon he would not be able to walk at all. The words he had written in his idyll on the passing of Arthur came back to him in all their pathos: "The old order changeth, yielding place to new. And God fulfills himself in many ways. . . ."

God fulfills himself in many ways! And man's destiny lies not in the ebbing of the past but in the flood tide of the future.

And now Tennyson was ready to put out to sea. Once more in the assembled company, when the dessert had been cleared, he put aside his pipe and picked up the manuscript of his verses as the evening shadows fell:

> For tho' from out our bourne of time and place
> The flood may bear me far,
> I hope to see my Pilot face to face
> When I have crossed the bar.

SWINBURNE

Great Poems by Swinburne

Atalanta in Calydon.
Erectheus.
Bothwell.
Mary Stuart.
Rosamund.
The Duke of Gandia.
Astrophel.
The Triumph of Time.
Dolores.
Tristram of Lyonesse.
The Queen Mother.
Hesperia.
Songs Before Sunrise.

Border Ballads.
The Sisters.
The Tale of Balen.
Birthday Ode.
Ode on the Proclamation of the French Republic.
The Last Oracle.
A Baby's Hands.
The Forsaken Garden.
A Ballade of Dreamland.
Les Noyades.
A Song of Italy.
A Century of Roundels.

Algernon Charles Swinburne

1837–1909

HE HAD THE MEASLES when he was a little fellow at Eton. His mother had been sent for. She sat by the bedside reading Shakespeare to him all day. At teatime she left him to have tea with his housemaster's family. Algernon begged the maid, whom his mother had brought along with her from home, to continue with the reading while he took his own tea. Suddenly a pot of jam descended upon the reader's head. "That's for your awful interpretation of Shakespeare!" he cried.

A howling, a stamping and then a bloodcurdling succession of shrill and staccato outcries. Mrs Swinburne and the tutor and his wife rushed into Algernon's room. A flaming torch of wild red hair, with two emerald-green eyes staring out of the tumbled curls, was dancing over the bed, a pair of pitifully small arms was flailing in the air, and an avalanche of verses came rushing out of a pallid mouth.

"The poor child's in delirium!" exclaimed the horrified tutor.

"Oh no," laughed Mrs Swinburne. "It's the way he always recites his *Hamlet*."

II

HE HAD inherited his passionate temper from his paternal grandfather, Sir John Swinburne, and his aristocratic sensibility from his mother, who was the daughter of the third Earl of Ashburnham. His poetical genius, however, came to him as a gift from the gods. For neither his father nor his mother possessed the slightest aptitude for poetry. Nor did any of his brothers or his sisters. As the eldest of the six children of Admiral Charles Henry Swinburne, he was destined—so his father hoped—for a naval career in the family tradition.

But the parents soon abandoned this idea of a seafaring life for their son. For the only part of him that ever seemed to grow normally was his head. Indeed, his head grew to an *abnormal* size while the rest of his body remained *subnormal*, so that when he entered Eton he looked like a pumpkin balanced upon a forked radish. His cousin, Lord Redesdale, who was an upper-class student at Eton when Swinburne arrived there, expressed the fear that the little fellow's head might snap off from the body and fall to the ground at any moment. His hat, even in his first year at Eton, was the largest in the school.

The size of Swinburne's head was further exaggerated by "the tousled mass of red hair standing almost at right angles from it. . . . Red, violent, aggressive red it was, unmistakable red, like burnished copper." One of his schoolmates at Eton related how on a foggy day, in a classroom approached by a sort of ladder, Swinburne's blazing head appeared as if coming out of the floor, late—as usual—for school. The teacher, interrupting the lesson, pointed to Swinburne's head and exclaimed, "Ah, here's the rising sun at last!"

At Eton Swinburne read much and studied little. He was generally to be found in the boys' library, "perched up Turk-or-tailor-wise in one of the windows . . . with some huge old-world tome, almost as big as himself, upon his lap, the afternoon sun setting on fire the great mop of red hair." He was happy so long as he was left alone; but let a fellow student tease him or a teacher order him to give up his independent reading for a prescribed lesson, and there was the devil to pay. He couldn't brook interference of any kind with his self-appointed program. And when the teachers insisted upon interfering with his program, in order that he might fulfill the scholastic requirements, he left school unceremoniously (1853) and returned to the indulgent bosom of his family. He was now sixteen years old.

At home his parents wisely refrained from crossing him. For they knew the consequences. From early childhood he had developed the trick, whenever he grew excited, of jerking his arms down from the shoulders and vibrating his hands quickly like a spinning top. If he happened to be seated at the moment, he would accompany this motion of the hands with a simultaneous vibration of the feet. His mother, alarmed at this violent agitation, had taken him to a specialist. And the specialist had advised her that her son was suffering from "an excess of electric vitality" and that the best way to cure him was to leave him alone.

To the end of his days Swinburne never got over these physical manifestations of his "excessive electric vitality." As he grew toward manhood, however, he found considerable relief for his superabundant vitality in mountain climbing and in swimming. Indifferent to every other kind of sport—he had never owned a cricket bat or attended any school games—he "could climb and swim forever." Strangely enough, for a poet with so fragile a body, he didn't know the meaning of fear. Shortly after his break with Eton he decided to climb Culver Cliff, a dangerous headland on the Isle of Wight, where the Swinburnes had a summer home. His only reason for attempting this "impossible feat" was that it had never been attempted before. "My mother," he wrote in a letter to one of his friends, "wanted to know why I had done such a thing, and when I told her she laughed a short, sweet laugh most satisfactory to the young ear and said, 'Nobody ever thought you were a coward, my boy.' I said that was all very well, but how could I tell till I tried? 'But you won't do it again?' she said. I replied, 'Of course not—where could be the fun?' I knew now that it could be done, and I only wanted to do it because nobody thought it could."

As to his early fondness for swimming, we have his own testimony in another of his letters: "The salt of the sea *must* have been in my blood before I was born. I can remember no earlier enjoyment than being held up naked in my father's arms and brandished between his hands, then shot like a stone from a sling through the air, shouting and laughing with delight, head-foremost into the coming wave. . . . I remember being afraid of other things, but never of the sea."

These, then, were the ingredients that went into the making of the young poet—a huge, beautiful head surrounded with an aureole of flame, a puny, pitiable body in compensation for which he had learned to dare and to defy, a passion for reading the great works of the past, an electric driving energy that made him atingle to every moment of his life and a rebellious yearning for independence—Victor Hugo, the French apostle of freedom, was his Moses, his Socrates, his very God. And over and above all these characteristics was the magic gift of a singing soul—a mystery as incomprehensible as the mystery of the moving stars.

III

FOR THREE YEARS Swinburne flirted with the idea of enlisting in the cavalry. He wanted to be a poet of deeds rather than of words. He had been fired with the vision of Balaklava (October 25, 1854), and it had become "the one dream of my life"—as he put it—to ride at the head of another such charge. "He saw himself," to quote Sir Edmund Gosse, "galloping to the destruction of kings on a charger as black as night." But his father "resolutely stamped out" his equestrian ambition. "A fine figure you'd cut on horseback with that minikin body of yours!"

And so there was nothing for him to do but to return to his books. In the winter of 1856 he matriculated at Oxford—only to find that the conventions of the college were as disagreeable as the restrictions of the preparatory school. He just couldn't fit into the measurements of the normal existence. He neither joined in the games nor appeared at the wine parties of his fellow students. It was rumored that the "queer duck" was sitting in his room and "writing poetry in five languages." When he went out for his exercise he was generally alone. His gait was peculiar—it was a mincing dance rather than a walk. "Swinburne," remarked one of his classmates, "seemed to be pirouetting through life in a perpetual minuet."

As for the dons of Oxford, they were little impressed with his personality and even less with his poetry. In his junior year he competed for the Newdigate prize with a poem on the Northwest Passage. The judges passed over his composition and awarded the prize to a Mr Francis Law Latham—a young man who as a poet "shot up like a rocket and came down like a stick."

Professors and poets rarely understand one another. His teachers despised Swinburne, and Swinburne despised his teachers. He had nothing but contempt for the academic life at Oxford. "An Oxford graduate," he said, "never dies, since he has never lived; he merely ceases." Swinburne himself didn't complete his course at Oxford. He left it, just as he had left Eton, before his graduation.

Disgraced for the second time, the imperturbable young poet yielded to his father's request and went to live as a private pupil at the home of William Stubbs, a scholarly clergyman in the agricultural parish of Navestock. Swinburne arrived at Navestock on a midsummer Saturday night. The next morning his breakfast was served in his bedroom, and his host left word that "inasmuch as Mr Swinburne must be tired from his journey, he need not attend the service in the parish church."

Swinburne finished his breakfast, got out of bed and pulled up the window blinds. It was a gorgeous day. "Not a bad idea to go out and get a few whiffs of that country air." He put on a pair of scarlet slippers and a crimson dressing gown—he had a partiality for bright colors—and stepped out into the garden with his giant mop of red hair uncombed.

The bell summoned the parishioners to their devotions. The

approach to the church from the village was such that it was necessary for the entire congregation to pass by the gate of the vicarage garden in order to get to the church door. Swinburne, a flaming scarlet from top to toe, sauntered up to the gate. He was curious to see what the villagers looked like.

But it never occurred to him that he too was an object of curiosity—nay, an apparition of terror. Here was a burning Satan come straight out of hell to bar their attendance from their Sunday worship. One by one they shambled timidly up to the vicarage and then stopped in their tracks as if petrified. Swinburne stared at the parishioners, the parishioners stared at Swinburne—and the church remained empty of its worshipers. The Reverend Mr Stubbs, amazed at the absence of his congregation, ordered the sexton to ring again. But still the church remained empty! At last one of the bolder spirits of Navestock, taking his life into his hands, shut his eyes tightly and made a bolt past the devil into the church. The rest of the congregation, relieved to see that their friend had not been burned alive for his rashness, followed him in a gallop.

"How oddly the Navestock yokel takes his Sunday service!" reflected Swinburne as he returned to his room.

"How oddly my young student boarder behaves of a Sunday morning!" laughed Mr Stubbs when he heard of the incident. And—how oddly he behaves at all times, observed Mr Stubbs a few days later. One evening the vicar and his wife asked Swinburne whether it was true that he wrote poetry.

"Yes," replied Swinburne, "I've dashed off a line or two in my spare moments."

"Won't you read some of it to us, please?" urged Mrs Stubbs.

Swinburne went up to his room and came back with a thick batch of manuscript—a huge historical tragedy in blank verse. He began to read it in the early evening and didn't get through with it until after midnight.

Then he looked up from his manuscript. "Do you like it?"

"On the whole, yes," replied his host. "But to be candid

with you, Mr Swinburne, I would tone down some of the love passages. They are—what shall I say?—a bit too intimate for an inexperienced young poet."

The vicar had expected a modest remonstrance from his pupil. What he actually got, to his amazement, was a long silent stare which ended in an unearthly shriek.

"Why, Mr Swinburne!"

But Swinburne had seized the manuscript and dashed out of the room.

That night there was no sleep in the vicarage. For every few minutes there were strange noises in the poet's room. Again and again the vicar, fearing for Swinburne's safety, knocked on his door. But the door was bolted from the inside.

It was not until very late in the morning that Swinburne came down from his room. His eyes were feverish.

"I'm sorry for what I've said last night, Mr Swinburne."

"Oh, that's all right."

"I hope I haven't discouraged you about that tragedy."

"I lighted a fire in the grate and burned every page of it."

"Oh, my God!" cried the vicar in consternation.

"But there's no harm done. I rewrote it word for word from memory."

IV

DISAPPOINTED in their son, Admiral Charles and Lady Jane Swinburne took him on a trip to the Continent in the hope that a wider acquaintance with the world might make him more worldly-minded. One afternoon in Paris, as Swinburne and his parents were riding in an open carriage in the Champs Élysées, they passed by the equipage of Napoleon III, the one ruler whom the young poet especially detested. The admiral and his lady stood up and bowed to the emperor, and the admiral tipped his hat. But Algernon remained seated and kept his hat on his head. Later on, when asked to account for his incivility, he replied: "Had I taken off my hat to Napoleon the Little, I would have been obliged to cut off my hand at the wrist. No, thank you, I need my hand for writing poetry."

He surrounded himself with the "portraits and the presences" of the "fighters, the liberators and the rebels" of the world. He struck up an ardent friendship with William Morris and with Dante Gabriel Rossetti. His friendship with Rossetti in particular was to fill his life with "cordial kindness and exuberant generosity." And also it was to bring him face to face with the greatest tragedy of his personal experience. Rossetti, that brilliant painter-poet with an English mind and an Italian heart, was married to a young woman who in her red-gold hair, her inexperienced enthusiasms and her restless absurdities was like a sister of Swinburne's. The three young bohemians became inseparable. Rossetti looked upon the playful but seemingly harmless intimacies of Swinburne and his girl wife with the affectionate tolerance of an older brother. When their playfulness became too boisterous he separated them gently as he would have separated a pair of romping kittens. Such was their relationship when on a February night in 1862 the Rossettis and Swinburne dined together at the Sablonière Hotel in Leicester Square. After their meal Rossetti escorted his wife home and then went out again. When he returned, some hours later, he found her dead. She had taken an overdose of laudanum.

The reason for her death remained a mystery. Rossetti absolved Swinburne of all blame in the matter. Indeed, Rossetti now became more attached than ever to his "little Northumbrian friend," as he affectionately called him. But to Swinburne, no less than to Rossetti, the tragic death of the young girl wife had been a vast and bitter experience. His character had grown up at last.

One other painful experience contributed to the maturing of Swinburne's character at about this time. He had met and fallen in love with a "graceful and vivacious" girl who seemed to reciprocate his attentions. She gave him roses, she played for him, she smiled upon him and flattered him; and he, in return, "placed his heart and his hopes under the palms of her feet."

But on the day when he suddenly proposed to her she laughed in his face—just as Lady Montagu had laughed in the face of Alexander Pope on a similar occasion.

Humiliated and enraged to see her "trampling his love to dust and death," he returned to his poetry and to his first and most faithful mistress—the sea. He celebrated his mystical marriage to the sea in his magnificent poem—*The Triumph of Time*. First he wrests out of his heart the love which he has offered to another and which has been trodden underfoot:

> Is it worth a tear, is it worth an hour,
>   To think of things that are well outworn?
> Of fruitless husk and fugitive flower,
>   The dream forgone and the deed forborne?

And then he turns exultantly to the arms of his newest—and oldest—love:

> I will go back to the great sweet mother,
>   Mother and lover of men, the sea.
> I will go down to her, I and none other,
>   Close with her, kiss her and mix her with me;
> Cling to her, strive with her, hold her fast:
> O fair white mother, in days long past
> Born without sister, born without brother,
>   Set free my soul as thy soul is free!

V

WITH HIS "virgin soul washed free by the sea waves," he now dedicated his entire life to his poetry. He published his first volume, *The Queen Mother*, and established a record with it; he failed to sell a single copy of the book. He came across the book of another "failure"—Walt Whitman—and found a kindred soul speaking to him out of "the barbaric yawp" of the rebellious poet of democracy. "Have you seen . . . Walt Whitman's *Leaves of Grass?*" he wrote to one of his friends. "I really think (it) is the most lovely and wonderful thing I have read for years and years." Like Walt Whitman, he loved to shock people. One Sunday evening, at a dinner party which included the presence of such notables as Thackeray, Lord Houghton and the Archbishop of York, he was requested to read some of his poetry. With impish perversity he selected *Les Noyades*, a most inappropriate poem for an archbishop's ears. The ladies began to giggle nervously; the churchman stared with a look of horror in his eyes; Thackeray nudged Lord Houghton in the ribs; and Swinburne, noting the confusion, kept raising his voice into a higher and ever higher crescendo of defiance. A terrific explosion was in the making when suddenly the butler, "like an angel from heaven," threw open the door and announced, "Prayers, my lord!"

VI

SWINBURNE rebelled against the old-fashioned prayers, the old-fashioned priests and the old-fashioned gods. In his "Greek tragedy," *Atalanta*, the first poem which fully revealed his "superhuman cleverness and superdiabolical audacity," he denounced the old gods in a choral ode of scorching invective and superb music.

> For the gods very subtly fashion
>   Madness with sadness upon earth:
> Not knowing in any wise compassion,
>   Nor holding pity of any worth.

As for Jehovah, the leader and the father of the gods, he is

> The Lord of love and loathing and of strife
>   Who gives a star and takes a sun away;
> Who shapes the soul and makes her a barren wife
>   To the earthly body and grievous growth of clay;
>   .   .   .   .   .
> Who makes desire, and slays desire with shame;
>   Who shakes the heaven as ashes in his hand;

Who, seeing the light and shadow for the same,
  Bids day waste night as fire devours a brand,
Smites without sword, and scourges without rod;
  The supreme evil, God.

Among the most helpless of all the pitiable creatures of this ancient God is man—a mixture of fire and sand and falling tears, made for a day and a night and a morrow of labor and heavy sorrow. He

    ... weaves, and is clothed with derision,
      Sows, and he shall not reap;
    His life is a watch or a vision
      Between a sleep and a sleep.

Swinburne is a rebel, yet he is not an atheist. The evil gods that he fights against are merely the destructive aspects of nature. They are the superstitious conceptions of a primitive mind—gods made after the image of man in his savage stage. Swinburne renounces these gods and the life which results from their worship. But he does not renounce God and he does not renounce life. Indeed, he proclaims a joyous acceptance of creation and a passionate response to the thirst for drinking the cup of life to the full. Life is so beautiful because it is so brief— a flash of golden sunlight that illumines the landscape between two winter nights. How should we know the comfort of the light were it not for the terror of the dark? How should we know the ecstasy of our love were it not for the apprehension of its loss? How should we know the music of pity were it not for the discord of suffering? For the human body, attuned as it is to the sweetness of attainment through the bitterness of toil, and for the human heart, whose tenderness is measured only by its sadness, this is the most beautiful and the best of all possible worlds.

And so let us drink life's beauty, and bathe in its sunlight, and defy its dangers, and fight against oppression, and breast the waves of good or ill fortune with a resolute heart. "This thing is God—to be man with thy might!"

[*209*]

Such was the poetic creed of Swinburne and such the philosophic program of his career. He turned his life into a springtime of song. For April was in his blood. In spite of his fragile constitution—he had developed frequent and severe attacks of epilepsy—he plunged into the turmoil of London and translated the effervescence of his experience into the music of his verse. Occasionally, for his health's sake, his friends lured him into the quiet of the countryside. And then he indulged himself in his favorite pastime—

> Sea-satiate, bruised with buffets of the brine,
> Laughing, and flushed as one afire with wine.

At one time his fondness for swimming came near to costing him his life. Overestimating the power of his puny arms and legs, he had allowed the waves to carry him out to sea. He was being tossed about "like a helpless cork" and had just about reached the limit of his endurance when he was fortunately sighted by a passing ship.

"As I was floating toward my death," he afterward told his friends, "I reflected with satisfaction that my volume of republican poems (*Songs Before Sunrise*) was all ready for the press."

These poems were violently attacked for their "fanatical paradoxes." But Swinburne was not afraid of attacks; on the contrary, he reveled in them. It gave him the keenest delight to throw the reading public into consternation with the bombshells of his unorthodox poems on politics and religion and love. His poetry, remarked one of his critics, was enough to send a blush to the cheek of Mrs Grundy. "Yes," retorted Swinburne, "and a dream into her heart." He constantly quarreled with his critics. "I defy castigation!" God had endowed his son with genius, complained Swinburne's father, but He had not "vouchsafed to grant him self-control." Swinburne had conceived a suspicion against all mankind. He was ready to pick a fight on the least provocation. For days at a stretch he would refuse to see anyone. His personality had become like an exposed nerve—

sensitive to the subtlest music of nature, hurt at the slightest dissent from his views.

He was becoming more and more eccentric. He would walk through the streets of London reciting poetry at the top of his voice. Once he spent the night at the house of an admiring family. The lady of the house, in order to do him honor, had filled his bedroom with Japanese lilies. In the middle of the night he roused the household with his delirious screaming. "They've poisoned me!" he screeched. "They've poisoned me with perfume!"

At last one of his closest friends, the barrister Theodore Watts-Dunton, took him in hand. He transferred him from the turmoil of London to the quietude of Putney, and here he kept him and cared for him just as a solicitous gardener would care for an exotic flower.

Swinburne remained with Watts-Dunton for thirty years. These were the serenest years of his life.

> I hid my heart in a nest of roses,
>   Out of the sun's way, hidden apart;
> In a softer bed than the soft white snow's is,
>   Under the roses I hid my heart.

The serenest years—and the most unproductive. His genius, like a hothouse flower, had lost its outdoor touch.

VII

WATTS-DUNTON protected Swinburne not only against the excitement of his former companions but also against the excitement of his former thoughts. Under the influence of his guardian the fighter against "all the oppression that is done under the sun" had become as "a child at play with his toys." Or rather, as the *ghost* of a child. He lived on as a legendary reminder of a once great poet. Occasionally a flash of his old-time humor would break through the cloud of his arrested genius. Referring one day to some of the contemporary poets of England, he remarked: "I can parody Robert Browning's discords with impunity, since Robert Browning can never revenge himself by parodying my harmonies." The sad thing about Swinburne, however, was that he was now reduced to parodying himself. His poems at this period sounded like a poor imitation of Swinburne. And his critical judgment had begun to fail along with the failure of his creative faculty. He tried to revaluate his former values and generally for the worse. He had once hailed Walt Whitman as "the singer from over the sea—the heart of the hearts that are free." But now, allowing his views to be molded by the well-intentioned but spiritually unenlightened Watts-Dunton, he characterized the Muse of Walt Whitman as "a drunken applewoman, indecently sprawling in the slush and garbage of the gutter amid the rotten refuse of her over-turned fruit stall."

Swinburne's sunset was not one of trailing glory. A haze had come up over the horizon to meet him and to obscure his passing. He had grown deaf in his old age, and he was now almost completely shut off from the world. He felt keenly about the loss of his faculties. "I am stale," he wrote to a friend, "a garment out of fashion." His character had grown gentle. It was far more lovable now—and far less amusing.

As he approached the icy years of his life he felt lonely, like a solitary fir tree in a forest of maples. One by one his friends died, but he lived on. He had become very fond of children, "the little citizens of heaven."

> If of such be the kingdom of heaven,
> Then it must be heaven indeed.

And thus he dreamed away the decline of his days, a legendary, lonely figure in a land of forgotten fame. One autumn evening a young lady was walking through a thick white mist on Wimbledon Common. Her shoelace had become untied, and she bent down to fasten it. "While I was doing so," she writes, "someone stumbled over me and cried out *Oh!* in a tone of passionate dismay. I looked up to find a white face immediately above me and a blaze of red hair which seemed to part the mist like a flame. In a flash a small, thin-legged man's figure tripped precipitately away, and the fog appeared to swallow him up as if he had been a vision. . . ."

The dying singer of our deathless songs was groping his way into the mists of eternity.

BRYANT

Great Poems by Bryant

Thanatopsis.
To a Waterfowl.
Forest Hymn.
The Fountain.
The Little People of the Snow.
Sella.
Voices of Nature.
The White-Footed Deer.
Autumn Pastoral.
The Prairies.
A Lifetime.

Death of Lincoln.
The Yellow Violet.
The Fringed Gentian.
Monument Mountain.
The Past.
Robert of Lincoln.
O Fairest of the Rural Maids.
A Summer Ramble.
The Evening Wind.
The Poet.
The Flood of Years.

Bryant

Poe

William Cullen Bryant

1794–1878

DR PETER BRYANT, "the good and learned" physician of Cummington, in the Berkshire section of Massachusetts, dabbled occasionally in politics and in poetry. Once, when he was serving in the legislature at the Boston Statehouse, Willard Phillips, an editor of the *North American Review*, suggested that he send him some of his poetry for examination. Dr Bryant happened to have in his pocket at that time a poem which his young son, William Cullen, had written. The boy was only seventeen years old, and the title of the poem was *Thanatopsis*.

Dr Bryant made a clean copy of the poem and brought it, without appending the author's name, to the editorial office of the *North American Review*. Mr Phillips was not in at the time. When he returned and saw the poem he could hardly believe his eyes. He rushed to the house of his coeditor, Richard H. Dana, and read the poem to him.

Mr Dana listened politely and then broke into a skeptical smile. "Phillips, you've been imposed upon. No one on this side of the Atlantic is capable of writing such poetry."

"But I know the man who wrote it! Doctor Peter Bryant, an old friend of mine. Why, he's sitting at this very moment in the Statehouse Senate."

"I think I had better have a look at him," said Dana. Putting on his galoshes and his overcoat, he trudged over to the State-house and asked an attendant to point out Dr Bryant to him. "I looked at him with profound attention and interest," remarked Dana afterward in a conversation with the Reverend Robert C. Waterston. "I saw before me a man of striking personality; but the stamp of genius was wanting. It is a good head, I said to myself, but I do not see *Thanatopsis* in it."

II

THERE WAS no stamp of genius either in Dr Peter Bryant or in any of William Cullen's earlier ancestors. Most of them were giants on the physical rather than on the mental side. His great-grandfather, Ichabod Bryant, was "of such enormous size and strength that he could place his hands upon the shoulders of any common man and crush him to the earth in spite of his resistance." Dr Peter Bryant, Cullen's father, could "take a barrel of cider and lift it into a cart over the wheel." His ancestors on his mother's side, too, were men and women of extraordinary vigor. Two days after Cullen's birth (November 3, 1794) his mother was down in the kitchen making a coat for one of her other children.

But Cullen inherited none of his family's physical power. By the mysterious alchemy of the heavens the iron of the Bryant bodily strength was in Cullen transmuted into the gold of poetical genius.

He was a delicate and sickly child. It took all of his father's medical skill to pull him through one dangerous illness after another. At an early age the symptoms of consumption manifested themselves. He was susceptible to colds upon the slightest change in the weather. At last his father resorted to a drastic treatment in order to harden the fragile little body. Early every morning throughout the summer he plunged Cullen into a cold spring near the house, "continuing the treatment, in spite of the outcries and protestations of his patient, so late into the autumn as sometimes to render it necessary to break the ice that skimmed the surface."

Along with his abnormally frail body went an abnormally precocious mind. "When but a few days more than sixteen months old," he tells us, "I knew all the letters of the alphabet."

He entered school at four. Although he liked his studies and tried to be attentive to his teacher, the "weakness of the flesh" sometimes got the better of him. "Once (in the classroom) I awoke from a sound nap to find myself in the lap of the schoolmistress and was vexed to be thus treated like a baby."

From his earliest days he loved to read poetry. And to write it. Every night when he said his prayers he added the words, "And please, God, let me be a poet." One of his earliest compositions was a transcription of the Book of Job into heroic couplets. The opening lines were about as unpromising of future greatness as any doggerel could possibly be:

> His name was Job, evil he did eschew,
> To him were born three sons; three daughters too.

His father looked at the poem, shook his head and said, "Someday you will be ashamed of this."

And indeed it was not long before Cullen grew ashamed of his early doggerel. He had found, in his father's library, Pope's translation of the *Iliad*, the works of Spenser and of Milton and the plays of Shakespeare. And then—glory of glories!—one day his father brought him a volume of Wordsworth's poems. Here at last was the man who spoke to the innermost heart. His poetry grew as naturally as the wild flowers in the forest. It was the language which Cullen could best understand and—he felt certain—could best employ. To do for America what Wordsworth had done for England—*this* from now on would be the primary object of his life. "Please, God, let me be the humble poet of the American landscape."

To his kindled emotions the poetry of Wordsworth was "wind

over flame." It took Bryant but a short time to develop from a commonplace writer of doggerel to the inspired poet of *Thanatopsis*.

III

IN THE FALL OF 1810 he entered Williams College, a new and struggling institution with a faculty of one professor and two tutors. The students were for the most part young men like Bryant whose parents couldn't afford to send them to Yale or to Harvard. Bryant soon became dissatisfied with the inadequate educational facilities of the college, "the pale-faced, moping students," and the "dark, dirty, dank and unwholesome cells" of the dormitory. He obtained "an honorable dismission" from Williams and returned to Cummington to prepare himself for Yale. He studied diligently for several months—only to learn that Dr Bryant hadn't the means to pay for his further education.

Keenly disappointed, Cullen decided to take up the study of law as the next best thing to a college education. He entered a lawyer's office at Worthington, not far from his home town, and three years later received his certificate as an "Attorney of the Common Pleas."

He settled down to his legal practice at Great Barrington—not so much because it was a favorable town for a lawyer but because it was a beautiful spot for a poet. "It was on the 3d of October (1816) that I made the journey thither. . . . The woods were in all the glory of autumn. . . . I well remember how much I was struck by the beauty of the smooth green meadows on the banks of that lovely river, the Hoosatonic. . . . I admired no less the contrast between this soft scene and the steep, craggy hills that overlooked it, clothed with their many-colored forests. I had never before seen the southern part of the Berkshires and congratulated myself on becoming an inhabitant of so picturesque a region."

Although he earned a fairly good living at his legal practice, he preferred making verses to making briefs. "You ask whether

[220]

I am pleased with my profession," he wrote to one of his friends. "Alas, sir, the Muse was my first love, and the remains of that passion . . . will always, I fear, cause me to look coldly on the severe beauties of the law." What he especially disliked about the law was the fact that it was "so rarely synonymous with justice."

It was his distaste for the law which indirectly led to the writing of one of his most beautiful poems. Some time before he had settled down in Great Barrington, while he was still undecided as to where to hang up his shingle, he was tramping one December day over the seven miles that separated his village from the neighboring village of Plainfield. Some of his friends had advised him to start his practice at that place. He felt "very forlorn and desolate." His future was uncertain, his profession unpalatable, his genius frustrated. "The sun," writes his biographer, Parke Godwin, "had already set, leaving behind it one of those brilliant seas of chrysolite and opal which often flood the New England skies; and, while he was looking upon the rosy splendor with rapt admiration, a solitary bird made wing along the illuminated horizon. He watched the lone wanderer until it was lost in the distance, asking himself whither it had come and to what home it was flying? When he went to the house where he was to stop for the night his mind was still full of what he had seen and felt." Buoyed up with a new strength and courage, he sat down and wrote the poem *To a Waterfowl:*

> Whither, midst falling dew,
> While glow the heavens with the last steps of day,
> Far, through their rosy depths, dost thou pursue
> Thy solitary way?

> Vainly the fowler's eye
> Might mark thy distant flight to do thee wrong,
> As, darkly painted on the crimson sky,
> Thy figure floats along.

. . . .

There is a Power whose care
Teaches thy way along that pathless coast—
The desert and illimitable air—
Lone wandering, but not lost.

. . . .

He who, from zone to zone,
Guides through the boundless sky thy solitary flight,
In the long way that I must tread alone,
Will lead my steps aright.

The scene changes. Time—several years later. Place—England. Characters—two young men. One of them, Hartley Coleridge, is the son of the great poet. The other, Matthew Arnold, is himself destined to become a great poet. Hartley Coleridge has just rushed into Matthew Arnold's house. "Matt," he cries excitedly, "do you want to hear the best short poem in the English language?"

"Faith, Hartley, I do."

Hartley reads the poem *To a Waterfowl* and then raises his glowing eyes from the paper. "Well, what do you think of it?"

"I am not sure but you are right, Hartley. Is this your father's poem?"

"Oh no. Father has never written anything like that."

IV

BRYANT'S POEMS were superb in quality but few in number. His duties as a struggling young lawyer kept him for the greater part away from the seductions of the Muse. And on top of his legal duties his fellow townsmen honored him—or rather burdened him—with the office of the town clerkship. His records may still be seen at the Town Hall of Great Barrington. One of these records is of particular interest. For it registers his own marriage to Fanny Fairchild, "fairest of the rural maids" of Great Barrington.

Bryant had met her at a village "sociable" and had fallen

in love at first sight with her "very pretty blonde hair, small slender stature, gray eyes, dainty foot, transparent and delicate hands and the wonderfully frank and sweet expression of her face."

On the occasion of their engagement Bryant wrote a prayer which served as a guide for the affectionate serenity of their married life:

"May Almighty God mercifully take care of our happiness here and hereafter. May we ever continue constant to each other and mindful of our mutual promises of attachment and truth. . . . May we lead a long, happy and innocent life, without any diminution of affection till we die. May there never be any jealousy, distrust, coldness or dissatisfaction between us—nor any occasion for any—nothing but kindness, forbearance, mutual confidence and attention to each other's happiness. And that we may be less unworthy of so great a thing, may we be assisted to cultivate all the benign and charitable affections and offices not only toward each other but toward our neighbors, the human race and all the creatures of God. . . ."

The great event of his marriage was shortly followed by another event of major importance. Bryant received an invitation from the Phi Beta Kappa society of Harvard to read a poem at the commencement. This in itself was a notable distinction for so young a poet. But more significant even than the honor of the invitation was the opportunity it gave him to take a trip to Boston—the first such trip of his life, although he had been born only about a hundred miles away from this city— and to make the acquaintance of its leading scholars and writers. He met, among others, John Quincy Adams, Edward Everett, William Ellery Channing, Willard Phillips and Richard Henry Dana. These men, "the earliest April blossoms" of the flowering of New England, made a profound impression upon Bryant. And Bryant made no less profound an impression upon these men. Especially delighted with the poet-lawyer of the Berkshires was Richard Henry Dana, the assistant editor of the *North American Review*.

In their background these two young men were as far apart as the poles. Dana was a descendant of Governor Dudley, a graduate of Harvard College and a member of the exclusive social set known as the New England Brahmins. Bryant, on the other hand, was the offshoot of an obscure family tree, a graduate of no college at all and, under the supercilious monocle of the cultured Bostonians, a rather awkward country bumpkin. Moreover, Dana was a Calvinist in religion and a Monarchist in politics, whereas Bryant had adopted the religion of Unitarianism and the politics of Democracy.

Yet they shared one thing in common—a passion, almost an adoration, for the poetry of Wordsworth. Together with Wordsworth, both Dana and Bryant felt that the world has an inner truth which is not outwardly apparent to the ordinary senses, and that to him who is blessed with this inner vision there is a time when "the earth and every common sight" seem "apparel'd in celestial light."

This mystical conviction of "a light beyond the veil" was the bond which united the two young men in a lifelong friendship. Somewhat older and considerably more worldly than Bryant, Dana became not only his intimate friend but his literary adviser. He urged him to publish a volume of his poetry; and then, when the book had been published and well received, he induced the young lawyer-littérateur to unhyphenate himself—that is, to give up his law in a small country town and to devote himself to his literature in a big commercial city.

Bryant was thirty-one years old when he took this momentous step. At the suggestion of Dana and some of his other friends he went to seek his fortune in New York rather than in Boston. For in New York, he was told, he would find it easier to secure a job in journalism. "Any deficiencies of salary, moreover," wrote Henry Sedgwick, one of his Berkshire friends who had settled in New York, "may be eked out by teaching foreigners, of whom there are many in this city, eager to learn our language and literature. In short, it would be strange if you could not succeed where everybody and everything succeeds."

Fortunately there came to Bryant at this time, in addition to the practical advice of his friends, the concrete offer of a position on the editorial staff of the New York *World*. He accepted the offer with alacrity. "I do not know how long my connection with this work will continue," he wrote to Dana. "My salary is one thousand dollars; no great sum, to be sure, but it is twice what I got by my practice in the country." The greater bulk of his duties consisted in the reviewing of books—an employment, to be sure, "not the most congenial to my taste, nor that for which I am best fitted, but it affords me, for the present, a certain compensation."

And, as he hoped, a greater amount of leisure for the courting of his Muse. In this hope, however, he was disappointed. From the very outset he was so submerged in his journalistic labors that he found very little time for his poetry. The gods, it seemed, had destined him for the planting of a few scattered flowers.

Few—but fadeless.

V

AT ABOUT THIS TIME a doubly severe blow fell upon him—the death of his father and of his sister. He had always worshiped his father—not only as the man "who taught my youth the art of verse" but as the physician who measured his success by the gratitude of his patients rather than by the size of his fees. "His patients generally paid him whatever they pleased, be it ever so little." Bryant's father died, as he had lived, in contented poverty. As for Bryant's sister, she died of tuberculosis, the disease which had always threatened but had never conquered Bryant himself. He had been deeply attached to his sister. Just before her death he had written a farewell sonnet to her. Death, he had said,

> should come
> Gently to one of gentle mold like thee,
> As light winds wandering through groves of flowers
> Detach the delicate blossom from the tree.

When death came—she was only twenty-two years old at the time—he dedicated an equally tender poem to her memory:

> In the cold moist earth we laid her, when the forests cast the leaf,
> And we wept that one so lovely should have a life so brief:
> Yet not unmeet it was that one, like that young friend of ours,
> So gentle and so beautiful, should perish with the flowers.

To forget his grief over his double bereavement Bryant plunged heart and soul into his work. Thin, pale, "almost diminutive in size," he yet possessed an enormous appetite for labor. And a prodigious capacity for friendship. "He had a strange fondness," observed a neighbor, "for talking with queer and common people—farmers, woodmen and stage drivers. He loved to crack his jokes with them. And," added his neighbor, "some of Mr Bryant's jokes were rather on the spicy side." He possessed a sense of humor—that saving grace without which a poet is likely to degenerate into a prig. There was no man whose laughter was heartier, even if it happened to be at his own expense. "His laugh . . . began with a queer chuckle, spread gradually over the whole face and finally shook him all over like an ague."

And it required a great deal of laughter to season the unpalatable dish of his daily drudgery. He was tied to a treadmill which gave him no letup and which, on top of it all, threatened at any moment to collapse. And before long it did. The publishers lost their investment and abandoned the paper.

Desperately he turned back to his law and obtained a license to practice in the courts of New York. Once more he was ready to

> . . . mingle among the jostling crowd
> Where the sons of strife are subtle and loud.

Luck was with him, however. He secured a position on the New York *Evening Post*—and remained with that paper to the end of his days.

VI

As USUAL, his editorial and his political duties—the *Evening Post* was a strong supporter of Andrew Jackson—kept Bryant so preoccupied for the greater part of the day that he had but a few minutes to spare for his poetry. He was not altogether contented with these conditions; but, as he wrote to Dana, "politics and a bellyful are better than poetry and starvation."

Politics and a bellyful, a trenchant but honest journalistic pen, a handful of immortal poems and an honored name—such, in brief, is the story of the rest of his life. Thanks to his Yankee thrift he was able before long to buy a controlling share in the paper. Under his influence the *Evening Post* became one of the leading exponents of American liberal thought. Bryant was active in the formation of the Republican party, in the nomination of Lincoln for the presidency, in the crusade for the emancipation of slavery and in the campaign for the recognition of the rights of labor. He was ready, not only with his pen but with his tongue and with his purse, to advance every free cause against the encroachments of tyranny. He proclaimed the principle of true Americanism—life, liberty and the mutual pursuit of happiness. Never, he declared, should anyone pursue his happiness up to the point where it interferes with the happiness of his neighbor. He regarded it not only as un-American but as inhuman

> . . . to blend our pleasure or our pride
> With sorrow of the meanest thing that feels.

Live, let live and help live—this, to Bryant, was the politics, the poetry and the religion of the New World.

He was the first of the national poets of America. He was American not only in his landscapes but in his language. "I observe," he wrote to one of his correspondents, "that you have used several French expressions in your letter. I think if you will study our own language that you will find it capable of express-ing all the ideas you may have."

He enjoyed the expression of his ideas in the simple Yankee prose of New England. Yet he was anxious, again and again, to abandon his prose for his poetry. "Here (at the office of the *Evening Post*)," he confided to Dana, "I am a draught horse, harnessed to a daily drag. I have so much to do with my legs and hoofs, struggling and pulling and kicking, that, if there is anything of the Pegasus in me, I am too much exhausted to use my wings."

And thus for several years "the poet and the journalist wrestled with each other in the affections of Bryant like Jacob and Esau in the womb of Rebecca." As time went on, however, and as the paper grew more and more prosperous, he resigned himself to his "mess of pottage"—especially so since it was honestly earned and generously shared with those less fortunate than himself. His prosperity enabled him to rescue his friends out of their doldrums, to buy a country estate for his family on Long Island Sound—"such a nook as a poet might well choose" —to take several interesting trips to Europe and to mellow into an old age that was free at least from care if not from labor.

Yet he was never too absorbed in his labor to neglect the duties—or rather, the pleasures—of hospitality at his spacious country home at Roslyn. "You shall come to Roslyn, you and your Sultana," he wrote to one of his friends, "and you shall receive a royal welcome. . . . Come on and we will make the most of you both and anybody else you choose to bring along with you. . . ."

And anybody else you choose to bring along with you—such was the all-inclusive cordiality of his home and his heart.

VII

HE IS an old man now but still hard at work. Every morning at seven, after a walk of three miles, he sits down to his editorial labors on the *Post*. The last few years of his life have been the busiest. In the middle seventies he has undertaken the most ambitious of his works—the translation of the *Iliad* and the *Odyssey*—and on the very threshold of eighty he has completed the task of "transplanting the flowers of Troy upon the banks of the Hudson."

His vigor is unimpaired, but his heart is sad. For the passing years have reaped a plentiful harvest of his friends. And last and most tragic of all, the hand of death has taken his wife. This blow is almost more than he is able to bear.

> What am I doing, thus alone,
> In the glory of Nature here,
> Silver-haired, like a snowflake thrown
> On the greens of the springing year?

Yet he carries on. "It is getting rather late in the evening now. Almost time to go to bed." But there are a number of things that are still to be done before he can take his rest. Editorials to be written in behalf of freedom, poems to be reshaped for eternity, speeches to be delivered for the inspiration of his fellow men. And it is at one of these inspiring speeches that he receives the summons for his own death. The statue of the great liberator Mazzini has just been unveiled at Central Park. Bryant, his "good gray head" uncovered to the sun, is delivering the final paragraph of his address:

"Image of the illustrious champion of civil and religious liberty . . . remain for eyes yet to come where we place thee, in the midst of millions; remain till the day shall dawn—far distant though it be—when the duties of human brotherhood shall be acknowledged by all the races of mankind."

A sudden dizziness due to the hot sun. Bryant stumbles, falls backward and strikes his head.

For three weeks he remains unconscious, and then (on June 12, 1878) his great and simple heart reaches its final beat.

POE

Great Poems by Poe

The Raven.
The Bells.
Israfel.
Annabel Lee.
Ulalume.
For Annie.
Sonnet—Silence.
Lenore.
The Sleeper.
Eldorado.

To Helen.
'Neath Blue-Bell or Streamer.
A Dream within a Dream.
The City in the Sea.
The Valley of Unrest.
The Coliseum.
Dream-Land.
To One in Paradise.
Tamerlane.
Romance.

Edgar Allan Poe

1809–1849

IN LOOKING BACK through history," wrote Edgar Allan Poe, "we should pass over the biographies of 'the good and the great,' while we search carefully for the records of wretches who died in prison, in Bedlam or upon the gallows." Poe had a tender fellow feeling for the picturesque denizens of the dump.

Poe's own life, to be sure, began in Boston—the most "proper" of American cities. A man born here could not be destined for the scrap heap if given half a chance. But Poe was given somewhat less than half a chance. He was born of a pair of strolling players, and he lost them both in his earliest years. As a compensation for the loss of his parents the fates presented him with a couple of foster parents. The wealthy and aristocratic Allans of Virginia, who adopted Edgar Poe, gave him their name and their affection but not their comprehension. They could never quite make out this wayward little Bohemian who had come to them from an alien world. They tried their best to prepare him for their own world of exclusive snobbery and conventional culture—and they failed. It was not in his blood.

As the first step in their effort to turn him into a Southern gentleman they sent him to an English boarding school. He returned to the States with an exterior polish, a dashing manner and a drawing-room etiquette. But he had also picked up the besetting vice of the English aristocrat—a passion for cards and for wine. And he had neither the purse nor the constitution necessary for the lavish indulgence of this vice.

Add to this a fiery but morbid imagination, a supersensitive heart, a feeble will and an impetuous tongue, and you have a young poet hardly suited to pass unscathed through the battles of life.

And, sure enough, his troubles began early. Shortly after he entered the University of Virginia he confronted his foster father with a gambling debt that sent the old gentleman into a fury. Poe was taken out of college and put into the counting-house.

His career among the money-changers was as brief as it was distasteful. He ran away from his desk and enlisted in the army. He gave his name as Edgar A. Perry. Within two years he rose to the rank of sergeant major. And then he escaped.

His guardian had traced him in his flight. He was bitterly disappointed in "this good-for-nothing son of those good-for-nothing actors." But he decided to give him another chance. He secured for him a congressional recommendation to West Point.

Poe entered the military academy at the age of twenty. But it soon became apparent that he was not fitted for the life of a commissioned officer. He could brook no discipline. He had become unruly. He showed an utter contempt for his duties. He was discharged in disgrace.

No one could make head or tail of him. Mr Allan threw up his hands in despair. He had committed the terrible error of taking under his wing no ordinary personality. Of all the lovely babies he might have adopted, he remarked bitterly, the rulers of the world in their jest had given him the one incomprehensible problem child of the generation!

II

THE CHARACTER OF POE was indeed beyond the comprehension of Mr Allan who, for all his wealth and aristocracy, was a simple-minded man. He never dreamt that his foster son was endowed with poetic genius. Nor did any of Poe's companions suspect the feverish activity that went on inside his head. For all his pleasant intercourse, Poe had as yet shared his heart with no one. In fact, it was said that he lacked the power of making intimate friends. There was a strange reserve about him, people remarked. Even at the university, where he had often acted as a ringleader in the frolics, "no one knew him at all." What was the reason for this inner aloofness? his companions asked themselves. And a few of them suggested that perhaps it was due to his inherent loneliness. He lived out of his environment, like a fish out of the water. He was a miscast and unhappy actor —a child of the gutter compelled to assume the role of an aristocrat. And in a sense they were right. He found no warmth in his uncongenial environment, no tribal sympathy, no parental love. Once, indeed, when a mere boy at school, he had known for an instant the tenderness of an older woman's understanding. She was the mother of a school chum. And she had spoken words of affection with a voice he had never heard before! But then she had died, and the few words of love he had known in his childhood remained nothing but an echo and a memory.

He lived alone in his memories and his dreams. And passing these memories and dreams through the filter of his morbid imagination, he transmuted them into poetry the like of which had never yet been heard in America.

When he was discharged from West Point he submitted these dream poems to the Baltimore papers. The editors of these papers looked quizzically at the author. He had written sheer nonsense, they thought. But it was such exquisite nonsense!

Penniless and out of tune with the world, Poe went on with his bizarre poetry—*Tamerlane*, the story of the man who conquered the world for his beloved and returned to lay it at her feet, only to find that in his absence she had died of a lonely heart; *Al Aaraaf*, the outlandish tale of another world; poems and stories that were no tales of all but fantastic visions set to a new music. Of course nobody could understand these poems. Yet all those who read them could hear the strange and haunting echo of a new music.

He published a slender volume of his verse—written during his student days among the cadets. The press reviewed the book favorably. It was a good beginning. The author might write a beautiful if not a magnificent poem once he had mastered his material. "I am certain that as yet I have written neither a beautiful nor a magnificent poem. But I will do so—I take my oath upon it—if only they will give me time!"

III

MEANWHILE he turned his attention to prose. He had decided upon a literary career and he realized that the way to fame and fortune lay over the adventurous highways of fiction. He submitted a weird thriller—the fantastic story of a shipwreck—in a prize competition and succeeded in winning the first prize. When the editors of the *Baltimore Saturday Visitor* expressed a desire to dine with the man to whom they had awarded the money Poe sent them the following reply: "Your invitation to dinner has wounded me to the quick. I cannot come, for reasons of the most humiliating nature. I haven't a decent suit of clothes to wear."

His foster father had broken off intercourse with him. One day Poe heard that Mr Allan was dangerously ill. He rushed to his bedside. But Allan, summoning his last flicker of strength, rose from his bed, grasped his cane and waved it menacingly, demanding that Poe leave the house at once. Shortly thereafter Allan died. By the terms of the will Poe was left not a single penny.

Yet he seemed to be on the way to success. The literary gentry in Baltimore were wagging their tongues about him. There were rumors that he was about to publish a volume of bizarre tales. "The young fellow is highly imaginative, though slightly given to the terrific."

They were willing to help him to a start. Thanks to their recommendation, he received an offer for an editorial position on the *Southern Literary Messenger* in Richmond, Virginia. He accepted the offer. Encouraged by the prospect of a steady income—ten dollars a week—Poe felt that he could now publicly announce his marriage which had taken place privately sometime earlier. He had wedded his thirteen-year-old cousin, Virginia Clemm, despite the endeavors of her relatives to postpone the match until the girl was older. They had braved the conventional opinion of the folk around them. Conventional opinions, conventional acts—these were but the passing shadows of the unimaginative world in which most men lived. Of what interest were they to Poe, who lived in the comforting solidity of his own fantastic world?

He was entirely unorthodox. He couldn't be fathomed. No sooner did he find himself more or less settled in life, with a growing reputation and a future, than he drank himself out of his security. He had a queer sense of humor. It was hollow and mocking. There was no laughter to it. Mr White, in dismissing him from his editorial job, wrote a cordial enough letter. "I cannot address you in such language as this occasion and my feelings demand. . . . When you once again tread these streets I have my fears . . . that you will again drink till your senses are lost. Unless you look to your Maker for help you will not be safe. . . . If you would make yourself contented with quarters in my house, or with any other private family, where liquor is not used, I should think there was some hope for you. But if you go to a tavern or to any place where it is used at table, you are not safe."

He left Baltimore to seek his fortune in Philadelphia. To seek his fortune and to find new misfortunes. For wherever he went he took his sensitiveness and his weakness along with him.

Yet his weakness, he insisted, was the direct result of his sensitiveness. It wasn't that he drank excessively, he explained, but that he couldn't drink at all. Physically as well as mentally he was different from other people. His nerves were so tense that the slightest stimulus moved him to the greatest excitement. "I pledge, before God, the solemn word of a gentleman that I am temperate even to rigor." If he took a single glass of weak wine or beer, he declared, it almost always ended in severe illness. His own excess was the average man's daily stint.

Thus he argued before the world. He couldn't drink much, yet he was compelled to drink a little. He appealed to "all the physicians in the world" that it required something stronger than water to translate his glowing fancies into living words.

But he had little opportunity to indulge his fancies. Occasionally the editors offered him a job as a book reviewer—a chore he heartily detested. "They want me to make myself the shifting toady of the hour and bow and cringe and sound the glory of third-rate ability with a penny trumpet! Then I would be feted alive. And then *perhaps* I would be praised when dead." But he couldn't be connected permanently with any publication not his own. He couldn't go on forever writing reviews in other people's magazines, compelled to express opinions backed by financial investment, required to shout "amen" along with the public to the "microscopical literary efforts of a hundred animalcula who call themselves authors."

Someday he would start a magazine of his own and work only for himself. And *then* he would give free wing to his fantasies. This was the subject of his hope and his despair. For there were times when he doubted whether he could ever find the proper channel to communicate to the mass of mankind the images that came to him in that borderline interval between his sleeping and his waking moments. Perhaps there was no one who had ever gone through his own strange mental experiences. Perhaps, indeed, there were no human words to express such experiences. "They are not ideas in my brain. They are not dreams. They arise from the soul in its utmost tranquillity.

They are not born of a waking state; they come not to one in sleep. They take shape at those mere points in time when the waking world blends with the world of sleep—at the split second when my mind hovers between dreams and consciousness—and who can say whether the human being is at that absolutely psychical moment awake or asleep?" Such a moment of exquisite delicacy can scarcely be experienced by the normal five senses. It lies in the province of an infinity of supersenses entirely alien to the physical state. "Is not such a moment the very origin of my life, the very essence of my genius? And, if so, is such an experience common to every man or is it confined only to my individual self?"

Lost in this haunted borderland, the poet tried to find an answer to his questions. He must transfer his own fluid moment into the frozen store of memory and survey his dreams with a practical eye. He must have faith in the power of words. He must demonstrate the fact that fantasies as well as thoughts could survive within the province of precise language. Otherwise he would be lost, like a ghost haunting the house of life and vainly trying to take his place in the reality of his fellow men.

"I must make my fantasies worthy of belief." He would introduce his readers into the highest reaches of impossible imaginings, leading them subtly and imperceptibly to accept the ghost for the substance, the myth for the truth, hardly aware of the point where they had overstepped the bounds of the solid world into the land of somber hues and twilight landscapes whose secrets were known to only one man.

And so he tried to capture the moments between his sleeping and his waking and translated them into pseudorealistic visions that seemed more real than reality. He published a book of these stories—*Ligeia, The Fall of the House of Usher, William Wilson*. . . . The public read them and understood. Now at last he would be able to enjoy all the good things to which a man of genius was entitled—love, fame, the dominion of the intellect, the consciousness of power, the thrilling sense of beauty, the free air of heaven. His troubles, he thought, were over at last!

IV

But his troubles had only begun. He was slandered by his fellow craftsmen—critics who were jealous of his success as a writer, writers who were incensed at his honesty as a critic. And climaxing all these difficulties came the discouraging succession of cant-ridden letters from the editors dispensing with his services. They would be glad to take him back, they always advised him patronizingly, if only he would stop drinking. They might as well have worded it, if only he would stop writing!

And then a still greater evil befell him. Virginia, his child wife whom he loved "as no man ever loved before," had ruptured a blood vessel while singing. Her life was despaired of. "I took leave of her forever and underwent the agonies of her death. She recovered partially, and I again hoped. At the end of a year the vessel broke again." Then again—again. "I became insane with long intervals of horrible sanity. During those fits of absolute unconsciousness I drank—God only knows how often or how much." And then he found a temporary cure for himself—found it in the definite verdict of the doctors that an early death awaited her. This certain tragedy he could bear like a man. It was the horrible oscillation between hope and despair that he could not have endured much longer.

But it was six years before she died—a slow and agonizing death for them both. He hovered around her couch with tender anxiety, and a shudder seized him like a convulsion at her slightest cough. There were nights when no one dared to speak to him. When the warm weather came he rode out with her in the twilight, and his watchful eyes eagerly searched her pallid face for the slightest change of expression.

"Dear Griswold," the man of pride was finally compelled to write to one of his friends, "can you not send me $5? I am sick and Virginia is almost gone."

Once more he had lost his editorial job, this time on *Graham's*

Magazine. Together with his invalid wife he left Philadelphia to try his luck in New York. He had ten dollars in his pocket. Upon his arrival in the City of New Hope he wrote a letter to Virginia's mother:

"My Dear Muddy, we arrived safe at the Walnut Street Wharf. . . . I took Sis to the Depôt Hotel. . . . Last night for supper we had the nicest tea you ever drank, strong and hot—wheat bread and rye bread—cheese—teacakes (elegant), a great dish (two dishes) of elegant ham and two of cold veal, piled up like a mountain in large slices—three dishes of the cakes and everything in the greatest profusion. . . . Sis is delighted. . . . She has coughed hardly any and has had no night sweats. She is now busy mending my pants which I tore against a nail. . . . We have got four dollars and a half left. . . . I feel in excellent spirits and haven't taken a drop—so that I hope soon to get out of trouble."

It was but a faint beam of happiness in the black vigil of their despair. Soon the winter came—and with it the coughing and the fevers and the sweats. Virginia lay on a bed that had no mattress or any other bedding except straw and a white counterpane and sheets. She was wrapped in the coat of her husband and she held a large furry kitten to her bosom for warmth. Her husband clasped her hands. This contact helped the circulation somewhat. Her mother rubbed her feet to keep them from frostbite.

She passed into eternity on the Lord's Day, while the church bells were ringing and the faithful were at worship. He escorted her poor little body to the grave in the black military coat that had kept her warm in her last moments. And as they lowered her to her rest he recalled the words he had written in his despair: "The star-shaped flowers shrank into the stems of the trees and appeared no more. . . . And Life departed from our paths; for the tall flamingo flaunted no more his scarlet plumage before us, but flew sadly from the vale into the hills. . . . And the golden and silver fish swam down through the gorge at the lower end of our domain and bedecked the sweet river never again. . . . And the lulling melody . . . died little by little away, in murmurs growing lower and lower. . . ."

V

AT LAST Poe had become famous as a writer of the bizarre. Famous but not prosperous. The entire literary world had been startled into recognition of his genius when he won the first prize for *The Gold Bug*, the short story of ciphers and secrets. But the prize brought him only one hundred dollars and an infinity of trouble. For the story had started a "cipher" fad. A host of admirers sent him cryptograms and challenged him to solve them. "I have lost in time, which to me is money, more than a thousand dollars, solving secret messages" with no other purpose than to demonstrate his analytical powers before so large an audience. And his audience grew even larger when he startled the world with *The Raven*. Yet with all his fame he remained as poor as ever—he had sold *The Raven* for ten dollars. And so he slunk through the world, a sad, solitary, hungry celebrity robed in black, meeting people with a cynical smile on his lips and "dreaming dreams no mortal ever dreamed before."

And in spite of his sadness and his hunger he kept on creating his strange visions and—let it be admitted—plagiarizing freely when the fire of his creation burned low. When other writers stooped to this sort of unpermitted borrowing he called it downright theft. When he himself did it—well, he did it, and that was that! For he lived in a world whose laws, whose customs and whose demands, he insisted, were quite beyond the sympathetic understanding of the average human mind. His cryptograms, his hoaxes, his pseudoscientific accounts of journeys in a balloon and his supernatural reports of conversations with the dead and of corpses come to life—all these were part and parcel of the phantasmagoria in which his spirit habitually dwelt. Wasn't all life a hoax, a fantastic vision plagiarized by some Divine Poet out of the epic nightmare of a diabolical mind? Then why should not he, a human poet, plagiarize the fantastic visions of other human minds?

He therefore felt no compunction when it was pointed out that his sea narrative of Arthur Gordon Pym was copied largely from an account of Morell's *Voyages* and that his startling essay on conchology (shells)—a subject on which he hadn't the slightest training—was an almost exact reproduction of a book written by Captain Thomas Brown.

Always posing, always pretending to a knowledge he didn't possess, always coloring his imposture with verisimilitude, living in a world of subjective fancies and self-made laws. Again and again in his stories and his articles he referred to foreign books which, upon investigation, were found never to have existed. Like other writers handicapped by insufficient education, he loved to show off his pseudo scholarship through the "quotations" of passages from languages he knew nothing about.

But he did not regard his fictitious quotations as impostures. He was an artist. He sought no facts; he sought only effects. He was a painter of the grotesque and the arabesque. He was interested not so much in the true as in the beautiful. "The sense of beauty," he wrote, "is an immortal instinct deep within the spirit of man."

To evoke beauty through the music of words—that, and that alone, was the purpose of his art. He called music "the most entrancing of poetic moods." In order to create these entrancing moods, these musical pictures of the grotesque and the arabesque, he employed the entire repertory of the literary magician's tricks—"novelty, quotation, repetition, unexpected phrases, quaintnesses . . . sentences and sentiments of sweet sounds" that were "simply beyond the reach of analysis." He maintained that those who persist in reconciling "the obstinate oils of poetry and truth" are "mad beyond redemption." No work of art, he declared, should ever point a moral or embody a truth.

What he tried to create, therefore, was *artistic* rather than *scientific* reality, *verisimilitude* rather than *verity*, a mere *semblance* of the truth rather than the *actual* truth. And this, he explained, was the justification for his artifices and his hoaxes and his pseudoscientific "discoveries" and his fictitious quotations. He was, in his poetry as well as in his prose, a writer of fiction. But he was also a creator, and therefore his fiction appeared at times to be even truer than the truth.

VI

AFTER THE DEATH OF HIS WIFE he continued to live in his rented cottage at Fordham. He underwent a critical illness during these "lonesome latter years." And then, as he slowly recuperated among his pet tropical songbirds and his dahlias and his heliotropes, his mind became wrapped in the clouds of mysticism. He began to lecture on the universe and planned the prospectus of a philosophy compared to which "Newton's discovery of gravitation would be a mere incident." He wrote the book and called it *Eureka—I Have Made the Discovery!* He regarded this as the greatest of his works. It was not enough that he had taken his place among the masters of poetry and fiction; he had now become—he believed—the leading philosopher of the century. But the critics thought otherwise. They regarded the book as the sad outpouring of a pompous obscurity, the pathetic attempt of a mortal failure to find an immortal soul.

But Poe was not yet ready to confess himself as a failure. He still clung to the hope of starting his own magazine ånd of "generally re-establishing myself in the literary world." He made a speaking tour of New England. "Those clear, sad eyes," wrote a reviewer of one of his lectures, "seemed to look down upon us from an eminence. . . . He smiled, but seldom laughed or said anything to excite mirth in others."

At a lecture on poetry which he delivered in Providence he met Mrs Whitman, a fellow poet to whom he became deeply attached. They were engaged to be married. But his conduct repelled her. Often he was found unconscious on the streets—a victim of laudanum or of alcohol. He was a pitiable object when in his cups. Staggering along the gutter, his eyes bleary and his clothes a bundle of mud-stained rags, he would lose himself in "sublime rhapsodies on the evolution of the universe," speaking as from some imaginary platform to multitudinous dream audiences of "vast and attentive visitors."

Finally, when he had drunk and drugged himself into popular discredit, Mrs Whitman broke the engagement.

But he still entertained the dream of that magazine he was going to start. In 1849 he left Fordham for Richmond to work out the plans for the project. And then this hope, too, was shattered—not through any external opposition but through the inadequacy of his own will. His mind had become tormented with the suspicion of some dreadful conspiracy against his life. He begged an acquaintance for a razor so that he might remove his mustache and thus effect a disguise against his pursuers. His friends feared for his sanity unless he could find a companion to watch over him. They were much relieved when he renewed his courtship for an old childhood sweetheart, now a wealthy widow. Once again an engagement was announced. Poe wound up his affairs and then left for his wedding in the South.

But he never reached his destination. They found him in Baltimore—in one of the election polls of the fourth ward—out of his mind, his traveling bag missing, all his money gone. It was believed that, under the influence of liquor, he had fallen into the hands of a band of electioneering ruffians who had drugged him and kept him prisoner until the day of election and who had then led him stupefied from one ward to the next to vote under various names.

They took him to the hospital. His face was drenched with perspiration. He talked deliriously for hours. And then his mind became somewhat clearer. He mumbled a few coherent phrases just before he died.

> O God! . . . Is all we see or seem
> But a dream within a dream?

LONGFELLOW

Great Poems by Longfellow

Longfellow

Whittier

Henry Wadsworth Longfellow

1807–1882

IN THE EARLY PART of the nineteenth century New England was a land of seamen, merchants, farmers and pioneers. They were hampered neither by the burdens of excessive wealth nor by the hardships of excessive poverty. Theirs was a land of living pines, not of dead pyramids. They were interested in staking out the future rather than in raking over the past. They were not stifled with titles. They were a hard-living, hard-fighting, stubborn and stalwart society, proud of their material and moral accomplishments. For they had tamed a continent and created a democracy. And yet they were despised for the very qualities which made them unique among the races of men. For the peoples of the Old World looked down upon the inhabitants of the New World as a rabble of road builders with flexed muscles and inflexible minds—men who wrestled with the vast acres of the soil but who felt little concern for the vaster acres of the spirit. The American brothers of Esau, said the Europeans with a contemptuous sneer, had sold their artistic birthright for a mess of pottage.

And the Americans were ready to admit the charge. Even the patriarchal families of New England shuffled back like prodigal sons to the Old World to receive the blessings of a European education. It hardly occurred to anyone that the soul of a gentleman might be nurtured in the wilderness of America. Morally and intellectually New England was a British colony long after she had won her political independence. But little by little she fought her fight and won her victory in the war of her *cultural* independence. The George Washington of this second and bloodless American Revolution was Henry Longfellow.

II

HE WAS BORN in the town of Portland, on the rugged coast of Maine. His ancestors were distinguished in the military and judicial records of New England. His maternal grandfather, General Peleg Wadsworth, was a Revolutionary War hero. His other grandfather was a famous judge; and his father, a member of Congress and a presidential elector. Tracing his family still further back, Longfellow was able to number among his ancestors no less than four members of the Mayflower party, one of whom was John Alden. The Longfellows came from the very top of the social cream of New England.

And Henry's education was aristocratic like his birth. From the very start he was brought up "in habits of respect and obedience, of unselfishness, the dread of debt and the faithful performance of duty." His first schoolmaster recorded of him at five, "Henry's conduct last quarter was very correct and amiable." At Bowdoin College, which he entered before he was sixteen, "he was always a gentleman in his deportment and a model in his character and habits." At eighteen he said that the only women he met were "something to be enshrined and holy —to be gazed at and talked with, and nothing further." He attended balls but never danced except with the older ladies, "to whom the attention might give pleasure." Here was the paragon of Aristotle's gentleman who adhered to the golden mean, "Nothing in excess." Such was the proper spirit for a philosopher but hardly for a poet. The contemporary poets of England—Shelley, Byron, Keats—could hardly have flourished in this Puritan atmosphere of New England. It was to young Longfellow's credit that his virtue failed to wear down his genius.

He had been reared in a home of books and music and literary gossip. It was therefore not extraordinary that he began to write poetry at an early age. At college he had definitely made up his mind to embark on a literary career. But his father, in a letter which he sent to Henry at Bowdoin College, cautioned him against such a course with the observation that there was not sufficient wealth in America to afford a living for a literary man. Yet the face of the cultured artist in Longfellow's father was hidden under the mask of the shrewd Yankee. He began his letter with a practical warning, and he ended it with a poetical criticism. "I observe some poetry in the *U. S. Literary Gazette*," he wrote, "which, from the signature, I presume to be from your pen. It is a very pretty production, and I read it with pleasure. But you will observe that the second line of the sixth verse has too many feet."

While Longfellow was trying to make up his mind as to his future career, Destiny stepped in to shape it for him. The chair of modern languages at Bowdoin had become vacant. An instructorship was offered to Henry upon his graduation provided he traveled through Europe and familiarized himself with the languages at firsthand. And Henry, on the principle that "as many languages as a person acquires, so many times is he a man," set sail for Europe with all the eagerness of the young poet.

He arrived in France and wrote from Auteuil that the situation was ideal. "I can at any time hear French conversation —for the French are always talking." He traveled over the country with a flute and mingled his literary with his musical studies. He toured Spain, Italy and Germany, and wherever he went his good spirits went as a shining light before him. His countenance was in itself "a letter of recommendation."

Equally striking with his personality was his ability to pick up languages. After three years of study abroad he returned to Portland an expert linguist. But now he displayed as great a proficiency in business as in languages: he refused to accept anything less than a full professorship at Bowdoin. "The Board of Trustees of Bowdoin College, Sept. 1st, 1829, Mr Henry W. Longfellow having declined to accept the office of instructor in modern languages, voted that we now proceed to the choice of a professor of modern languages—and Mr H. W. Longfellow was chosen."

Henry was only twenty-two at the time. So far every gift of the gods had been bestowed upon him. And now came another supreme blessing. One Sunday in church he noticed that Mary Potter, a former schoolmate whom he had not seen for several years, had during his absence grown into a beautiful young woman. With professorial dignity he got his sister to introduce him to Miss Potter and with poetical ardor he induced Miss Potter to become his wife.

Love can live on bread crusts buttered with caresses. On the meager salary of eight hundred a year the young professor and his wife settled down in a house under the rural elms while all living things around them "sent up a song of joy to meet the rising sun."

III

LONGFELLOW was restless. He was not content to remain a mere professor of modern languages at Bowdoin. He wanted to become an influence in the shaping of the infant literature of his country. The Europeans charged that the Americans were swallowed up in their schemes for material gain and indifferent to everything else. Longfellow was sensitive to this criticism. He experienced the self-consciousness of a pioneer of letters working among the pioneers of the soil. He would join forces with his fellow adventurers of the spirit—Cooper, Bryant, Irving, Whittier—to call his countrymen to arms. He would prove to them that the true glory of a nation consisted not in the extent of its physical conquests but in the horizons of its mental and its moral achievements. His countrymen were building up a splendid body of civilization. But it was a body without a soul.

Longfellow wanted to dedicate himself, along with his fellow educators, to the building of the soul of American culture. Above all things he wanted to create an American literature for an American public. But for the present his professorial duties consumed the greater part of his time. These duties had now become more arduous than ever. Professor Ticknor, the distinguished teacher of modern languages at Harvard, had resigned his post. And Longfellow had been offered this chair, again with the proviso that he "travel and broaden himself" in the cultural centers of Europe.

On this second European journey the young linguist, accompanied now by his lovely wife, traveled everywhere through "an enchanted fairyland of uninterrupted happiness." Mary Longfellow wrote home many a joyful letter describing their meeting with the Carlyles in London, their visit to the palace of the Swedish king and their tasty excursions among the dishes of Copenhagen dinner society. It was so good to be loved and admired and toasted as the wife of the brilliant young professor of Harvard—so good to be simply alive!

But suddenly the series of letters was interrupted by a brief note from Henry: "Our beloved Mary is no more."

IV

SHE DIED on a Sunday morning in Rotterdam—without pain and with complete resignation. She had given birth to a premature child. For three weeks she had suffered extreme physical and mental torture. Henry had remained at her bedside, holding her hand and watching over her as her life breath ebbed gradually away. Toward the end she had passed beyond suffering although she was still conscious. A few minutes before her death she had put her arms around his neck. "Dear Henry, do not forget me." And then she had closed her eyes with a peaceful smile. "I am not dead, I do not sleep. I have awakened from the dream of life."

Such was the sudden blow that bowed the poet's head. He collected her clothing and sent it home to her sister with a note that the suffering he had undergone in performing this simple duty was more than he could describe. He realized that the world considered grief unmanly and that it was suspicious of a sorrow expressed by outward signs. Hence he sealed his unutterable emotion under a mask of cheerful composure. But there were hours "when it seemed to me that my heart would break. . . ." A thousand associations called up the past. Often a mere look or sound—a voice—the odor of a flower . . . "And yet, my dear Eliza, in a few days and we shall all be gone." And others will have taken our places, sorrowing as we sorrow now. And we shall say, how childish it was for us to mourn things so transitory. . . .

And when he finished the letter to the sister of his departed wife he plunged into his studies of Germanic literature and in a twelvemonth returned home to take up his duties as Smith Professor of Modern Languages at Harvard.

He came to Cambridge in the winter of his twenty-ninth year and established residence in the historic Craigie House. This famous old colonial dwelling had served as the headquarters of General Washington during the siege of Boston in the Revolutionary War. It stands on Brattle Street in a block of houses known as Tory Row. Here had lived the wealthy aristocracy— the loyalists and the royalists of New England, the proprietors of West Indian plantations, the owners of ships and the masters of slaves.

After the war the house had passed into the hands of Andrew Craigie, apothecary general of the northern department of the Revolutionary Army. He had built additions to it and had made it a haven of hospitality for distinguished visitors from foreign shores. But he died in poverty, leaving a widow who was compelled to rent out its spacious rooms to boarders.

Mrs Craigie became a legendary character among the college students. She walked about in a white turban, played half-forgotten tunes on the pianoforte and read Voltaire. When

Longfellow came looking for lodgings she drew herself up with dignity and led him through many rooms, describing the history and tradition of each and then shutting each door behind her with the words, "But you can't have *this* room." Finally she designated a room he *might* have, commenting, with a sad emphasis on the faded glories of the past: "This was General Washington's chamber."

During the following summer the splendid old elms in front of the house were attacked by cankerworms. Mrs Craigie sat reading by the open window as the worms crawled down the leaves and fastened themselves to her dress and her turban. When Longfellow came upon her and asked whether she had taken steps to destroy the worms she looked at him and declared in a solemn, rebuking voice: "Young man, they are our fellow worms; have they not as good a right to live as we?"

Such was the quaint atmosphere in which Longfellow lived and taught and entertained and wrote. He sat at a round table with his scholars and guided them graciously through "certain indiscreet" phrases of the French writers. He drove to Boston and to Brookline, where he was in great demand at the whist parties. And he never failed to dance with the elderly ladies at the fancy balls. "Everybody flocks around the younger ladies. *Somebody* has to be nice to the older ones."

And he was a favorite with them all, young and old alike. Dressed in his blue frock coat of Parisian cut, his handsome waistcoat, his faultless pantaloons and his primrose "kids," he was one of the most charming young men of New England. And one of the most vivacious. He was always "on the wing." Like a butterfly flitting from flower to flower, he tripped from one lady to another, admired and courted by all.

Finally he selected one of them for his heart and his home. It was seven years after he had come to Craigie House that he entered upon his second marriage. This second Mrs Longfellow, the daughter of a Boston merchant whom he had met in Switzerland shortly after the death of his first wife, was a young woman of "rare intelligence and deep, unutterable eyes." For their wedding present the Longfellows received a deed to the Craigie House which the young lady's father had bought for them.

And now fame began to fly into the Craigie House with rustling wings. Longfellow had published a volume of poetry which re-echoed the spirit of Goethe and the rhythms of the Scandinavian sagas. In one of his daydreams he had heard the surf beat of a ballad verse and had beheld the homely beauty of the blacksmith's chestnut tree. He had looked upon the toiling masses and felt their eager yearning to reach higher—ever higher—*Excelsior*. In every daily task he had found a homily for a universal philosophy of faith. And it was not the philosophy of a "favored son of fortune" who had never thought and suffered. Longfellow had drained the cup of sorrow to the dregs. Indeed, it was through his sorrow that he had attained his wisdom.

And it was through his poetry that he was eager to share his wisdom with the rest of the world. His university teaching was secondary—and irksome. "This college work is like a great hand laid on all the strings of my lyre," he complained. Its endless routine threatened to stifle the freshness of his song.

Finally he announced his retirement from the faculty. He wore his flowing academic gown for the last time on commencement day, and "the whole crowded church looked ghostly and unreal," as a thing in which he had no part. He watched the pompous parade of the scholars, wrapped in their medieval robes and steeped in the traditions of the past, and he felt more convinced than ever that he must burst the bars of his academic learning and breathe the fresh air of the New England balsam woods. Close the tombs of the dead past. Open the doors of the living present. The words of his own poem came back to him: "Wisely improve the present. It is thine."

V

THE PRESENT was alive and vibrant and aflame with hopeful energy right here in his own country—in every American city, town, village, home. No need to seek for your inspiration in other lands and under other skies. "I have traveled a great deal," remarked Henry Thoreau, "—in Concord." This universal philosopher and cosmopolitan soul had been carefully tilling the little plot of his own home. For home is the place where human harvests grow. America for the native pioneer is the God-given acre of his own present life. Shame on the tillers who neglect their own soil! "Let us have no more nightingales from our poets who can everywhere see the woodchuck and no more poems on Rhenish castles while the smoke of the wigwam mingles with the misty pines."

To Longfellow it seemed as natural to build American tales out of her own folklore as to construct American shelters out of her native pine. There was no tradition of the German Black Forest which could outmatch the haunting legends of the Catskills; no city of Europe more solemnly picturesque than the Boston of the Puritan fathers; no epic of the Scottish clans more poignant than the expulsion of the Acadians from their native land of Nova Scotia.

Sing too in American rhythms of the native Indians—of Black Hawk and his friends with their red blankets and their shoulders greased in vermilion. Dream at your Craigie study and give form to the wind and a spirit to the leaf shadow. And above all sing the music that sounds like a mighty oak tree felled in the forest. Hang out the crepe for a departed European past. Unfurl to the skies the flag of the living American present.

And so, as he walked through the temple of elms along the quiet shades of Brattle Street, he swung his white gloves to the rhythm of Hiawatha. With his heart attuned to the thunder of the bison on the plain, he shot the arrows of his songs into the air and let them fall to earth, he knew not where. He passed by the "Mausoleum of Harvard University," with its dusty books about an ancient world, and stepped beyond it into the world of men—and into the sunlight of fame.

For his tales of the New World—*Evangeline, Hiawatha, The Courtship of Miles Standish*—had become household treasures wherever English was spoken. By common consent he had been crowned as the Poet of the People. "It is not by depth or novelty of thought that I interest you. . . . I do not propose to solve the enigmas of existence. . . . I shall not win you with the expression of an exceptional experience. . . . I entertain the simple feelings; I instruct the natural emotions of men of good intent every-where."

Yet Longfellow was the scholar as well as the poet. While he rejected the dead body of the past he preserved its living soul. He took the rich wine of the Old World and poured it out for the banquets of the New. And "the atmosphere was filled with magic" as he related the ever-new, ever-living romances of a bygone day. He sat in the Wayside Inn of his fancy and watched the eternal procession of its guests—the musician, the poet, the merchant, the Talmudic scholar, the student, the priest. And as he looked out of the window upon the great dignified oaks of his household gods he had a smile and a cheering word for all the weary and discouraged wayfarers—the cobbler, the farmer, the drayman, the peddler bent under his heavy pack, the soldier marching to the battlefield of the Civil War.

He was the poet of home, of serenity, of peace. And yet again and again there was mist and snow and sorrow within his own heart. Death had made a series of forays into his household. But as often as Death had taken away, Life had returned to replenish his store. "Two angels, one of Life and one of Death, passed o'er our village." When his father and his mother were gathered into the night, Alice and Edith and laughing Allegra came calling in the dawn.

But one summer day the scales of this justice were sorely tipped against him. It was the sort of day (in 1861) when a poet looking out upon the sunlight gives his thanks to the Creator. Mrs Longfellow was seated in the library curling her children's hair with an iron heated at a wax taper. Her dress caught fire, and within an instant she was a mass of flames. She fled from the hall to save her children. Her husband rushed from his study at her screams for help, seized her in his embracing arms and partially succeeded in smothering the fire. She was carried to bed in great suffering. The following day she died.

The poet walked through Craigie House from room to room, wringing his hands. He was almost insane with grief. The over-brimming cup of his good fortune had excited the envy of the gods. "I was too happy," he moaned again and again, "too happy!"

She was placed in the coffin with the unburned side of her face uppermost. White and fresh and beautiful it seemed in repose. He never forgot that last glimpse of her.

Nor did he ever forget the tragedy of his loss as he passed down the hallway of the years "in the long sleepless watches of the night."

> There is a mountain in the distant west
> That, sun-defying, in its deep ravines
>   Displays a cross of snow upon its side.
> Such is the cross I wear upon my breast
> These eighteen years, through all the changing scenes
>   And seasons, changeless since the day she died.

VI

As THE YEARS drifted into eternity like the melted snows, he remained inwardly sorrowful but outwardly serene. It had been his hope that the passage of time might neither impair his mind nor rob him of his power to sing. In this hope he was not disappointed. The flowers of his fancy retained their fragrance throughout the autumn of his life. After the death of his second wife he had undertaken a labor of love—the rendering of Dante's *Divine Comedy* into English verse. For he too, like Dante, had beheld the vision of his Beatrice in heaven. He translated this epic at the rate of a canto a day. At the beginning of his daily task he entered the cathedral of the great Italian's heart and bowed his head in unashamed prayer.

He paid a final visit to Europe and received an ovation ac-corded to no other American before him. A laborer stopped him in the street and recited his *Psalm of Life*. When he called at the palace of Queen Victoria the servants hid behind the curtains to catch a glimpse of the venerable man whose face, fringed with silver-white hair and beard, "glowed like a beautiful carnation" and whose "hope-inspiring poems" they knew by heart.

When he returned to Cambridge he was hailed as its first citizen. He retired to his study and mused among the relics of the past—the inkstand on which he rested his pen and which had once belonged to Coleridge, the wastepaper basket where Moore had consigned the rough drafts of his poems, the fragments of Dante's coffin. Often he would look up at the fast-fading portraits of the present—the crayon likenesses of Hawthorne, Sumner and Emerson, scholars and dreamers like himself, who met his glance from the wall in respectful questioning silence, as if to say, "What will become of us all?"

And he rubbed his palm over the armchair that had been shaped from the wood of the old chestnut tree on Brattle Street and presented to him by the children of Cambridge when the city elders had decreed that the tree must be felled. This spreading chestnut tree, as it stood by the smithy's door, was also a thing of the past. But here it had come to life again in another shape and for another use. Brought back to life through the efforts of the school children, the citizens of the coming years, it was a symbol of the future scooped from the heart of the past, even as the old poet who sat in its aged arms.

VII

ON THE fiftieth anniversary of his class at Bowdoin College he came among his old schoolmates and read them a poem for the occasion in a voice failing with the years but young with hope. And he threw down a challenge to death. "We who are about to die salute you—unafraid." The old classmates gathered in their former study rooms and strolled over the campus grounds and chatted awhile and prayed awhile—and then bade one another farewell. For they knew that the class of 1825 would never gather again. Old age had taken its toll.

But to the poet old age was no less an opportunity than youth. The stars shine only in the night—they are invisible by day. There was labor yet to be extended upon the house beautiful of the human spirit, melodies yet to be sung after the evening shadows fell. Why, he was only seventy-five—he had lived but an instant in the day of eternity. Outside his grandchildren were playing in the street and the birds were making music in the neighboring fields. There would always be children playing in the streets and birds singing in the fields.

The village clock struck the hour. The poet roused himself from his slumbers and looked silently at the marble busts of the company placed around the room. There was a kindly twinkle in old Goethe's eye, and a voice seemed to come from his lips: "Take me, O great Eternity!"

The poet rose to his feet and drowsily snuffed out the lights of the candles. Then he went upstairs to sleep.

WHITTIER

John Greenleaf Whittier

1807–1892

Hᴇ ᴄᴀᴍᴇ of a Quaker stock. Which means that he came of a *fighter* stock. The stories that he heard as a child about the early Quakers were stories of militant pacifists, of spiritual ad‑ venturers, of resisters against evil in whatever form and at whatever sacrifice. The hero of Whittier's childhood was George Fox, the shoemaker of Leicestershire who had refused to remove his hat in the presence of kings and who, in the face of ridicule, imprisonment, violence and even death, had commanded the masters of the world to release their slaves. "One day," Whit‑ tier's father related to him, "George Fox was struck in the face when he addressed a hostile crowd in the public square. He was knocked down, kicked and trampled upon until he fainted. When he regained consciousness he stood up, wiped away the blood from his face and finished what he had to say."

That was the sort of man to follow! When Whittier grew up he would try to be the American George Fox.

II

Hɪs ꜰᴀᴛʜᴇʀ managed to wrest but a scant living out of the rocky soil of Massachusetts. Here, in a homestead on the out‑ skirts of Haverhill, he raised a family of two boys and two girls.

John, the second of the children and the first of the boys, was born on December 17, the "snowbound" season of 1807.

His childhood consisted of many chores, a small measure of play and a tincture of schooling. His teacher, Joshua Coffin, was a man gifted with a sense of humor and a flair for story-telling. To the prescribed curriculum of the three Rs he added a fourth—Romance. He filled the little heads of his pupils with a veritable Arabian Nights entertainment of American folklore. Several of these stories were later to become immortalized in Whittier's *Legends of New England.*

On Sunday (Whittier's Quaker parents called it *First day*) afternoons the entire family gathered in the living room for the reading of the Living Book. At the age of seven Whittier was able to repeat long passages and even entire chapters of the Bible by heart. His father, proud of his son's precocious memory, would make him display it at the quarterly meetings of the Quakers. His audiences listened to his recitations with amaze-ment. "Thee will be a great man someday," they said.

And indeed it was his ambition to be a great man. A man like George Fox. Perhaps even a greater man than George Fox. He would like more than anything else to be a poet, a *fighter poet*, like the prophets in the Bible.

He began to write poetry as a mere child. And from the out-set he showed a partiality for rebellious themes. Among the heroes of his early poems he selected William Penn, the "founder of a new freedom" in America; William Leddra, the Quaker martyr who had been executed on Boston Common (1659); John Milton, his "nearest conception of a real man"; and Lord Byron, the "bright bold star" who had fought for freedom but whose personal conduct, apologized Whittier, had best be "shaded by deep oblivion."

Whittier regarded his earlier poems as spiritual and literary exercises. He did not as yet dare to step forward as a poet be-fore the public. Later, when his thought and his expression became more mature, he would submit his work to the editors of the local papers.

But his sister Mary anticipated him. In the early summer of 1826, without her brother's knowledge, she sent one of his poems to the office of the *Newburyport Press*, a paper to which the elder Whittier was a subscriber.

The editor read the manuscript, thought it "passing good" and printed it. Whittier was busy mending a stone wall by the roadside when the postman delivered the paper containing his poem. "His heart came into his mouth" when he thus unexpectedly found himself face to face with his first printed thoughts.

But this was to be followed by a still greater surprise. A few days after the publication of his manuscript the young farmer poet, besmeared with dirt, was crawling under the barn in search of a hen that had stolen her nest. Suddenly his sister came running up to the barn. "Hurry, John, there's somebody to see you!"

"Somebody to see me? I wonder who?"

"You'll never guess, John. It's the editor."

"What editor?"

"Mr Garrison, the editor of the *Free Press!*"

"Oh, good gracious!" cried Whittier in dismay. "Just look at me!"

Stealthily he sidled into the house to change his clothes. In his hurry he put on a pair of trousers that were several inches too short for him. And then, diffident, tremulous, eager, he stepped into the living room to be introduced to the editor.

Such was the first meeting between William Lloyd Garrison and John Greenleaf Whittier—the two young men who were destined to become famous as the prophet and the poet of the black man's freedom.

III

GARRISON not only befriended Whittier but guided him into the literary world. He introduced him to other editors—Robert Morris, Abijah Thayer, Robert Greene. Whittier began to go into "society" and to meet people. One day, at a Boston gathering, he found himself talking to that "strange inhabitant of another planet"—an actress. She invited him to visit the theater, an invitation which sent the Quaker poet scurrying back to his farm in a cold sweat. A course of education that would widen his horizon, advised his literary friends, would be a good thing for him. And for his poetry.

But higher education was a luxury in the Whittier family. There was, to be sure, an inexpensive private school in the neighborhood—the Haverhill Academy. But even that was beyond the Whittier means.

Fortunately, however, a young man who worked on the Whittier farm enabled them to solve the problem. This young man had once served as a cobbler's apprentice. He now taught Whittier how to make ladies' slippers, and with the money earned at this trade Whittier was able to meet his academic expenses.

And now, having stooped as a cobbler in order to rise as a scholar, Whittier fell in love with his cousin and classmate, Mary Emerson Smith. This was the first of many romances in Whittier's life, yet he was fated to remain celibate to the end. The same terror that had gripped him at the invitation to the theater was to take hold of him again and again at the invitation to love. Unlike his hero, Lord Byron, who was all fire, Whittier was a peculiar combination of passion and ice. He had the prophetic fervor for justice and the puritan aversion to play.

And his fervor for justice kept him always on the firing line in the endless human battle for freedom. Unable for financial reasons to enter college, he went into journalism after only two years at the academy. Thanks to the recommendation of Garrison, he secured a position as editor of the *Philanthropist*, a liberal paper published in Boston. "With the unescapable sense of wrong burning like a volcano in the recesses of my spirit," as he wrote to his friend Thayer, he launched upon his editorial duties "with a heart free from misanthropy" and with a pen "eager to dispense good will to all."

For eight months he wrote editorials in defense of the aristocracy of the mind as against the aristocracy of wealth. And then he was obliged to give up his literary job. His father was ill, and John's presence was needed on the farm. Shortly there-after his father died, and the support of the family fell upon John's none-too-sturdy shoulders. "From now on," he said, "I am afraid I shall have to hoe potatoes instead of writing poems."

But he was mistaken. Another offer for an editorial position—this time with the munificent salary of five hundred dollars a year! It was almost too good to be true. He eagerly accepted the offer and went to Hartford, Connecticut, to assume his duties as editor of the *New England Review.*

He remained with this paper for a year and a half, a period in the course of which he made an important discovery: he had a talent and an appetite for politics. He espoused the cause of the underprivileged. He defended their rights in his editorials and his verses. "Woe to those," he exclaimed in one of his poems,

> Who trample down the sacred rights of man
> . . . . . There will come a time
> Of awful retribution. Not a groan
> Bursts upward from the persecuted heart
> But reaches unto heaven. No martyr's blood
> Reeks up unheeded to the circling sky.

Thus far, however, Whittier's liberalism was abstract rather than concrete. He had not as yet found a definite cause for which to fight. He was anxious to enter into the political arena. But for what purpose? There was at that period (in 1830), so far as Whittier could see, no great national crisis in America, no crusade that would try men's souls. On the other hand, there was a rather serious crisis in Whittier's personal affairs. He had been rejected in his suit for the hand of Mary Smith. A young poet, especially a poet with the acid of rebellion in his pen, was not a suitable provider for a young lady who cared more for the comforts of the flesh than she did for the conquests of the spirit. For a time she tantalized him with the bait of her flirta-tions and then she cast him away to marry a more promising suitor—Judge Thomas of Covington, Kentucky. Whittier addressed a number of bitter poems to the "moonlight transit of her fickle smile," upbraiding her for her heartless desertion of

> This broken toy, a lovesick man,
> The freshness of whose hope is dead—
> An idler in life's caravan—
> A scribbler for his daily bread.

And then once more he was obliged to interrupt his "scribbling." His health, never of the best, gave way under the strain of his disappointment. Resigning from the *New England Review*, he returned to end his "despondent days" on his Haverhill farm.

IV

HAVING LOST HIS HAPPINESS, Whittier at last found his cause. He threw himself into the fight for the abolition of slavery. His health was as yet far below par, and his spirits were not much higher; but an irresistible call had come from Garrison. "My brother," Garrison had written to him (in 1833) "there are upwards of two million of our countrymen who are doomed to the most horrible servitude. . . . This is the time to let the oppressed go free. . . . The cause is worthy of Gabriel—yea, the God of hosts places Himself at our head. Whittier, enlist! Your talent, zeal, influence—all are needed."

And Whittier "heard and answered, *Here am I!*" From a poetical "scribbler" he became a political agitator. He wrote and issued at his own expense a pamphlet against slavery. As a result of the publication of this pamphlet he not only consumed his savings but lost his opportunity for a living. The publishers of the more popular magazines turned their faces away from him. They regarded him as a man with a tainted pen. His former friends began to cross to the other side when they met him on the street. There was even talk of tar and feathers. Yet he went on with his work. His associates in the abolitionist movement had discovered that he possessed an eloquent tongue.

They elected him as a delegate to the first antislavery convention, to be held in Philadelphia. Among the other Massachusetts delegates to this convention were his old schoolteacher, Joshua Coffin, and William Lloyd Garrison.

With his tall, slim figure, his black beard, his black flashing eyes, his pale, austere features and his not ungraceful gestures, he made a profound impression upon the convention. But the convention made an even profounder impression upon him. For this assembly at Philadelphia was the parent of the American Antislavery Society. Whittier felt that here he was at the striking of one of the decisive hours in history. Years later he referred to his participation in this "birth of the new freedom" as the most significant act of his life. "I set a higher value on my name as appended to the antislavery declaration of 1833 than on the title page of any of my books."

With the abolition of slavery as his crusade Whittier plunged into the turmoil of local and national politics. Twice he was elected to the Massachusetts legislature, only to resign from his second term because of his ill health. And even then, though unable himself to take an active part in the daily debates and excitements of the political assemblies, he gave freely of his voice and his pen and his heart to those statesmen who shared his political views. It was at the urging of this shy and uneducated poet politician that the shy and scholarly Charles Sumner was induced to give up his sheltered position at the Harvard Law School and to become the storm center of politics at the national capital. On the day when Sumner was elected to the Senate Whittier was so ill that he didn't expect to recover. Yet he made haste to send him his congratulations. "Sick abed," he wrote to his fellow fighter for abolition. "Yet I heard the guns (of your triumph)—Quaker as I am—with real satisfaction."

And sick abed though he frequently was throughout this period of his life, he became one of the moving spirits in the abolitionist cause. On at least two occasions, when he was well enough to be up and about, he was hooted and hunted and stoned through the streets—once in Concord and once in Newburyport. But he didn't retreat. His motto was always, "Forward and sunward!"

From 1835 to 1838 the crusade for abolition had reached its height. Whittier fed the fires of this crusade with his militant poems—*The Hunters of Men, Toussaint L'Ouverture, To William Lloyd Garrison, Stanzas for the Times, Our Countrymen in Chains, Massachusetts to Virginia*—dozens of other flames of indignation kindled by the flint of his determined purpose against the steel of oppression. Some of these poems were recited from Maine to the Rockies. The entire North literally rang with his impassioned words:

> What, mothers from their children riven!
> What, God's own image bought and sold!
> Americans to market driven,
> And bartered as the brute for gold!

And it was not only against institutions that he dared to raise his voice but against individuals as well. When Daniel Webster, one of his childhood heroes, deserted the cause of the abolitionists Whittier castigated him in a poem which has become part of American political history:

> So fallen! so lost! the light withdrawn
> Which once he wore—
> The glory from his gray hairs gone
> Forevermore!
> Of all we loved and honored, naught
> Save power remains—
> A fallen angel's pride of thought,
> Still strong in chains!

V

WHITTIER reached the climax in his political activities when a Philadelphia mob burned down the office of the *Pennsylvania Freeman*, an abolitionist paper of which he was the editor at the time (May 17, 1838). In this fire he came near to losing his life.

But he did not lose his ardor. For several years he continued his tireless crusade in the antislavery cause. And then he withdrew once more to the countryside. Not out of fear but out of sorrow. For he began to realize that the peaceful agitation of the abolitionists was being rapidly whipped up into the tempest of a civil war. With his Quaker faith to sustain him he had hoped to see slavery "abolished by the power of moral truth." But now that he saw the approaching tidal wave of bloodshed he turned away in despair. No cause, he felt, could justify the murder of his fellow men.

And so he returned to the peace and the poetry of rural New England. He settled down in a little cottage at Amesbury, added at one end of it a garden room which he filled—in season —with harebells and laurel, spent his afternoons exchanging gossip with the farmers as he sat on a sugar barrel in the village store and devoted his mornings to the perpetuation of the romance of New England in homespun phrases and simple tones. His rhythms were often crude and his rhymes not always faultless. Yet the best of his poems—*Skipper Ireson's Ride, Songs of Labor, The Barefoot Boy, Among the Hills, Telling the Bees, Sweet Fern, My Playmate, The Meeting, Snow-Bound*—possess that quality which is more important than elegant rhythms and faultless rhymes. They are *alive*.

And they are American. Whittier was the first singer of Yankee pastorals unadulterated by the borrowed fripperies of the British muse. His landscapes have the color and the scent of New England—the haycarts and the dusty roads, the clover and the honeysuckle and the goldenrod, the spicy pinewoods and the salt-sea tang, the clamdigging and the berrypicking and the husking of the sweet corn—and, over it all, the wood thrush weaving the landscape together with the shuttle of its native song.

Such, in the poetry of Whittier, is the American scene in which the "barefoot boy" grows up into the democratic man.

These poems of the American scene found an enthusiastic response. From persecution the public turned to adulation.

The bread-and-water days of Whittier's poverty were over. His *Snow-Bound* earned him ten thousand dollars in royalties. The earnings on his other poems, too, kept pouring in—not, indeed, with an overwhelming rapidity but with a steady and sufficient accumulation to make him feel like a rich man.

Whittier was delighted with his good fortune. For, Quaker though he was, he loved life. He thoroughly enjoyed the adoration of his public, especially of his *female* public. To the end of his days he remained a harmless philanderer. Again and again he returned to his favorite game of proposal and refusal. Time after time he brought himself to the verge of marriage and always withdrew at the very last moment. He liked to think of himself as a solitary island surrounded by a sea of admiring ladies.

And of these admiring ladies there was no end. They sent him snips of their dresses and locks of their hair. One of them, the poetess Gail Hamilton, addressed him as "my dear Sheik" —he was a white-bearded sheik of sixty at the time—and reminded him wistfully of a visit she had paid him when "you and I walked into Paradise, shut the gate and threw away the key." Another of his "Pilgrims," as he called his female admirers, presented him with a scarf and with a marriage proposal on his sixty-ninth birthday. Still another of his admirers— he was now eighty and she fifty-six—wrote to him coyly:

"It seems especially fitting, Dear Mr Whittier, that I should tell thee today once more how much thy affectionate interest has been to me since the gracious bestowal of it so many years ago. *There is more, much more that I would say*, but 'no words outworn suffice on lips or scroll.' "

For many years he encouraged these offerings on the altar of his vanity. But there comes a time when "even preserved roses," as the Persian proverb has it, "begin to cloy the appetite." Whittier had had too much of adoration. He began to suffer from sacrificial indigestion. After all, he was a simple Quaker who wanted peace. He begged his Pilgrims to leave him alone. He even put a "burglar alarm" on his front door to warn him when the ladies were coming and to give him a chance to escape by the rear door. If they managed to get in before he managed to get out, he met them with his hat on his head and told them that he was just on the point of leaving when they arrived. Sometimes he would roam the streets for hours in order to avoid his devotees. "I have had hard work to lose him," he once complained to his sister, "but I have lost him." And then, with a helpless smile, he added: "But I can never lose a *her*."

And so he lived through the unquiet years of his afternoon, the victim of a belated fame. One day a woman neighbor came to see him on a matter of business. He told her that he couldn't give her his undivided attention just then since there were two other women in the parlor waiting for him. "What, more of them?" she exclaimed. "Was ever a man so beset?"

"Have you any remedy to suggest?"

"Indeed I have. Why don't you marry *one* woman so she'll keep all the *rest* of the women away?"

"I'm afraid I'm not the marrying kind," he laughed. "You see," he went on by way of explanation, "when I was in love I had no money. Now that I have money I'm not in love."

VI

HE WAS NOW too old to love and too old to hate. Like an extinct volcano, he remained unperturbed while the stream of history flowed by his door. New times, new injustices, new causes—but Whittier paid no attention to them. He had already fought his fight. Now that slavery was abolished he believed that the millennium had come. "In the quiet of his country home," wrote William Dean Howells, "Whittier . . . keeps fully abreast of the *literary* movement, but I doubt if he so fully appreciates the importance of the *social* movement. Like some others of the great antislavery men, he seems to imagine that mankind has won itself a clear field by destroying *chattel* slavery, and he has no sympathy with those who think that the man who may any moment be out of work is the victim of *industrial* slavery."

But, Howells goes on to add, "This is not strange." For "few men last over from one reform to another." After all, why expect the fire of youth in the heart of old age?

Whittier was paying the price of a protracted old age. He had outlived his own greatness—not only as a crusader but also as a poet. In his own lifetime he had come to be worshiped as "one of those great dead gods of another day."

He spent the last few years of his life in the resigned contemplation of his past dead glory. "It is a satisfaction," he wrote to one of his friends, "to sit under a tree and read our own songs."

And one day in his eighty-fifth year, as he sat thus recalling the dreams of his old songs, Death took him mercifully by the hand and led him into a dreamless sleep.

WHITMAN

Great Poems by Whitman

Walt Whitman

1819–1892

A NAVY-YARD HORSECAR is lumbering over the cobblestones at the foot of Capitol Hill in Washington. It is near sundown on a stifling July day. The air is rancid with the midsummer perspiration of a packed carful of laborers returning home from their work. Inside the car, near the door, stands a young woman holding one child by the hand and another—a babe of about eleven months—against her breast. The infant is hot and fretful. Its interminable howling annoys the passengers and drives the mother to the verge of distraction.

The car stops to let on a number of new passengers. One of them, a middle-aged, bearded and florid-faced giant of a man, swings with an awkward but agile step onto the rear platform. He stops near the conductor and begins to talk to him in a low voice. Evidently these two men are intimate friends.

There is something fresh and fragrant about the bearded passenger. "He has the look of a man who has just taken a sea bath." He is dressed in workingman's clothes, but his shirt, though open at the throat, is spotlessly white. His head is covered with a broad-brimmed white hat. His face is "suffused with serenity and goodness and physical and mental health." He looks calm and cheerful and cool in this suffocating caldron of human fretfulness.

The car, with its grumbling workers and howling infant, is tugging slowly toward the top of Capitol Hill. The atmosphere inside has become unbearable. The flushed and exhausted mother is ready to burst into tears. The car stops at a street corner to let off several of the passengers. The rear platform is almost empty now. The bearded man reaches inside and, in spite of the mother's protests, takes the infant out of her sweltering arms and into the open air of the platform. The child, astonished at its sudden adventure, stops its screaming. With its chubby fists planted against the stranger's breast it throws its little head back and gazes into the man's face. The result of the examination is apparently satisfactory. For the child snuggles up against the stranger's shoulder and within a few moments is fast asleep.

Another stop. The conductor gets off for his supper and a bit of rest. "Pick you up on the way back, Pete!" shouts the bearded man as, with the sleeping babe in his arms, he assumes the duties of the conductor. Leaning against the dashboard on the rear platform, he keeps an eye on the passengers, pulls the bell to leave them off the car and exchanges a parting good word with each and every one of them as they step down from the platform.

"Queer chap," remarks one of the passengers to another as they leave the car together.

"Yeah, queer chap and the author of a queer book."

"What's the name of the book?"

"*Leaves of Grass.*"

II

THE TITLE of his poems, *Leaves of Grass*, was one of the happiest of Walt Whitman's inspirations. For this title represents the perfect symbol for the Poetry of Democracy. The leaves of grass, like the common people, are the simplest and the sturdiest of growing things. Disregarded, trampled underfoot and flourish-

Whitman

Kipling

ing best in the obscurest places, the grass bows but never breaks under the lash of the angry winds. While the higher and the hardier plants break down, the lowly grass keeps growing and spreading everywhere. Walt Whitman might have paraphrased the words of Abraham Lincoln: "God must love the blades of grass and the common people, or he wouldn't have made so many of them."

Leaves of Grass could have been written only by an American son of poverty—the obscure member of a democratic race. Walt Whitman boasted an ancestry that was both poor and obscure. He got his blunt and sturdy honesty from his American father, his Quaker gentleness from his Dutch mother and his rebellious hunger for justice from both branches of the family. His paternal as well as his maternal ancestors had served in Washington's army. And there seemed to be a rebellious strain even in the women of the Whitman family. His great-grandmother on his father's side was quite a legend among her neighbors. Smoking a pipe and swearing like a trooper, she had been the terror of the village hoodlums and the guardian angel of the Negro slaves' children. It was from her that Whitman inherited his stubbornness as well as his kindness and his fellow feeling for the underdog.

The second of nine children, Walt Whitman was born (May 31, 1819) at West Hills, Long Island—or, as Whitman preferred to call it, Paumanok, "the island with its breast against the sea." In his infancy he was rocked to sleep by the beating of the sea surf on the headlands near his home. This irregular rhythm of the wind and the waves got into his blood stream and found an echo many years later in the unmetrical cadences of his poetry.

When Walt was four years old the Whitmans moved to Brooklyn. For his father had decided to give up farming in favor of carpentry as a better means of livelihood. But the children were sent to spend their summer vacations with their grandparents at West Hills. Here Walt "adventured" for hours at a stretch and became intimately acquainted with the rivers and the fields and the forests and that most beloved of all his comrades, the everlastingly resounding sea.

In the skimpy school hours of the winter months young Whitman applied himself to the four Rs—readin', 'ritin', 'rithmetic and restin'. Especially the fourth. "This boy is so idle," said his schoolteacher, Benjamin Halleck, "I am sure he will never amount to anything."

Walt's father agreed with Mr Halleck. It was useless for the boy to continue with his education. Let him rub shoulders with people and learn to do an honest day's labor. And so, at thirteen, he took Walt out of school and apprenticed him to a printer.

But in the printing shop as in the classroom the youngster continued to devote himself to the fine art of doing nothing. "If the boy caught an ague," his employer once remarked, "he would be too lazy to shake."

It was not mere laziness, however, that kept him wrapped up in the perpetual enchantment of his daydreams. "I loafe and invite my soul." While his body was quiescent, his mind was active. "I lean and loafe at my ease observing a spear of summer grass." His eye and his heart were constantly open to the world about him. Though he had left school, he was still educating himself. Indeed, he had entered upon a higher course of education—higher than any of the courses to be found in the colleges. The antennae of his mind were reaching out to come into contact with reality. The *real* reality. He was trying, subconsciously perhaps at the start, to find a clear way "through the dimness" called *the mystery of life*. What is the grass? What are the stars? And what am I?

And for the present there was a definite and insistent answer at least to the last of these questions. I am a creature that must be fed and clothed and sheltered. In other words, he must make a living for himself. For a time he tried carpentry and disliked it. He then turned to schoolteaching, and this too he found distasteful. Finally he drifted into literature and knew at once that this was where he belonged.

He was only twenty-two when he wrote his first book—a

melodramatic temperance novel. And it almost proved to be his artistic undoing, for it was a financial success. Within a short time the publishers had disposed of twenty thousand copies. A reception such as this, at so early an age, was enough to turn the head of any young author. Walt Whitman seemed destined for popular mediocrity as a scribbler of sermons in fiction. His sense of humor saved him, however. He gave a beer party to his friends in order to celebrate the success of his temperance story and then entered upon the slow steps of his development from a second-rate novelist into a first-rate poet.

III

IN ORDER to solve the bread-and-butter problem during the years of his apprenticeship to the Muse he accepted an editorial job on the Brooklyn *Daily Eagle*. The pay was good and the work congenial. "There is a curious kind of sympathy," he wrote in one of his editorials, "between the editor and his public. . . . Daily communion creates a sort of brotherhood . . . between the two parties. As for us, we like it."

He liked his work, but he liked his leisure even more. Again and again he would urge his readers to relax. "Let us enjoy life a little. Has God made this beautiful earth . . . all for nothing? Let us go forth awhile and get better air in our lungs." He loved to be out in the air whenever possible. Though not athletic himself—"I am more of a floater than a swimmer"—he enjoyed watching the athletic games of other people. Indeed, he enjoyed watching anything and everything about him. Watching and absorbing—slowly, methodically, thoroughly. He was never in a hurry. He couldn't understand why people should "run after ferries with hats flying off and skirts flying behind." His own favorite pastime when he crossed the ferry from Brooklyn to New York was to stand aside and look at the people. "Crowds of men and women attired in the usual costumes, how curious you are to me! . . . I, too, am one of the crowd. . . . The men and the women I see are all near to me."

This was the thought that kept recurring to him again and again. The united kinship of human life. All men draw their sustenance from the one spiritual fountain which is God, just as all plants derive their strength from the one common breast of Mother Earth.

All men are interrelated members of one body—mankind. White men, red men, yellow men, black men—all are brothers under their skin. It was this thought that he tried to emphasize in the editorial pages of the *Eagle*. And it was because of this thought that he lost his position on the paper. One day he had become involved in an argument with an influential politician on the question of slavery. Rumor had it that he had kicked the proslavery gentleman down the steps. At any rate, Whitman was told to look for another job.

He found his new job in New Orleans. And when he came to this Queen City of the South he entered upon "the most interesting episode" of his life. Unfortunately we can only guess as to the nature of this episode, since he has drawn the veil of silence over it. But one thing seems certain—that he became "intimately acquainted with a woman of a different social rank" than his own. He met her, apparently, at a ball in the suburb known as Lafayette. It was an evening in May. Walt Whitman, at the insistence of his friends, had put on formal clothes—probably for the first time in his life. As he drew the white kid gloves over his large hands he burst them, so that they looked like "cracked dumplings." Folding his hands "nonchalantly" behind his back, he watched "the Creole beauties, the free women of color, the graceful forms and lovely faces in plain, fancy and mask dresses." As he looked at these women, "each one lovelier than the other," he caught a glimpse of "what I conceived the very pink of perfection, in form, grace and movement, in fancy dress." He managed to get an introduction to her. . . .

And this is all we know with regard to the entire episode. Walt Whitman had written a full account of his visit to New Orleans, but he later destroyed all the pages in which he had referred to this "solitary romance" of his life. This romance resulted in no marriage, either because the lady in question was already married to another man or else because her family objected to Walt for financial or for social reasons. But he became the father of at least one of her children. Many years later he wrote to John Addington Symonds about this episode and mentioned a grandson with whom he kept in constant touch. But he begged Symonds never to "disclose the secret" to anybody else. To do so, he said, "would indisputably do a great injury to someone."

This, then, is all we know of his "one brief hour of madness and joy"—this, and a poem or two in which he hinted about his New Orleans experience.

> Out of the rolling ocean, the crowd, came a drop gently to me,
> Whispering *I love you, before long I die,*
> *I have travel'd a long way merely to look on you, to touch you,*
> *For I could not die till I once looked on you.*
>
> .   .   .   .
>
> Again we wander—we love—we separate again,
> Again she holds me by the hand—I must not go!
> I see her close beside me, with silent lips, sad and tremulous.
>
> .   .   .   .
>
> Return in peace to the ocean, my love,
> I too am part of that ocean, my love. . . .

And that ocean is one indivisible stream of inseparable life. For a brief space it may "carry us diverse, yet (it) cannot carry us diverse forever."

Be not impatient—a little space—— And in the meantime, "I salute the air, the ocean and the land every day at sundown for your dear sake, my love. . . ."

His mysterious romance at New Orleans proved to be the final ingredient of sunlight and sadness necessary for the flowering of his poetical genius. It was shortly after his return from New Orleans that he began to write his *Leaves of Grass*.

IV

THE FIRST EDITION OF *Leaves of Grass* came out in 1855. It fell like a feather upon a sea of contemptuous silence. There was only one man in America—Ralph Waldo Emerson—who recognized something of its greatness. Having come across a copy of the book, Emerson wrote to its unknown author: "I am not blind to the worth of the wonderful gift of the *Leaves of Grass*. I find it the most extraordinary piece of wit and wisdom that America has yet contributed. . . . I find incomparable things, said incomparably well. . . . I greet you at the beginning of a great career. . . ."

While Emerson was still under the enchantment of his first reading of the *Leaves of Grass* he sent one of his own admirers to visit Walt Whitman in Brooklyn. "*There* you will see a poet you can *really* admire. . . . Americans abroad may now come home: unto us a man is born."

Later, however, Emerson found the language of Whitman a little too pungent for his delicate New England palate. He could stand Whitman's doctrine of equality; he himself had advanced it, with a somewhat dainty timidity, in his democratic poem *The Mountain and the Squirrel*. But what he could not tolerate was Whitman's disconcerting frankness. The Sage of Concord was too cultured a gentleman "to expose the unexposable and to mention the unmentionable"—at least in the open pages of a book. There was no need, he felt, to emphasize bluntly the obvious fact that there are puddles on the earth as well as stars in the heavens. When Emerson reread some of Whitman's outspoken sex poems he repented of his earlier wholehearted endorsement. He advised Whitman to omit these poems from the next edition, pointing out to him the danger that the "unnecessary inclusion of the sex element" might attract the wrong readers and repel the right readers. To all of which criticism the younger poet replied that there was no unnecessary element in his book, that every poem was just as important to the book as every organ is important to the body and that in spite of Emerson's advice—which he most deeply respected—he remained "more convinced than ever to adhere to my own theory."

Emerson gently decided to leave Whitman to his own theory. But he was now inclined to agree with the editor of one of the literary journals (the Boston *Intelligence*) that Whitman was an escaped lunatic. He failed to realize, as at first the entire world failed to realize, that here was no prurient dabbler in forbidden things but a poet of universal sympathy. Whitman spoke of the various parts of the body in the same spirit in which God had created them. Whitman's poems are a glorification of life—of every phase of it. To the pure all things are pure. Whitman found beauty and holiness everywhere because he examined everything with an attitude of holiness and beauty. A hasty stroll over the *Leaves of Grass* should demonstrate this fact.

This book of Whitman's poems is, like the life of its author, foursquare. It is founded upon the principles of *equality, pity, religion* and *love*.

We have already referred to Whitman's doctrine of equality. He worships the "divine average"—that is, he reveals the divine essence that inheres in the everyday life of the average man. His aim is "to teach the average man the glory of his daily walk and trade." No one, however lowly, need fear that he is unworthy to live and to enjoy life. Let no one presume to lord it over others and let no one allow others to lord it over him. "Resist much, obey little." Do not bow to superiors, for no one is your superior. You are the equal of any. All are the children of the earth, and in the final reckoning the impartial mother plays no favorites. All things are the related parts of God. They are the leaves of the undying tree of life. The selfsame immortal sap flows through the veins of the entire universe. "I know that the spirit of God is the brother of my own and that all the men ever born are also my brothers and the women my sisters and lovers." The greatest and the least are tending toward the same goal, and all alike will reach it in the end. "Have you out-stripped the rest? Are you the President? It is a trifle; they will more than arrive there, every one, and still pass on." Whitman believes in the evolution of the individual as well as of the race. Each human soul undergoes a lengthy process of education—before its appearance upon this earth, throughout its earthly existence and after its passage into the next world. Each soul must pass through every grade of this education. Those who during their lifetime upon earth appear to belong to the humbler classes are merely, for the time being, going through a lower grade than their fellow pupils in the democratic school of eternal life. But in the long run every human soul will reach the highest grade in this universal school and graduate into the presence of God. Walt Whitman's democracy is not merely a political or a social doctrine. It is a religious faith—a supreme conviction that each and every one of us will attain to perfection in the end. Just what this "perfection" may be, Whitman does not pretend to know. "But I know that it will in its turn prove sufficient and cannot fail."

It cannot fail the young man who died and was buried,
Nor the young woman who died and was put by his side,
Nor the little child that peeped in at the door, and then drew back
    and was never seen again,
Nor the old man who has lived without purpose, and feels it with
    bitterness worse than gall. . . .

The glory of an immortal life awaits them all. "I do not call one greater and one smaller. That which fills its period and space is equal to any." The great Camerado will be there to greet us all with His kindly smile of infinite love.

Whitman's doctrine of equality is due to his great sense of pity. He feels akin to all the sufferers of the world. "Whoever walks a furlong without sympathy," he writes, "walks to his own funeral dressed in his own shroud." Unable to injure any living creature, Walt Whitman cannot conceive of a Creator whose sense of pity is less than his own. He salutes all the inhabitants of the earth. His good will extends to all things created. "Health to you, good will to you all . . . in America's name!"

Walt Whitman was perhaps the most compassionate of modern poets. And because of his compassion he was constantly preoccupied with the problem of death. Always he spoke in its praise. Death, he said, is the great Physician whose white hand brushes away the last vestige of human pain. Whatever may be our burden in the glare and the turmoil of the world, the poet comforts us all alike with the lovely and soothing promise of "night, sleep, death and the stars." Do you weep at the brevity of your life and the intensity of your suffering? "Weep not, child, weep not, my darling; something there is more immortal even than the stars, something that shall endure longer even than lustrous Jupiter, longer than sun or any revolving satellite or the radiant sisters the Pleiades." And what is that something? Your ultimate happiness, your triumphant destiny, your undying soul.

Walt Whitman rarely went to church, but he was one of the most religious of poets. As we have already noted, he made a religion of Democracy. He transplanted the pantheism of Spinoza into the soil of American republicanism. The United States of America—the United Body of Mankind—the United Soul of the Universe. The body and the soul, he said, are one; and death is merely an extension of life. "I laugh at what you call dissolution," for "I know I am deathless." This conviction that all men are deathless, and that all human lives are equally important ripples that play upon the surface of the universal ocean of life, is everywhere expressed with a finality that becomes a gospel in his *Leaves of Grass*. This new Gospel of American Democracy glorifies the dignity of man. Every human creature is a high priest who can, if he will, speak face to face with God. A new era will begin when the human race becomes aware of this fact. A new religion, greater and more inclusive than the old, will flush the world with love. For each individual life will then recognize its kinship with the whole. Walt Whitman sings the song of a new world, a new race, a new devotion, a new faith. "I say no man has ever yet been half devout enough, none has ever yet adored or worship'd half enough, none has begun to think how divine he himself is and how certain the future is."

With this faith implanted in his heart Walt Whitman offers the hand of friendship to all men. He sings to them "the evangel poem" of comrades and of love. "For who but I should understand love with all its sorrow and joy? And who but I should be the poet of comrades?"

Love, to Whitman, is a reunion—a meeting again with those to whom we have been united in a remote past. "Passing stranger, you do not know how longingly I look upon you. You must be he I was seeking or she I was seeking (it comes to me as of a dream). I have somewhere surely lived a life of joy with you."

In his communion with other people Walt Whitman found a joy that passes understanding. He did not merely *sing* of comradeship. He was one of those very rare men who actually *lived* it. He identified himself with the whole world and tried to give of himself to everybody. He had a passion for cultivating the friendship of the humble. He extended the comradely hand to those who couldn't "get on" in the competitive struggle of life. He drove a coach during an entire winter for a coachman who was ill. Following his own prescription as set forth in the preface to the 1855 edition of *Leaves of Grass*, he loved the earth and sun and the animals, despised riches, gave alms to everybody that asked, stood up for the stupid and the weak, took off his hat to nothing known or unknown and entered into close fellowship with all those who were poor in the possession of friends.

His was the American Gospel at its best.

V

DURING the Civil War he offered his life to the service of humanity—not on the battlefields but in the hospitals. His brother George, who had enlisted in the 51st New York Volunteers, was

wounded at the Battle of Fredericksburg. Walt went down to
nurse him at the Soldiers' Hospital in Washington. When he
arrived there George was already well. But Walt remained in
Washington to look after the other wounded and dying soldiers.
This was his daily occupation to the end of the war. Never was
nurse more skillful or minister more tender. Walt became the
companion of the sick soldiers, their secretary, their attendant,
their comforter, their friend. We have a picture of the "Good
Gray Poet" from the pen of a man who accompanied Walt on
one of his hospital visits:

"Never shall I forget that visit. . . . There were three rows of
cots, and each cot bore its man. When he appeared, in passing
along, there was a smile of affection and welcome on every face,
however wan, and his presence seemed to light up the place as it
might be lit by the presence of the Son of Love. From cot to cot
they called him, often in tremulous tones or in whispers; they
embraced him, they touched his hand, they gazed at him. To
one he gave a few words of cheer, for another he wrote a letter
home, to others he gave an orange, a few comfits, a cigar, a
pipe and tobacco, a sheet of paper or a postage stamp, all of
which and many other things were in his capacious haversack.
From another he would receive a dying message for mother,
wife or sweetheart; for another he would promise to go on an
errand; to another, some special friend, very low, he would give
a manly farewell kiss. He did the things for them which no nurse
or doctor could do, and he seemed to leave a benediction at
every cot as he passed along. . . ."

He performed miracles, the doctors said—miracles of healing.
A few courageous words, spoken in his gentle voice, would at
times bring back to life those who had resigned themselves to
death and whom even the doctors had given up. Many of the
soldiers remembered him years later as "the man with the face
of the Saviour."

In his work among the wounded soldiers he made no distinction between friend and foe. All the stricken men, whether
of the North or of the South, were his "brothers in distress."

One of the most beautiful of the poems which he wrote during the Civil War describes his feeling at the sight of a slain enemy:

Word over all, beautiful as the sky,
Beautiful that war and all its carnage must in time be utterly lost,
That the hands of the sisters Death and Night incessantly softly wash
    again, and ever again, this soil'd world;
For my enemy is dead, a man divine as myself is dead;
I look where he lies white-faced and stiff in the coffin—I draw near,
Bend down and touch lightly with my lips the white face in the coffin.

Whitman received no pay for his ministration to the sick and the dying soldiers. In order to support himself during this period he secured a clerical post in the Indian Bureau of the Department of the Interior. Some busybody, however, called the attention of James Harlan, the secretary of the interior, to Walt Whitman's "pernicious poetry." One evening, while Walt was making his usual rounds of the hospitals, the curious Mr Harlan walked into the poet's office, found a copy of *Leaves of Grass* on the desk and read enough of it to shut the book with a complete miscomprehension of the poems and with a muddle-witted prejudice against their author. The next morning, when the poet arrived at his desk, he found the following note awaiting him:

"The service of Walter Whitman will be dispensed with from and after this date."

The gods, wrote an Eastern sage, are forever walking through the cities of men. But the eyes of men are too blind to see them.

VI

IN 1873 Walt Whitman suffered a paralytic stroke. The seeds of this illness, said his doctor, had been planted in his body during the long vigils and the laborious sacrifices in the soldiers' hospitals. He recovered partially from his paralysis, but he was never himself again. His body remained broken to the end of his days. He limped his painful way through the cities of men, an obscure, lonely and at times hungry god. With a basket over his arm he peddled his books from door to door. One winter day, as he was thus trying to exchange nuggets of gold for crusts of bread, an elderly widow, Mrs Mary Davis, took pity on him. She invited him into her cottage, offered him a warm breakfast and decided then and there to take care of him for the rest of his life. A few of his admirers bought him a little box of a house in Camden, New Jersey, the town in which his mother had died and in which he was anxious to end his own days. The furniture was of the scantiest—a bed, a dry-goods case to write on, a couple of chairs, a table on which stood an oilstove to cook his food, nothing more. After a while, however, Mrs Davis moved in as his housekeeper and brought her own furniture along with her. He now lived "like a prince in his own domain."

A prince in a ramshackle hovel. The house was "on the other side of the railroad tracks." The street was shabby, noise-ridden and infested with the offensive odors of a near-by guano factory. But in the back yard there was a pear tree under which he would sit on summer evenings. And on the front doorstep the children would come to play and to wait for the pennies that he tossed them—whenever he could spare them—out of the window.

Thus he spent the last few years of his life—receiving his friends in the downstairs "parlor" as long as he was able to move around and in his upstairs "study" when his strength had given out. Both "parlor" and "study" were cluttered—chairs, tables, mantelpieces, floor—with hundreds of copies of his unsold books.

On his seventy-second birthday (May 31, 1891) a group of his friends hired a caterer and gave the poet a "banquet" in his home. "We had a capital supper," he wrote, "chicken soup, salmon, roast lamb, etc., etc., etc. I had been under a horrible spell from 5 to 6, but Warry got me dress'd and down (like carrying down a great log) . . ."

This was his last birthday on earth. A few months later they got him dressed and carried him—to his first birthday in heaven? Speaking of the afterlife to the agnostic Robert G. Ingersoll, Walt Whitman had once declared, "Well, Bob, I don't know—for anybody but *myself*. But for *myself*—I am as certain of it as I am that we are all here!"

KIPLING

Great Poems by Kipling

Recessional.
The Vampire.
The Ballad of East and West.
The English Flag.
Danny Deever.
Tommy.
Fuzzy-Wuzzy.
Gunga Din.
To the Unknown Goddess.
La Nuit Blanche.
My Rival.
A Code of Morals.
Loot.

Mandalay.
Route-Marchin'.
The Ballad of the King's Jest.
Boots.
The Undertaker's Horse.
The Fall of Jock Gillespie.
The Last Suttee.
The Grave of the Hundred Dead.
Delilah.
The Lovers' Litany.
The Song of the Women.
The Widow at Windsor.

Rudyard Kipling
1865–1936

T HE EDITOR of the San Francisco *Examiner* looked up from the article he was reading to the young reporter who had just handed it in to him. The reporter was nervous, unimpressive, diminutive and extremely young—actually he was twenty-four, but he looked no more than sixteen. He blinked at the editor through glasses that were of an unusual thickness.

"So this is the best you can do, Mr Kipling?" growled the editor.

"I'm afraid so, sir."

"And they tell me you've published several things in India."

"Yes sir. *Departmental Ditties, Plain Tales from the Hills,* one oɪ two other trifles." And then timidly: "They seemed to like them in India, sir."

"I dare say!" The words shot out in a derisive staccato. "They'd like anything in India." The editor looked back from the reporter to the article, which he summarized in a single word—"Rot!"

"I'll try to do better next time, sir."

"There 'll be no next time!" And then, relenting somewhat, the editor lowered his voice to a tone of fatherly advice. "I'm sorry, Mr Kipling, but you just don't know how to use the

English language. You'll excuse my bluntness, but the *Examiner* is not a kindergarten for amateur writers."

And thus ended the American journalistic career of the young Englishman who had already, at the age of twenty-four, written *The Man Who Would Be King*—"one of the best short stories," to quote Mr H. G. Wells, "in the history of literature."

II

JOSEPH RUDYARD KIPLING—like Thomas Woodrow Wilson, he later dropped his first name—was "the son of a beloved family, artists and booklovers together." He was born (December 30, 1865) and spent his early childhood in Bombay, a city of acrid odors, multitudinous noises and "thundering" colors. He absorbed into his very blood and marrow this atmosphere of passionate contrasts seething under the glare of the oriental sun.

But he was able to temper this oriental excitement with a sound and solid British education. When he was five years old his father—a professor of sculpture at the Bombay School of Art—took him to England and placed him, together with his sister, under the care of a relative at Southsea. For the next seven years the nearsighted and undersized little fellow was subjected to the rigid discipline of a conservative Victorian household. And then he was transferred to the even more rigid discipline of the United Service College, a private school managed by military officers for youngsters who intended to enter the Indian service.

At school Kipling was distinguished only for his precocious mustache, an "early spring growth" of black hair that had sprouted on his upper lip at the age of twelve. Aside from this "premature mark of maturity" Kipling showed nothing, either physically or mentally, to single him out from the other students. He took after his headmaster, Cormell Price, whom he greatly admired and who himself as a youngster had carried off "no honors, either with his head or his arms or his legs." Kipling went through his classes quietly and unobtrusively, thankful for the "blessed affliction" of his poor sight, which kept him away from the outdoor games that he hated but which did not prevent him from reading the books that he loved.

And he read continuously and omnivorously—"scores and scores of ancient dramatists . . . Hakluyt's voyages . . . French translations of Muscovite authors called Pushkin and Lermontoff . . . an odd theme, purporting to be a translation of something called a *Rubáiyát* . . . hundreds of volumes of verse . . ." and those fascinating books written by scientists about the ancient forgotten epochs "when all the planets were little new-lit stars trying to find their places in the uncaring void. . . ." For his all-inclusive education the body of the poet child had traveled from India to England; and his mind from the here and now to the outermost limits of time and space.

When he graduated from the United Service College (at the age of seventeen) he felt that he had had enough of academic training. He wanted to get out into the larger university of the world. Accordingly his father, who was now the curator of the Lahore Museum, got him a reporter's job on the *Civil and Military Gazette*. After five years of apprenticeship on this paper Kipling found himself promoted to the assistant editorship of the Allahabad *Pioneer*.

He disliked his life in India, but he loved the life of a journalist. He had "sold his heart to the old Black Art we call the Daily Press." In his spare moments he dashed off a number of poems and stories just long enough to fill up the empty gaps in his paper. These poems and stories were miniatures of the world seen through the eyes of a reporter. Thanks to the limitation of space Kipling had learned the so-called trick of "shorthand literature." In a few colorful phrases he could recapture the "sweltering heat under which the mercury climbs to the top of the glass and the printing presses grow red hot . . . the drenching rains, the fever, the cholera, the blinding sandstorms . . . the oils and spices and puffs of temple incense . . . the villages blotted out by the jungle . . ." the squalor and the superstition and the generosity of the native bhisti . . . the stupidity and the vanity and the valor of the British sahib . . . the very soul and substance, in short, of the "blisterin' bloomin' country known as Injia"— that testing field of human character, where "there is neither East nor West, Border, nor Breed, nor Birth, when two strong men stand face to face, tho' they come from the ends of the earth."

For several years he stuck to these miniature paintings of the colorful life in the Punjab. He collected his stories and his poems into two slender volumes, and the echo of their publication reverberated as far as London. Time for him to leave India and to see the world. He was anxious to become a journalist on a larger scale. And so he borrowed several hundred rupees and set out upon his travels. He explored China and Japan; he examined the ceremonies and the cities of his "yellow brothers" with his nearsighted eyes and his farseeing mind, and he concluded that "all stations are exactly alike." And then he sailed for San Francisco where, as we have seen, he tried to establish himself as a reporter and failed.

He never forgave America for this insult to his dignity. To the end of his days he looked down upon the American men as an inferior race of barbarians. As for the American women— but that, as Kipling would say, is another story.

III

HAVING TRAVELED across the United States from San Francisco to New York, he incorporated his impressions in a travel book filled with spice and venom, and then he set sail for England. Here he met a young woman—an American woman, be it noted—and married her. For Kipling held the women of America in the greatest admiration. To be sure, a woman at best—he maintained—is a dangerous toy to play with. "Man is fire and woman is tow, and the Devil he comes and begins to blow. . . ." But "in America the tow is soaked in a solution that makes it fireproof, in absolute liberty and large knowledge. . . . Nothing is too good for an American's daughter. . . ."

[300]

The "American's daughter" of Kipling's choice was Caroline Starr Balestier, who at the time of Kipling's visit to England was staying there with her brother Wolcott Balestier, the London representative of the New York publishing firm of John W. Lovell. When Kipling and Caroline were married they went back to live in America.

And for a time Kipling actually liked it. He built a spacious, rambling bungalow on a hillside at Brattleboro, Vermont. He and his wife arrived at their new home in the midwinter (February 8) of 1892. The temperature was 32 below freezing—quite a plunge from the Allahabad swelterings of 118 in the shade. Kipling found the moonlight sleigh ride from the railroad station to his bungalow "beautiful beyond expression." In the distance, just above the horizon, towered the blue-and-silver peak of Mount Monadnock, "like a giant thumbnail pointing heavenward." When they entered their bungalow they were greeted with a blazing welcome from the Vermont pine logs which their neighbors had lighted in the fireplace.

The young poet named his bungalow *Naulahka*, the Jewel—after a novel which he had written in collaboration with his wife's brother, Wolcott Balestier. Here the Kiplings lived for almost five years, perhaps the happiest years of their life. Their neighbors took pride in pointing out to visitors the very unimpressive little fellow who rode out in his very impressive big carriage with its richly liveried coachman. For the most part, however, he preferred walking to riding. Strangers who met him on the country roads mistook him for "some weather-beaten farm hand, bent from too much hoeing on the Vermont hills."

His early stoop was due to his nearsighted eyes. Unable to sweep over faraway vistas, he had accustomed himself to bend his eyes downward so that he might the more closely observe the details of the life about him. He went on frequent hunting trips into the woods—not gun hunting but "eye hunting." He loved the woods, he said, "for their own sake and not for the sake of slaughter." There was nothing quite so glorious, he thought, as the sun-and-pine-drenched perfume of the New England countryside. Especially in the summer. "The New England summer," he said, "has Creole blood in her veins."

The New England winter, too, he found glorious—with its steel-blue days and its snow-sifted nights. For his outdoor exercise on the winter days he had invented a game of "snow golf." In order to be able to locate his golf balls, as he trudged after them in his rubber boots, he painted them red. His favorite indoor amusement during the long winter evenings was the production of plays in a miniature theater which he had set up at Naulahka. In the course of these plays he would improvise verses that would set his small audiences into gales of laughter. But he never allowed these "extemporary verses of his amateur hours" to be published or even to be written down.

As for his professional hours, he worked at his desk every morning from nine to one. And during this working period he was never disturbed. For in order to enter his study one had to pass through a smaller room—it was called *the dragon's chamber*—where Mrs Kipling sat with her knitting needles and with a sharp lookout against any unwelcome intruders.

It was in this study that Kipling wrote some of his best work—scores of stories and poems, *Captains Courageous* and the two *Jungle Books*. An interesting and touching story is told about the manuscript of the first *Jungle Book*. Kipling gave this manuscript as a present to the nurse who had cared for his first-born child. "Take this script," he said, "and someday if you are in need of money you may be able to sell it at a handsome price." Years later, when the nurse was actually in want, she sold the manuscript and managed to live in comfort for the rest of her life.

With the publication of the *Jungle Books* the young poet—he was not yet thirty—had come close to the high-water mark of his fame and his fortune. Millions of readers the world over had tasted his literary cocktail of sublimity and slang and found it to their liking. Kipling received more offers from magazines than he was able to accept. On one occasion the editor of the

Ladies' Home Journal, Edward W. Bok, requested Kipling to write a story for this magazine. The English poet, who disliked the *Ladies' Home Journal*, mentioned an exorbitant figure as his fee for the story. In this way he believed that he would scare off the editor. To his astonishment, however, Mr Bok agreed to the price. Kipling dashed off his story (*William the Conqueror*), threw it into the mailbox and thought that this was the end of the matter.

But it wasn't. A few days later he received a note from Mr Bok. The story was excellent and all that. But wouldn't Mr Kipling please make a minor yet very necessary change in the copy? The story contained a reference to whisky and champagne —two beverages that were taboo in the *Ladies' Home Journal*. Wouldn't Mr Kipling be gracious enough to substitute a couple of milder drinks for the whisky and the champagne?

The reply was prompt and short. No, Mr Kipling would *not* be gracious enough. "Either you take the whisky or you return the story."

The editor was obliged to give in. He published the story together with its intoxicating drinks.

"And thus," laughed Kipling when he recounted the incident, "I was the first man ever privileged to pour a glass of whisky into the pages of the *Ladies' Home Journal*."

Kipling was not an easy man to get along with. He never backed away from a quarrel. Indeed, his residence in America came to an end as a result of one of his quarrels. It started in a dispute with a neighbor about a boundary line on his Brattleboro estate. This dispute flared up into a disagreeable court trial, with all its attendant disgusting publicity. When the trial was over Kipling left America (August 1896) to settle down in "the blessed plot" of England.

Three years later he paid a final visit to the United States. This visit left him with nothing but painful memories. He hated "the long, narrow pig trough of New York . . . with her roar and rattle, her complex smells, her triply overheated rooms and her much too energetic inhabitants." Contributing to his general unhappiness on this occasion was a severe illness—an attack of pneumonia which almost cost him his life. And when he recovered his eldest child, Josephine, died. This was the little girl whose nurse he had presented with the manuscript of the *Jungle Book*.

Kipling spoke little of his child's death. Throughout his life he kept his deepest sorrows to himself.

> How can the wise man's words impart
> The burden that breaks the wise man's heart?

IV

WHEN Kipling lay critically ill in New York the German Kaiser sent several cabled inquiries about his health. The Kaiser was, of course, quite majestically unaware of Kipling's literary merits. But he had heard that this young British poet was the mouth-piece of a new aggressive credo—an unchristian doctrine that was after the Kaiser's own imperialistic heart. This credo, briefly summarized, represents "an appeal to, and a vindication of, the white man as brute." It is the "white man's burden," declared Kipling, to conquer and to oppress the "dusky men"—not only for the white man's glory but for the dusky men's good. Kipling's belief in the superior man was but the English version of Nietzsche's faith in the superman. The "white brute" is another name for the "blond beast." This passionate faith in the white man's superiority and in his destined supremacy bristles throughout the poems and the stories of the so-called "middle period" of Kipling's writing. It finds its first expression in his blustering poem *The English Flag:*

> First of the scattered legions, under a shrieking sky,
> Dipping between the rollers, the English Flag goes by.

This doctrine goes on, swaggering and shrieking from page to page, until it bursts out into a passionate glorification of war as one of the two noblest pursuits of man:

KIPLING

Two things greater than all things are—
The first is Love, and the second War.

Kipling's love for his country has now become transformed into hatred for every other country. His patriotism has descended to the jingoism of those who could sing such songs as the following:

We don't want to fight, but, by jingo, if we do,
We got the ships, we got the men, we got the mun-naye too.

No wonder the Kaiser was so anxious about the health of this brilliant apostle of brutality!

The Kaiser might have felt differently, however, had he known that Kipling would live to temper his aggression with the saving grace of compassion. For as the young poet grew older he also grew sadder and wiser. He no longer glorified the strident victories of the British soldier. Instead he began to emphasize his sturdy virtues—his determination, through thick and thin, "to do his duty, to live stoically, to live cleanly, to live cheerfully." Conquest may go too far; pride may degenerate into arrogance and imperialism into imperiousness. The seeds of today's victory may grow into the weeds of tomorrow's defeat. Against our own overmastering ambition, O Lord, protect us. It is a far different Kipling from the old tub thumper of the battlefield that we now find in the sober, solemn measures of his Victorian prayer, the *Recessional:*

The tumult and the shouting dies;
The Captains and the Kings depart;
Still stands Thine ancient sacrifice,
An humble and a contrite heart.
Lord God of Hosts, be with us yet,
Lest we forget—lest we forget!

"I started as a average kid," writes one of Kipling's tommies in *The Return*, "I finished as a thinkin' man." The same may be said of the England as envisaged in Kipling's imperial dream. It started as the despot over a horde of conquered tribes. It grew up as the leader in a commonwealth of co-operating nations. Rudyard Kipling, Tommy Atkins, Terence Mulvaney—every mother's son of England had at last become acquainted with the secret of her true nobility:

> An' last it come to me—not pride,
> Nor yet conceit, but on the 'ole
> (If such a term may be applied),
> The makin's of a bloomin' soul.

V

THE SOUL of Kipling, like the soul of England, had become refined through suffering. He had refused the laureateship because he wanted to be free to speak his mind. He had won the Nobel prize for literature (1907) only to realize that prizes and power were but drifting smoke. Towns without people, heads struck off by shellfire, "the pore dead that look so old an' was so young an hour ago—these are the things which make you know."

And these were the things that made *Kipling* know. He learned at firsthand the meaninglessness of aggression and the meannesses of war. When the First World War (of 1914) broke out it was the Kipling of the *Recessional* who spoke up against it.

> Once more we hear the word
> That sickened earth of old:
> "No law except the Sword
> Unsheathed and uncontrolled."

He lost his son in this war, and his heart was desolate for the desolate hearts of all the old men who had lost their sons in the war.

> Our world has passed away
> In wantonness o'erthrown.
> There is nothing left today
> But steel and fire and stone!

Steel shells for human lives. Bullets for bread. Fratricide for faith. Hatred for hope. A merciful Providence spared Kipling from living into the nightmare of the Second World War. He died in 1936, when only the distant rumblings of the Nazi aggression were heard beyond the horizon. But he had left to the British world, to the *entire* world, his last courageous Will and Testament:

> No easy hope or lies
> Shall bring us to our goal,
> But iron sacrifice
> Of body, will and soul.
>
> There is but one task for all—
> One life for each to give.
> What stands if freedom fall?
> Who dies if England live?